Yc

RISE
A NOVEL OF CONTEMPORARY ISRAEL

BY

YOSEF GOTLIEB

Rise

Published by
'Atida Press
The Olive Group
PO Box 40520
Mevasseret Tzion, Israel 91404
www.olivecommunications.net
info@olivecommunications.net

PUBLISHER'S NOTE:
This is a work of fiction. Names, characters, places, and incidents either are of the author's creation or are used fictitiously, and any resemblance to actual persons, living or dead, business establishments, events, or locales is entirely coincidental.

Copyright © Yosef Gotlieb, 2011. All rights reserved.

No part of this book may be used or reproduced in any manner without written permission from the publisher, except in the context of reviews.

ISBN 978-965-7557-01-3 (pbk)

Printed by
Alon Sefer
Kibbutz Tzora, Israel 99803

FOR MY CHILDREN,
TALI AND AMIHAI,
WHO AFFIRM HOPE

DEDICATED TO ALL WHO STRUGGLE FOR A
BETTER WORLD

צֶדֶק צֶדֶק תִּרְדֹּף לְמַעַן תִּחְיֶה וְיָרַשְׁתָּ אֶת הָאָרֶץ
אֲשֶׁר יְהוָה אֱלֹהֶיךָ נֹתֵן לָךְ.   דברים טז כ

Justice, justice pursue, so that you may thrive and inherit the land that the Lord your God is giving to you. [Deuteronomy 16:20]

CHAPTER ONE

Lilah spent her first few days back in Israel opening the airy, spacious apartment at 3 HaGaon Street that she had inherited from her parents; she had been brought there as a newborn and was raised there. It was the home Naftali had come back to after he refused to continue being a captive to Lilah's self-exile in the United States. It was there that Ido, their son, had been born and later returned to join his father.

The unpretentious but ample apartment was tucked into a small neighborhood, a veritable urban village a few short blocks from the northern Tel Aviv shore. Yonatan, Lilah's brother, and she had enjoyed a happy and comfortable childhood within these walls; the Hassons had been an especially close family. Their father, a physician, had emigrated from his native Istanbul to Palestine and married their mother, a teacher and landscape painter originally from Warsaw. Like many others of their generation, they were intellectuals who were dedicated to the establishment of a modern egalitarian society and a secular state for the Jewish nation.

Their home had been a place of welcome. There was a large living room and dining area partitioned by a long row of high, book-lined shelves. In the dining area, there was an extendable table capable of comfortably seating twenty people for dinner. It had been custom-made when Lilah was a little girl and its grooves and nicks held fond memories of holiday meals and stormy intellectual meetings. The large kitchen, a converted porch with a stone hearth, was half-hidden off the main room. Throughout, the walls were lined with oil paintings, works of Lilah's mother's hand.

The expansive common areas gave way to the private seclusion of the bedrooms. The master bedroom was flanked by two other rooms – Lilah's and Yonatan's – the latter having been inherited by the fallen soldier's nephew, Ido; he was born shortly after his uncle had been buried. Each bedroom had its own special features. Ido's room overlooked the enclosed courtyard of the building. It was thick with trees, a would-be forest that ignited the imagination; wild animals and wizards could lurk there in the mind of a boy. Lilah's room had a view of the sea, which she watched at dusk when the sun slid anew into the Mediterranean. When she was young, Lilah would lie on her bed and look out the windows for hours. The images that cut across the horizon ultimately honed her keen photographer's eye.

As she dusted and swept, consigned old clothes to storage bins and emptied the cabinets of goods no longer used, she understood that she had stepped over the chasm: What she had built in Boston, all that she had achieved in those thirty years had been left behind so that she could return, finally sealing the tomb –Yonatan's death – that had caused her to flee.

As she scoured the enamel sink in the kitchen that had seemed so huge to her when she was a girl, Lucian was much on her mind. She recalled six months earlier, a crisp, crystal-clear night in January on Cape Cod. "What do you mean, you're going back?" Lucian had asked incredulously after she told him of her decision: Thirty years an expat, she was going home.

She remembered Lucian looking as if he had been struck, the wrinkles of his broad Nordic face growing cumulous. "But why, Lilah, why? You are so one of us," Lucian asked, his stately pose slackening, aching.

Lucian was an elegant silver-haired patrician who had mentored Lilah and cultivated her those three decades. She had arrived at his institute in 1979, a twenty-two-year-old waif laden with troubles. Now, back in Tel Aviv beneath a pile of weekend newspapers under the coffee table, she came across a copy of her first picture book, a photo essay on the people of the Yucatan. In the forward, Lucian had written: "Lilah appeared at our editorial offices like a lily after rain, drooping from sorrows she would not discuss, big brown eyes with lace-like lashes, beautiful dark hair gracing a delicate porcelain face. Her English had a mysterious Mediterranean lilt. She claimed to have once been a soldier, though one could only imagine her, in bell-bottom jeans and a paisley blouse, to have been engaged and wounded only on the battlefield of love...She wanted to become a photographer..."

She became a photographer, a world-class one.

The revelation about her relocation was made at Lucian's weekend home on a Friday evening, just before they left to attend an exhibition of her photos from the *Women of the Ports* collection. There would be a reception in honor of Lilah Kedem's new work at Camera Distincta House, near the Museum of Fine Arts in Boston. Friends and admirers of the award-winning photographer would be coming from far and wide to sing her praises.

No one anticipated the announcement that evening that she was returning to Israel. She had traveled to and had lived in many places during those three decades, but had always returned to nest and create there, in New England. No one ever contemplated that she thought of any place else as her home. Lilah Kedem was an international figure, an artist and advocate for people on the margins – peasants in the Yucatan, refugees from Somalia's internecine wars, female dockworkers in macho Gdansk, orphans of genocide in the Sudan – all of whom she captured in her photos and the picture books composed from them.

That she was of Israeli birth was overlooked in the chic, cosmopolitan circles that her career required her to frequent. Yet she had decided to assert it that evening as she stood before the room full of admirers at Camera Distincta. The air seemed to stand still and dismay was evident when she said, simply, earnestly, "It is time for me to return to my son, to my husband

and to the land of my birth, my homeland, Israel."

Lilah, past fifty, was still comely as she stood demurely before the crowd at the Camera Distincta reception. She was dressed tastefully but without pretension, her figure sleek and fit. Subtle strands of gray mingled in the brown mane draping her Modiglianiesque neck. Her large, dark eyes glimmered in the stage lights.

Lucian looked crestfallen, brooding throughout that evening and acting coolly toward Lilah during the coming weeks. When spring came, and with it signs that Lilah was serious about the move, he had made one snide comment too many, a remark about her going back to "that man that left you and Ido." Lilah seethed. "Why can't you understand?" she had snapped at him, "I was the one who left. I was the one who fled from everything that had been dear to me." As she stood weeping, Lucian softened and embraced her and accepted what she had stated as her cardinal truth: "Thirty-one years is too long a time to waste living a tragedy."

The tragedy happened on January 29, 1979 when Yonatan fell in a barrage of bullets during the dead of night while his unit pursued *fedayeen* on the border near Gaza. Lilah and Naftali had not been married a year and she was pregnant with Ido when the three black angels in army fatigues, officer's epaulets on their shoulders, arrived at the door of the Hasson home at 3 HaGaon Street, to inform the family that the lieutenant had fallen. After they told the Hassons what had happened to brave Yonatan, the officers hoped to console them by telling them he would be buried a hero.

Lilah took no comfort in that. She had rather her brother live a thousand years as a healthy coward than be dead forever in a hallowed grave. She could not be consoled. "I cannot be in the land that took Yoni," she declared the night she announced to her parents she was leaving Israel and taking her son with her – with or without his father – a week after Ido had been born.

Naftali was torn by Lilah's ultimatum. How could he leave their homeland? His parents, though, made it plain that he could not let Lilah raise his child alone in some foreign country. Inquiries were made and family friends in Boston helped make arrangements so that Naftali would leave with his wife and son: He would study in Cambridge. The young family then departed so that Lilah could elude her memories.

Naftali felt sundered and tolerated Boston only long enough to finish his bachelor's and master's degrees and start his doctorate. When a position as a lecturer in political science opened at Tel Aviv University in 1983, he took it and accepted Lilah's parents' offer to move into 3 HaGaon Street. They were as interested as their son-in-law in enticing their daughter to return home with their grandson.

But Lilah could not abide. It was not only that she had planted herself and their son in a congenial New England refuge. It was not just that her career was beginning to bud. It was the shambles, the emotional wreckage within her, left by her brother's death, that barred her from coming home.

Naftali tried to preserve their family. He journeyed to Boston two, sometimes three times each year for holidays or vacations. As he watched Ido grow, he found it insufferable to be the father he wanted to be from afar. He wanted to draw him back home, with or without Lilah in tow.

Throughout their separation, neither Lilah nor Naftali had broached the possibility of divorce. By unspoken agreement, they acquiesced to be suspended by forces of both attraction and centrifuge. The family remained bipolar, stretched between Cambridge and Tel Aviv, taxing their resources and assailing their emotions.

It was Ido who took the first step out of the conundrum, deciding that he would go back to Israel for good after he finished high school in Cambridge. His summers and vacations had always been spent with his father at 3 HaGaon Street, even after his mother's parents had died. Throughout his schooling at the elite academies of New England, Ido had kept his Israeli identity firm. Between lacrosse and archery practice, there were courses in Hebrew civilization and language at Hebrew College in Brookline. He insisted on speaking only in Hebrew to Lilah. Of his two sets of friends, it was his Israeli buddies with whom he was most intimate.

And he would go into the Israel Defense Forces along with them – and no fool stuff either. He aimed for an elite unit. Lilah's attempts to preempt the inevitable – she knew that Naftali's son could have it no other way than to be a fighter in the Israel Defense Forces – were abandoned the summer after his graduation. By then Lilah had had a good look at her son. He was now a man: tall and muscular, with a face that looked like Michelangelo's David. And like the biblical king, his natural place was Judea. She knew that he had to follow his heart home.

Petrified, but intent to be dutiful, Lilah accompanied Ido right up to the gate at Tel HaShomer – the same induction center where many years earlier she had accompanied Yonatan when he entered the IDF. After they had given up their son at the army base as they walked back to Naftali's car, Lilah refused his hand when he offered it. She was furious with him and didn't speak with him for months. But she, no less than he, had gone and handed her son to his destiny, ignoring her premonitions.

Ten years later Naftali still adored her and she still loved him and that manifest truth had brought them together, yin and yang, the previous autumn. Naftali had been invited to speak at the "People of Decision" conference at Yale University. On the concluding day, a freak blizzard had paralyzed the Eastern Seaboard and all international flights had been cancelled. Stranded, Naftali called Lilah to see if she was home and asked if he could take the train up and stay with her in Cambridge.

The five days they spent together in relative seclusion were as close to romance as any they had had since their marriage. Despite the incessant beeping of Naftali's BlackBerry, they enjoyed being together: long talks over wine late into the night, the museums, jazz bars around Cambridge. Lilah began wondering: Could this work?

Their interlude together was not flawless. Naftali, a public man, had his responsibilities. That Saturday night after Lilah had worked her contacts and gotten tickets to a dance performance at Symphony Hall, Naftali was called away for a meeting with a senior Palestinian official who had also been stranded by the snow.

During the hours he was gone, when she found herself sitting in the concert hall alone, disappointed and piqued, she realized that she had been studying him. She saw in him compulsion, his work all-consuming. She watched the way Naftali clutched his cellphone like a life raft, his eyes rising and falling between the phone's display and her whenever they spoke across a table. He awaited the email updates from his staff in Jerusalem like a general hankering for dispatches from the front.

"Don't you ever turn off anymore?" Lilah finally asked him, exasperated on the Monday morning before he left. Even her phone was ringing with calls from his staff, tired of waiting for the busy signal of his BlackBerry to clear.

Naftali said nothing in response. He looked up at Lilah, forlorn. She saw in him a longing and, perhaps, she thought, an opportunity of redemption for her.

Lilah flew to Israel in February. Ostensibly, she was coming to scout locations for the final shots of *Women of the Ports*. She had decided on Israeli venues to complete the collection. The ostensible was true enough, but so was the yearning that Naftali's Boston visit had inspired in her. It had lingered as had the question, "Could this work?"

And here she was.

The air hotter than it should be for June, Lilah sat on the dining room floor, clearing out the buffet and packing old knickknacks in newspaper. She drank from a glass of iced tea while reading an article entitled "Israel's Economy Now Owned by the Twenty," referring to the concentration of the national economy in the hands of twenty families that presided over empires consisting of real estate, banks, mining operations and communications companies. When she had come in February, she watched admiringly – and with apprehension – from the visitor's gallery as Naftali stood at the Knesset rostrum and like some Athenian orator, thundered against the Nationalist government policies that served the Twenty. Professor Naftali Kedem, a political economist known at home and abroad, was widely respected for his scholarship – and his resolve. Four years earlier, he had been elected chair of the fledging New Democratic Party – the government's nemesis. He was popular in many quarters. His adversaries, though, held him in disdain.

Although the parliament was brimming with business that demanded his attention, Naftali made time to be with Lilah during her stay. Over late dinners, during the Saturday they spent in the Galilee in deep conversation as they gazed out over Lake Kinneret, he spoke about the intensity of his life: the struggling against the extremism threatening the society, the growing technocratic mindset that had settled into the university, the disaffection and materialism pervading the nation's culture. He intimated that it was a lonely struggle and voiced fears of growing old alone. Lilah had the sense there was still a hope he was harboring, something about the two of them, a wish, a yearning.

Lilah, too, bared her soul to him. She peered into his distinguished profile, one that might have been embossed on an ancient coin of some Mediterranean civilization and began thinking that yes, perhaps things could be restored between them. She saw anew what she had once loved in him: his intellectual depth, his commitment to a better world. He was an estimable man in whom increasing numbers of voters were placing their trust, a unifier preaching hope – once the scoundrels in power were dislodged. Her son thought the world of him and in her heart Lilah did too.

But she was uneasy after that day in the Knesset, anxious as she watched Naftali turn toward the government benches and intoned from the rostrum, "The people of Israel will no longer be treated like a mindless herd. You have fed the elephants and left us the crumbs: a failing educational system, double-digit unemployment, corruption that engulfs us like a sea. The people of Israel will sweep the government from office," he warned to the uproarious howls and hoots of the Nationalist parliamentarians and their allies. He trod on the toes of powerful men. It frightened Lilah.

Ignoring the catcalls from right-wing solons and the summons of journalists swarming like hornets, Naftali had boldly guided Lilah through the crowd and led her to a corner of the parliament building in search of a moment of calm with her. Lilah felt her heart thumping as she passed through the crowd, her hand held firmly in his as he led her to an alcove overlooking Jerusalem. There, she found herself breast to breast with him, his clean-shaven face a breath away from hers. As she looked into his wise, brown eyes she said, "You are amazing Naftali. I am so, so proud of you. But I worry."

Naftali's eyes moistened and speaking softly, plaintively he said, "Come home, Lilah, come home to stay." Lilah looked into Naftali's face in the harsh light of the Knesset hallway and succumbed to his appeal.

She had finally buried her brother deep in her heart and Lilah hoped that by her return, she might repair the broken vessels of her life, her estrangement from Naftali and Ido and from the society that had succored her before Yonatan's death, before the world had shattered.

Those first days back, worried about Naftali's fervency and the waves he had begun to make, and wondering how things would be for her now that she had returned, Lilah took a walk each evening along the beach. Along that same stretch of sand, she had in her youth cast many wishes upon the sea. She looked into the blackness and saw the stars pulsing in the great expanse above and sensed that there would be many stations quick in coming; her homecoming would be eventful. She tried listening to the cosmos – hoping for a whisper about what lay ahead.

It was time to finish *Women of the Ports* and Lilah intended for it to shine. And so on her fifth day back in Israel, Lilah awoke well before dawn and with a thermos of strong coffee to fortify her, she packed up her cameras, lenses and film – she had remained a celluloid enthusiast, favoring the craft of her hand on the lens and the focusing of an image on film to the automated expediency of digital formats – and departed for Jaffa, the ancient port south of Tel Aviv, eager to begin the shoot in that venue.

At 6:00 a.m., wearing blue jeans and a work shirt, she drove along the shore to Jaffa. She set up shop on the Crusader-period walls of an Old Jaffa monastery that overlooked the water. Lilah tracked back and forth until she found just the right angle to frame passersby against the backdrop of the sea. She set up one camera on a tripod and hung another around her neck.

The day began to warm up with blossoming sunshine. The streets and alleys of Old Jaffa awakened to the shrill calls of the seagulls and the scratch and clap of sandaled feet on stone. Devout yeshiva students on their way to morning devotions rushed past Arab laborers sleepily headed for their workplaces. The tape-recorded calls of a muezzin whiningly summoning the Moslem faithful to prayers starkly reminded Lilah she was back in the Middle East.

Jewish and Arab merchants yawned as they rolled up the shutters in front of their shops. Traffic picked up and buses and cars filed up and down the roads. Nearby, an artist worked on a watercolor that was mounted on an easel, while a group of birdwatchers from abroad gazed through binoculars at flocks rising and falling over the sea.

Lilah went to work; nothing could distract her. Energetically, with unbroken concentration, she crouched and stretched and chased down advantageous positions like a panther searching for the perfect prey. Lilah captured moments on film by treating her subjects as if she and they were inextricably coupled, the only beings on the planet. Lilah worked rapidly but with great care and subtlety; often, the subjects she photographed did not even notice her.

There were others, however, into whose faces she would stare long and hard until she elicited a reaction of surprise, defiance, silliness or embarrassment. On seeing the camera aimed at her, one woman opening a tiny café waved Lilah away as though shooing a mosquito. An ultra-Orthodox man hid his face behind his hat when he saw Lilah and her camera, lest he become party, even unwillingly, to a violation of the biblical prohibition on making graven images.

When it came to her work, Lilah was uninhibited. She let the camera capture whatever drew her interest. Then, when the light and shadows were right, she would reach out and eternalize the moment.

It was a good day for shooting and Lilah fired away. Her favorite shot was of an old Arab woman gracefully walking while balancing a basket filled with fresh fish atop her head. She was carrying the heavy basket from the docks where she had been given the early-morning catch by a fisherman whose hard-life face resembled hers – her son, perhaps. She effortlessly balanced the basket on her head. The woman's face was furrowed by a clutch of wrinkles, but her unusual blue eyes shone like bright windows into a long-ago youth. The old woman had a long, thin nose, high cheekbones and a taut mouth. Her white hair was hidden by a long white scarf. She wore an ankle-length dress that hung on her like a sheath.

Lilah was shooting at a furious rate but instead of reacting to the camera focused on her, the old woman tranquilly maintained her pace, gliding forward in her well-worn sandals, her face expressionless.

Three rolls of film later, a little after 10:00 a.m. and the heat striking like a hammer, Lilah decided to conclude the session. Her denim shirt and slacks were soaked. She gulped thirstily from a water bottle and mopped herself dry with a towel. Hungry, she stopped at the little café where the reluctant subject had waved her away. Lilah's smile and apology for the intrusion won the woman over. They chatted amicably as Lilah consumed a breakfast of cheese *bourekas* and salads.

It was nearly noon when she returned home. Exhausted, she showered and decided to take a nap before developing the film. She was already in bed, the ceiling fan whirling ineffectively overhead – she preferred that to the mechanical frigidness of the AC – when Ido phoned to say he could get away from his base that evening and would be coming for dinner. She was elated.

Lilah spent the afternoon preparing an elaborate meal including her son's favorite dishes. In high school, he had been a member of Food for Humanity and had become a vegetarian. Lilah made the cauliflower au gratin and mushroom casseroles that were his favorites and hoped that Ido would like her gazpacho, a new recipe. She prepared garlic bread and an elaborate salad, stuffed artichokes, and an almond-slivered rice pilaf. She topped off the project –running out for the ingredients and then the cooking – by baking a carrot cake, Ido's dessert of choice for as long as she could remember.

Lilah counted the minutes from sundown onward, anticipating Ido's arrival. She wanted the evening to be a success. It was her homecoming, her attempt to heal the strains their family had endured by her estrangement from this place. Lilah opened a bottle of wine and poured herself a glass, nursing the chardonnay as she waited, listening to Leonard Cohen on the stereo as she idly thumbed through a design journal. When she heard the jingle of the keys, she dashed to the door.

In green fatigues, Ido loomed large in the door. He was smiling broadly and Lilah leaned up to kiss him. It was no easy task. He was strapping and had come straight from maneuvers, his hair wind-blown and his darkly tanned face unshaven. His mountainous body was hunched with fatigue and his uniform was sodden with sweat and dust. How gallant he looked, Lilah first thought. But then his visage startled her. The pose he struck, the features of his face recalled her fallen brother all too well.

Ido stepped into the apartment, put down his backpack and wrapped his strong arms around his mother, hugging her tightly. He was determined to make the evening as relaxed and loving as possible. In his mind, this was his place, his home, which he would now share with her. The geographic oscillations he had suffered growing up were gone and if his mother was willing to finally join his father and him here in Israel, he wanted to welcome her. He had written her that before she came. Their embrace was long and warm. Whatever anxiety Lilah had had about her first encounter with Ido instantly dissipated.

Ido sunk into the cushions in the living room, pulled off his scruffy, worn boots and lay back, letting out a slight groan. He moved slowly, stiffly, unfolding himself from his soldierly exhaustion. Lilah brought him a glass of orange juice.

"You look great, *Ima*," he said, his voice trailing off in exhaustion. "You look as though you never left," he said between sips. "So," he probed, "are you glad to be back? It's just like Boston here, isn't it?" he teased.

"There's no place like home," Lilah replied. "Dinner's ready, though you probably want to take a shower first," she said, reaching into his bag to take out his laundry, as she used to do many years earlier whenever he returned home from camp or an overnight. He pulled himself up and took the towel that his mother had brought him and headed for the bathroom.

Ten minutes later, he reappeared in denims and a T-shirt, refreshed. He was lean and muscular and handsome, reminding Lilah of Naftali at the same age. They sat at the dinner table and made small talk about relatives and friends as they ate. The conversation ebbed at times, particularly when the subject of Ido's army experiences came up. Whenever that happened, he diverted the conversation back to safer, less threatening ground. Lilah was relieved when he did so, glad not to know too much.

She asked about his social life, if there was anyone special in his life. He replied vaguely and asked her about her travels and *Women of the Ports*. He ate prodigiously and the wine relaxed them both. By the time Lilah brought in the gifts she had brought back for him from her photo shoots in Halifax and Mindanao, they were both in expansive moods.

At eight o'clock, as though programmed to do so, Ido got up from the table in time to seat himself in front of the television for the nightly news. Lilah cleared the dishes and put up water for coffee. She sliced the cake she had baked and poured the coffee, placing everything on a tray.

By the time she walked back into the living room, Ido had curled himself into the spot on the cushions that had been his niche since childhood. He was sound asleep, snoring. Lilah looked down at him with affection. Suddenly, though, she realized that he looked much older than the last time she'd seen him. A wrinkle was etched into his forehead and a bald spot peeked through the crown of his head. He had begun to gray at the temples, too early she thought for a thirty-year-old.

Lilah turned off the television, threw a light blanket over Ido and went back into the kitchen to wash the dishes and start his laundry. She knew he was asleep for the night. She was wide awake though and decided it would be a good time to work in her darkroom, the enclosed part of the back porch, and develop the film she'd shot that morning. She ensconced herself there, immersed in her craft.

Lilah preferred to develop the prints manually rather than feed them into the automatic developer. She worked slowly and assiduously, completing each stage of the process before moving on to the next. Little by little, the images began to stare out at her from the solution-filled trays. Lilah scrutinized the prints. The most technically proficient of the lot were two frames of yeshiva students hurrying to synagogue for morning prayers. Of course, they were unsuitable for *Women of the Ports*. She considered enlarging them to include in her private collection.

Photos she had taken of a Bukharan woman selling fishing tackle were very appropriate and Lilah spent time getting the prints just right. But the best photos were of the old Arab woman with the deep blue eyes, walking with the basket of fish on her head. The more Lilah studied the photo, the more she was moved by it. The old woman carried herself with great nobility, though the heavy creases on her face suggested she had known no shortage of troubles. Technically, with strong lighting and high contrasts, the three prints of the fishwife made them an excellent choice for the little remaining space in the book. Lilah dried the prints and placed them in an oversized envelope, to be couriered to Lucian in Boston.

It was nearly three in the morning when Lilah finished

drying the photographs and composing the letter that would accompany them. She straightened up the darkroom and checked to make sure that Ido was sleeping soundly. Then she sorted and folded his laundry and placed it in his backpack. Lilah went to bed exhausted but content with her day. Memories of Old Jaffa lulled her to sleep.

ೞ ❖ ೞ

Lilah opened her eyes with a start. It was already after nine. She had intended to fix Ido a big breakfast and see him off, but he was, of course, long gone. The note he left said that while he had to leave before daybreak, "I haven't had such a good night's sleep in months." He added, "you're still the best cook – and mom – around." A smile crested on Lilah's face as she hurried to begin her day.

She was out of the house within 45 minutes, clutching the envelope to her editor. The most reliable international courier in Tel Aviv was on the other side of town near the old bus station, next to which the foreign workers congregated and street merchants made commerce. Lilah found a place to park the car and then elbowed her way through the throng, trying to ignore the bazaar's cacophony of sights and sounds.

Lilah emerged from the sweltering humidity of the crowded street and was now grateful for the air conditioning that enveloped her as she entered the building where the courier service was located. As she passed the kiosk in the lobby, something seized her eye: Splashed across the front page of one of the dailies was a large photograph of an Arab woman lying lifeless on the ground, a basket of fish spilled beside her. Disbelieving, Lilah picked up the paper and stared at the photo. She then opened the envelope that she was about to send to Lucian. Comparing the image of the woman in the picture she had taken the day before in Jaffa with the person lying in a pool of blood in the newspaper photo, she realized it was the same person. But where Lilah had captured her in life, the newspaper photo showed her lying lifeless with circles drawn on her chest around three bullet holes.

Lilah walked away in a state of distraction, fixated on the picture. The news dealer called after her. She stared blankly at him and then realized that she hadn't paid for the paper. Lilah dug into her purse, found a bill, handed it to the vendor and walked away, taking no notice of the proffered change. She leaned against a column, reading and rereading the caption under the photograph: "Arab woman, 73, killed in Jaffa – 'Sons of Gideon' claim responsibility."

The brief story that accompanied the photo reported that an elderly Arab woman had been gunned down in Jaffa at around noon the previous day. The police had not yet determined a motive behind the slaying, nor had any arrests been made. Apparently, there were no witnesses to the murder, which had occurred in a secluded alley. The police were investigating a communiqué issued by the "Sons of Gideon," a previously unknown group, which claimed to have killed the woman at random "to teach the Arabs who the masters of this country are," and who assured a similar fate for all non-Jews and "Jewish traitors" in the Land of Israel.

The newspaper reported that the police were inclined to accept the authenticity of the communiqué, which was received even before the murder had been reported.

Chapter Two

Lilah thought of a photo she had seen of window panes falling after the airplanes crashed into the World Trade Center on 9/11. She remembered riffs from a Rolling Stones song, *Shattered*, that she had played over and over after her brother's death.

Lilah sat on a bench near the beach where she had gone to gather her thoughts after the initial shock of the newspaper photo. She was stunned, could not comprehend it: Why would someone kill an elderly woman carrying a basket of fish? What kind of threat did she pose? What crime could she have committed to deserve being killed? The victim, identified in the article as Fatima Abed, was unknown to the police. Her family claimed she had no enemies. She was born and had lived in Jaffa her entire life and had had a brood of children and grandchildren. There was nothing else distinguishing to report about her. How ironic, Lilah thought, given the silent glory she had discerned in the woman and had captured in the photos.

"I feel shattered, as if I am falling," Lilah wrote in a letter she did not send to Lucian, "as if I have been blown out of those Manhattan towers by a bomb I had no idea was there."

While Lilah sat on the bench and gazed out at the sea, a kilometer away, on Salameh Street in Jaffa, a well-built man with alert eyes, vigorous if no longer young, was getting out of his car. He opened the trunk and removed a worn, leather briefcase. Eli Zedek keyed on the car alarm, and then activated the vehicle's immobilizer.

Handsome, with olive complexion and soft brown eyes, he was dressed casually though neatly in slacks and a button-down shirt worn loosely around his waist to conceal his weapon. He moved purposefully across the street and entered the headquarters of the Israel Police's Central District. He passed through the lobby with the fluidity of someone who had been there many times before.

The desk officers knew not to challenge him. None were quite sure which agency he worked for, and he moved through the most restricted areas with a nod from the unit's top officers. Eli made his way with understated power, without pretense but with clear intent. The reality was that the quiet man with the look of Mediterranean romance had even higher national security clearance than the district commissioner himself.

Eli did not "belong" to any specific security service. His institution had no formal name, no budget other than his salary. His twelve operatives and the secretary, all with high security clearance were paid through the Shin Bet, the state security service. Tax records listed Eli as the proprietor of a small firm dealing in software and based in an obscure office in Holon rented by the Defense Ministry.

If someone was intent on learning more about Eli's work and followed him for a week, he would see that Eli, besides his stops at government offices and field sites, was readily admitted through the ring of heavy security at the Prime Minister's Bureau. There, he would pass unimpeded into the office of the premier's defense advisor, a man named Amos. It was to him that Eli Zedek, the specialist on domestic extremism, reported.

During the 1980s and into the early nineties, the Israeli security establishment, well-schooled in dealing with Arab terrorism, was confronted by a new plague: Jewish ultra-nationalists who responded violently to Arab attacks on Jews. "Not a bad thing," Eli had said to the recruiter when he was first approached to join the team investigating bombings in which the mayors of Ramallah and Nablus were maimed by a shadowy group of West Bank settlers. A few months earlier, the Islamic College in Hebron had been invaded by gunmen determined to avenge the slaying of a yeshiva student. The attack left three students of the college dead and scores wounded. There had been other anti-Arab violence, acts of revenge for attacks against Jews: vandalism, harassment, property destruction and threats, and the security establishment was concerned about the growing lawlessness among adherents of *Gush Emunim*, the settlers' movement in Judea, Samaria and Gaza.

When the anti-Arab vigilantes proved themselves coolly effective, high priority was placed on squashing any incipient underground that might be in the works. Plans to bomb the Dome of the Rock, one of Islam's holiest places, was discovered and derailed before it could be attempted. Had they done so, it would have ignited a firestorm against Israel. In 1991, when ultranationalists were rumored to be organizing provocations aimed at disrupting the Israel-Palestinian peace dialog, Eli's name had come up when the security services realized the radical Jewish Right was becoming a threat.

After completing his military service with the rank of captain, Eli made good on the promise he had made to his father and enrolled at the Hebrew University. While completing his bachelor's degree in computer science, he worked as a Shin Bet field agent and had chalked up some impressive achievements, infiltrating and breaking up a gang of Jewish and Arab criminals trading in weapons. He had been accepted to a doctoral program in cybernetics and was about to begin his studies when his superiors asked him to create a database that would monitor the Jewish provocateurs.

Eli was a patriot and vaguely supported the West Bank Jewish settlement movement. He felt no great regard for Arabs; the experiences of his family in Libya and the results of Palestinian terror had had their effect on him. Eli would not have chosen the assignment. The real threat to the State came from Arabs, not Jews, he reasoned. Then, at the end of February 1994, an event occurred that shook Eli badly. An American-born settler, a follower of Rabbi Meir Kahane and his outlawed movement, massacred twenty-nine Arabs praying at the Cave of the Patriarchs in Hebron.

After that, Eli agreed to accept the assignment.

The position evolved and soon he was developing strategies for the containment of the extremists – and he and his team were responsible for preventing them from realizing their aims. A cover was invented: a small, fictitious software house. From that, Eli and the team he directed became an autonomous sphere in the security services orbit. His work became his life with little time for diversions, and he spent his days living more in the shadows than in light.

Eli had an apartment near his office. During the day, he was in the field, in the West Bank, in Jerusalem and anywhere else in the country his work took him.

He spent his evenings in the office developing profiles of prospective extremists and modeling how and where they might strike.

Eli's life was a solitary one. He ignored best he could the vagaries of solitude. He swam as often as possible and read a great deal, mostly biographies and history. He visited his father and sister and her family most weekends. He set aside special time with his five year-old nephew, Lior, each week. Other than these diversions, he devoted his every effort to his work.

Eli had just finished giving Lior a bath and dressing him for bed when the phone rang the previous evening. The caller identified herself as the duty officer at the Prime Minister's Office. She informed Eli that there had been a murder in Old Jaffa and that Jewish extremists had phoned the E-Netnews website and the newsroom of the English-language daily, *The Jerusalem Post*, to claim responsibility. Given the nature of the crime, such developments, according to situation room protocol, were to be reported immediately to Eli.

Eli's pulse quickened whenever such news reached him. He felt a tightening in his plexus. Crimes of a sectarian nature – whether perpetrated by Arabs against Jews or by Jews against Arabs – struck a blow against the State. And the State, for Eli Zedek, was an object of reverence, nearly sacred.

It had been that way for him for more than forty years, ever since security operatives sent by Jerusalem had spirited his family from their native Benghazi in June 1967, hours before his father, Simon was to be executed for "Zionist activities."

Eli, a boy of nine, remembered that night: a sudden sharp knocking on the door of their home and the exchange of whispers between Deborah, his mother, and an unseen visitor – desert jinn, Eli feared when he saw the alarm in his mother's eyes. His mother urgently dressed Eli and Dinah, his sister, for a journey. He vividly recalled his final sight of her: her rouged face, pillowy soft, thick black hair that tumbled out from under a kerchief, small earrings in the shape of a *hamsa*, large, honey-colored eyes that led inward to some dwelling place deep and timeless, full of faith and full of love. Eli remembered feeling as if he were bathing in the warmth of his mother's eyes when the moment suddenly crashed. He and Dinah were bundled off in the care of the men, the Israeli agents, who would spirit them and their father to Israel before Simon was executed.

A "woman of valor" Simon would sigh whenever his late wife, Deborah, was mentioned. She had kept their children, their home and his secrets safe so he could go about his activities. She had intended to join them but the authorities had found her before she could and vented their rage by taking her life.

Eli, after he understood that his mother had been martyred and that he would never be immersed in the soothing amber pools of her eyes again, had a dream that would recur for many years. He saw his mother beneath a palm tree by a river as he was being swept away by the swift current. Her face was full of sorrow as she reached out toward him. Chariots thundered toward her. She threw Eli kisses as sentinels took her by the forearms and dragged her away.

The dream stopped haunting him once he resolved that Israel was his mother now and that he would never let her be dragged away. Like the Biblical Deborah who had summoned the forces of her people to overcome evil, Eli became a protector of Israel – he would never forsake her.

The dark sinewy youth from hardscrabble streets in south Jerusalem had earned grades good enough to get into *Layada*, the capital's elite high school where he excelled scholastically. Eli declined an offer to enter the army's track for gifted conscripts combining academic study with scaled-back service. Instead, he applied and was accepted into a covert, elite infantry brigade that "carried the fight into the enemy's territory." He became an intelligence officer in a unit that engaged in espionage and sabotage against Palestinian military installations in southern Lebanon. His unit spearheaded the Israeli invasion during the 1982 First Lebanon War.

During the second year of his officer's commission, at the age of twenty-two, he was badly wounded while on a mission "somewhere abroad," presumably in a neighboring Arab country. The exact nature of the operation would remain classified. Eli's father, once a dentist and community leader in Libya and reduced to being a hospital orderly in Jerusalem, speculated that his son had been sent to rescue other Eli Zedeks and their families. This in his eyes restored the family's honor. For Simon, as for others, Eli was and would always be a redeemer.

Eli was kept waiting. He had come to see Chief Inspector Mordechai Carmi, the head of the Central Investigations Unit, at the Salameh Street command, a stone's throw from the site of yesterday's murder, which was the matter that occupied him now. Eli assumed that Carmi was intentionally keeping him waiting to show him that at least here, he was boss. Carmi had built his career in the police command by dint of loyalty to higher-ups. He was a flunky of the kind that Eli did not suffer well.

"Come in, Zedek," Carmi said gruffly. "I'm sorry that you've been kept waiting, but I'm very busy these days. Why didn't you call my secretary for an appointment?"

"This matter is somewhat urgent. It's about the Jaffa murder. I believe that you received a call from Amos," Eli said.

"What murder was that?" Carmi asked in a low grunt. The mention of Amos irked him. Amos was Eli's colleague and they were in constant contact with each other. Amos barely knew Carmi by face or name.

"Of the elderly Arab woman in Old Jaffa yesterday morning," Eli said.

"Oh, right," said Carmi inattentively as he studied a document on his desk. "There was something unusual about it, wasn't there? You always do your homework, Eli. Why don't you remind me?"

"The woman was apparently killed at random, possibly by Jewish extremists."

"That's it. And that's why you're involved. I forgot that you take care of the Arabs," he said, smiling facetiously. "I am not sure, though, that this is one of your cases. It's probably a revenge killing – you know, an Arab thing. In any event, I have two good investigators on the case, and I am sure they will have it wrapped up soon. In fact, I've asked them to have a preliminary report on my desk by the end of work today. If you're interested," Carmi said, concocting a smile, "I'll have the secretary put a copy in the mail for you. Or we can fax it to you, whatever."

"I'll pick it up myself say around five this afternoon, if that's alright."

"Suit yourself," Carmi said dryly.

Eli left the office feeling he had wasted several hours of his time on a case that was probably criminal, not security-related. All he had to show for his efforts was the aggravation Carmi caused him and a police report that would probably provide him with little more information about the murder than that contained in the morning newspaper.

ଔ ❖ ଓ

Lilah returned home swamped by exhaustion. She crawled into bed, hoping to expunge the incident from her mind. She slept fitfully for most of the afternoon. When she awoke, the sheets were damp with perspiration.

It was Friday, nearly dusk. Naftali would be coming at seven, the first full evening they would spend together since Lilah's return and she felt aflutter. She quickly straightened up the apartment, took a shower and intent on looking of appeal to Naftali, she took the time to groom herself well, applying lotions and body creams and brushing out her hair. She chose her lingerie carefully and put on a svelte black dress that flattered her figure. She wore a long beaded necklace from Madagascar and matching earrings and placed a flower comb she had brought back from Vietnam into her hair. She daubed her neck and wrists with a jasmine perfume Naftali had once given her and alternately jittery and hopeful, waited for him to arrive.

Naftali arrived punctually. He brought flowers, Birds of Paradise, Lilah's favorite. He was freshly shaven and "out of uniform," casual in khaki trousers, a knit shirt and leisure shoes he had purchased during a recent conference in Barcelona. He had taken a nap. He was at ease.

They drove out to Abu Ghosh, the Arab village off the Tel Aviv-Jerusalem Highway where a friend of Naftali's, an influential Arab writer and New Democratic Party member, had a discreet *pundak* known for great grilled meats and fish and Middle Eastern salads. On a Friday night, with most of the family clientele home around the Sabbath table, the restaurant was visited by patrons seeking quiet and intimacy. There, Lilah and Naftali could have some privacy.

The head waiter led them to a corner of the restaurant behind a half wall, shielding the parliamentarian and his companion from the eyes of the other diners. Still, someone caught a glimpse of Naftali and after they had placed their order, an older man with a well-groomed brush mustache and walking stick approached their table shadowed by a bodyguard.

"Good evening Naftali," he began somberly, "and good evening to you as well," he said genteelly to Lilah. He turned and faced Naftali. "Do allow me to say that while I respect your perseverance, I hope and expect that your continuing efforts to unseat us will continue to be for naught," he said, a portal to their ensuing chat during which phrases like "malfeasance" and "exploitative practices" and "supercilious approach" were pointedly exchanged. Lilah promptly understood that the two adversaries were butting horns, that their polite articulations aside, this was not leisure-time banter but a salvo in an ongoing political battle.

"See you at the Knesset when we reconvene on the 18th," the man said after he and Naftali stated their irreconcilable differences concerning a law the Naftali's New Democratic Party was sponsoring. The bill would markedly increase the royalties that corporations would have to pay the state treasury on revenues from minerals mined in Israel.

"Have no doubt," the man said acidly to Naftali, "the government will maintain its policy and protect the interests of Israel's corporate community."

"I have no doubt," Naftali began, grim-faced and resolute. "That's consistent with your position of protecting the magnates and foreign companies even at the expense of the state coffers. Your stance is well known," Naftali continued, his tone denunciatory.

The man nodded. Lilah discerned on his face a small smile, sardonic with a dash of worry in it as he parted from their table.

Naftali sighed and absently placed several tablespoons of *tabouleh* salad on his plate. "He's a well-known lawyer for the rich, a free market radical. He's one of the leaders of the Nationalist Party and pursues the conservative agenda with undying zeal, even if it brings the country to ruin," Naftali explained across the table to Lilah. "The Nationalists – if that's what you can call them, they don't serve the nation, only their friends and themselves – they're still the largest faction in the parliament," Naftali explained as the waiter refilled their wine glasses, "but hopefully that will soon change."

As Lilah watched him tear a piece of pita and scoop up the salads seemingly nonplussed by the incident, she felt frightened by the arena in which Naftali battled. This wasn't kids' stuff, opposing the government, challenging corporate interests. It seemed risky, worrisome.

As Naftali dished out *labeneh* and *tehina* on her plate and his, he looked so natural to Lilah in these surroundings: walls of Jerusalem stone, the low ceilings and intimate lighting, acoustic music sung softly in both Hebrew and Arabic. A wisp of Naftali's hair dangled over his brow. Lilah brushed it aside and touched his face and looked into his eyes. Something welled up in her: deep affection and great regret, thirty years of a fractured relationship.

"I love you," she said, then paused. "And I am sorry," she lamented.

He understood, his eyes told her. He understood, they said.

The entrees were brought to the table. They settled into the eating and the conversation enlivened. Naftali spoke animatedly about a colleague recently returned from a trek he had been on in Nepal. Eventually, he realized he was doing all the talking and that Lilah had drawn inward. She seemed anxious, pecking like a sparrow at her meal.

"Is something wrong?" Naftali asked. His voice ebbed intimately, inviting her confidence.

Lilah hesitated before speaking. "Yes, I suppose," she replied.

"Well?" Naftali asked. He pushed away his plate.

Lilah began slowly, "I was in Old Jaffa yesterday shooting the last few photos for my new book and that old woman was one of the people I photographed. I took her picture just before it happened," Lilah heard her voice tremble, her eyes moistening.

"Which woman?" he asked, calmly. He removed an empty pipe from his clutch bag. He no longer smoked – it had been more than ten years since his last cigarette – but he still carried the pipe. It pacified him.

"The old Arab woman in Jaffa," she said, surprised by the question. "The woman who was murdered, shot to death by that terrible group."

Naftali looked at Lilah, reading her eyes. "Yes, I heard about it," he said matter-of-factly, then paused, waiting for her to express what was on her mind.

"Don't you think it's terrible? Her only crime was being an Arab."

"Yes, it is terrible," Naftali agreed. "Unfortunately, those kinds of incidents are becoming more prevalent, though it's been a while since the extremists have actually killed anyone."

"Aren't you upset about it?"

"Of course, but it's hardly a surprise anymore."

"How can a murder not be surprising, especially when it involves someone completely innocent of any wrongdoing?"

"Lilah, you've been away. There has been a history to all this. Extremism has been under the surface of things here for a while."

"And you don't find that completely opposed to everything this country is about? My parents must be turning over in their graves."

"I am certain that they are, mine too. But terrorists from the other side have been killing our people for a long time, and our fanatics are grateful for an opportunity to reciprocate. The extremists are, for now, a small malignancy, germs that feed on social ills. The surest way to stop it is to cure those ills. That's my central concern."

"It's just so unbelievable," said Lilah, almost a cry. "One moment this grandmother is alive, going about her business, and the next minute she's shot down in cold blood.

"I'm sorry," Naftali said. "I see that it's upset you. In a way, she wasn't so anonymous for you."

"No, she wasn't. She was special, even if nobody celebrated her," Lilah said, trying to keep her surging emotions in check. "She touched me. I felt her essence," she said, thinking of that moment. "It was just so indiscriminate, so unjust."

The waiter asked if he could clear the table. "Thank you, Sayeed," said Naftali. The plates were cleared, the table tidied.

Lilah waited for him to leave, then resumed. "Do you know if they've caught the murderers yet?"

"I haven't heard. I don't have any inside information, just what I hear in the press. It could take a while before they get a lead."

"Whoever did this should be severely punished," Lilah said forcefully.

"I agree. Of course," Naftali said, "but there is a whole set of issues to take into account." He spoke tentatively, wanting to tread lightly in discussing the matter. There had been an unspoken understanding that on her return, Naftali would buffer her from the jagged edges of life in contemporary Israel.

"I guess," she continued, "I really feel badly about the victim. I'd like to do something."

"Something like what?" Naftali asked.

"I don't know. Something human, you know. She must have a family. Maybe they are going to need money."

Naftali looked empathically at Lilah. He smiled with affection. "You want to reach out to them?" he asked tenderly. "You want to show, in some way, that the extremists do not represent the Jewish people?"

"That's right. I want to show them that Israelis condemn what happened…"

"Lilah, the Arabs in Jaffa are Israelis, too. His eyes glanced upward toward Sayeed tending a nearby table, his back to them. "With your Hebrew as rusty as it has become, his is better than yours," he said quietly.

"Yes, sure, I know they are Israelis, the Arabs here, of course. They are citizens, as they should be. But they are a minority and we Jews know what that's like." She thought for a minute, and then continued. "I want to make a gesture to the family," she said, "I want them to know that these goons don't speak for the Jews." She hesitated for a moment, and then asked, "What do I do? Just send a condolence card?"

Naftali thought, and then suggested, "You said you have pictures of the woman. Perhaps her family would like copies of them."

Lilah considered the suggestion, and then enthused, "That's a great idea," she said, "I could enlarge the prints for them."

"They might appreciate that. That's something they wouldn't be expecting in the mail."

"I could bring the prints to the family. You know, put a face behind the gesture. Yes, I think I'd like that."

The millstone having fallen, Lilah was relieved, enthusiastic, free to enjoy the evening.

Naftali spent the night with Lilah at 3 HaGaon Street. They drank wine and then went to bed. They made love with greater agility and passion than Lilah thought their middle-aged bodies could muster. Auspicious she thought as she lay in his arms, he sleeping as peacefully as a tot.

A new beginning, Lilah thought contentedly as the Tel Aviv sea breeze toyed with the window drape in her room.

Pleased with the reproduction of the print she had enlarged and framed over the weekend, Lilah drove to Jaffa Sunday morning. She felt that she was doing a good thing, and that perhaps this good turn would bring others.

Naftali had contacted a party member from Jaffa who in turn contacted the local *waqf* and obtained rough directions to where the Abed family lived. It was, he conveyed, not easily found and Lilah would have to inquire when she got there about precisely where the family home was.

Lilah squeezed through the rising tide of people and edged her way down the cramped sidewalk, holding the framed picture wrapped in gift paper close to her. Along Yehuda Hayamit Street, Arabs and Jews seemed to pass each without enmity. There were well-dressed Jews and well-dressed Arabs, poor Jews and poor Arabs intermingling on the street. There were people whose origin could not be determined from their appearance. How could such a senseless killing have taken place here?" Lilah wondered.

She asked someone where the Greek Orthodox monastery was; the Abeds lived nearby. She was directed to turn down a street. The old, dilapidated buildings there seemed to be crumbling before her and few people were about. Some children were playing in the street. Several eyed the invader suspiciously. She walked along the road past some young Arab workers unloading bags of cement from a truck. They stared coldly at her. As she progressed along the street, narrowing into an alley, the buildings seemed to draw closer to one another, casting an ominous shadow. Lilah felt like an intruder. Her pace quickened.

She turned onto another street. Although it was empty, Lilah felt as if a thousand eyes were peering at her through the windows of the buildings. A teenage girl walked out of one building, laughing playfully as she traded a comment with someone inside. Her eyes caught Lilah's. She gazed stonily at the stranger.

Lilah decided to overcome her fear. "Excuse me, can you tell me where the Abed family lives?"

No answer.

Lilah repeated the question, more clearly enunciating her words.

Still no answer.

Lilah felt at a loss, her eyes darting about in search of someone who might help her. The girl evidently had a change of heart, and though her face and tone remained expressionless, she raised her skinny arm and pointed at a rickety shack on the beach at the end of the street. She then walked away.

Lilah looked down the desolate stretch. The row of concrete buildings abruptly ended, and strong sunlight bathed the open area. Suddenly, the sounds of the sea, waves crashing, the call of seagulls, seemed deafening. The sea salt felt rough on her skin.

At the end of the beach was a small, fenced-off sandlot. A shack stood in the middle. Clutching the gift like a shield, Lilah walked stiffly toward it.

Assembled from bits of scrap metal, wood and stone, the hovel was supported by feeble planks and stacks of bricks of various colors. The windows, covered by plastic sheets, consisted of assorted frames and panes scavenged from other buildings. A television antenna poked out of the roof. A rusted, abandoned refrigerator stood in the yard and heaps of trash were strewn about. Gulls swooped low and pecked at the offerings. Cats chewed at an assortment of unidentified objects. Why the municipality had not condemned the structure was anyone's guess, thought Lilah.

As she strained to take in the various pieces of the shack, she saw an old man sitting very straight, almost regally, on a crate in the front of it. The man was dressed in worn trousers and a shirt and was conspicuous for the *keffiyeh* he wore. His hands held onto a cane wedged between his legs. He took a look at Lilah, then gazed in the opposite direction. Lilah was frightened. She wasn't visiting just any grieving family of strangers – that would have been hard enough. She was entering a different world – one in which not being welcomed was expected. Slowly, she gained control of her fear. She reminded herself that she had visited many places in her life, many more foreign than this.

The sun hid behind a cloud, leaving her feeling less exposed. She seized the opportunity to walk over to the shack.

"Good morning" she called out skittishly to the old man, her voice overly upbeat. "Is this the home of the Abed family?"

The man did not respond. Lilah repeated the question, and then without turning his head toward her or acknowledging the question, he shouted coarsely in Arabic toward the shack.

A teenage boy appeared. He was dressed like any other Israeli youth his age – in a tight-fitting T-shirt, blue jeans and Nikes.

"Hello," said Lilah. "Is this the home of the Abed family?"

The boy nodded.

"My name is Lilah Kedem. I'm a photographer," she continued. The boy seemed to be listening, although he said nothing.

"Well," Lilah began, suddenly unsure about what she wanted to say. "Did you know the woman who...?" she asked, immediately feeling foolish for asking the obvious.

"She was my grandmother," he said.

"I'm very, very sorry about what happened to her," Lilah heard herself stammer. "It was a horrible, inhuman attack and I hope that the murderers are soon brought to justice."

The boy listened impassively, silent.

"I met your grandmother on the day she was shot. Actually," Lilah corrected herself, "I didn't really meet her. I was taking photographs of people that morning and when she walked by me, I decided to photograph her. She was a lovely subject."

The boy remained wordless as he listened. Pain began to creep across his face.

"After I heard what happened, I made a copy of the photograph I took of your grandmother. I thought your family might want to have it."

Lilah clumsily held out the package to the boy. He looked down at it, unsure of whether to accept it or not. He seemed nervous but eventually took it and stared at the object in his hand.

"Go ahead, please, open it," Lilah said softly.

The boy slowly pulled the gift wrap from the framed photo and gazed at the photograph. He stared at it for a few moments.

He turned and slowly approached the old man, Fatima Abed's widower Lilah presumed, who had remained fixed in the same position he had been in when Lilah had first spotted him. The youth held out the picture and showed it to the man. The man did not turn his head, but Lilah could see him shift his eyes and glance at it. Suddenly, in one fierce paroxysm of movement, the man dropped his cane and snatched the photo away from the boy. Lilah looked on aghast as he broke the frame over his knee, then tore the photograph in two.

The boy reacted instantly. His face turned stony and he said to Lilah, "My grandfather is angry. You should leave now."

Lilah was stunned. She stood frozen for a long moment, her mouth agape, staring at the teenager and the old man. Then she turned and walked away hurriedly.

Lilah did not know that someone had been watching her the entire time as she stood in front of the Abed home. Sitting in his car on a nearby corner was a man, Eli Zedek. No new evidence or leads had surfaced and he had come to the area in the hope of picking up some clues about the case.

Watching her through binoculars Eli was transported. He recalled his mother. The woman he was watching looked something like he remembered her, noble and earnest. As he observed the righteous eyes of the winsome woman, he was flooded with memories bitter and sweet: yearning, lamentation, longing.

Eli shook off the reverie and refocused. He wondered what this woman, so out of place thought she was doing. He would like to have known what exactly she had handed to the boy. Whatever, it was, he concluded, the act was woefully naïve. She should have known her kindness would be met by the old man's contempt. Such gestures were for naught, their hatred for the Jews was boundless.

CHAPTER THREE

Lilah fled Jaffa, stung and humiliated. The rebuff was so unexpected. Such hatred was simply not in her frame of reference.

After arriving home, while she loaded the laundry into the washing machine, the affront she felt gave way to anger. As she dusted the shelves in the living room, the anger turned into indignation. Finally, after she had vented her consternation by sweeping out the apartment for a second time, she settled on contrived indifference to buffer her contused soul from the events of the morning.

Naftali phoned in the afternoon to ask how the condolence visit went. He had taken a break from stormy negotiations at the Finance Ministry relating to a land privatization bill the Nationalists were trying to bulldoze through the Knesset. He called to be supportive, provide some positive reinforcement for Lilah's having ventured further into the thistles of Israel today.

Lilah was loquacious. She described the difficulty of finding parking in Jaffa, the poor signage she encountered, and how she was surprised by the colonnades at the Greek Orthodox monastery, which seemed to her more in the Byzantine style than in the Greco.

"Lilah, but how was the visit? How did it go?" he asked again, ignoring the summoning of an aide telling him the negotiations had resumed.

Lilah stated the facts, describing what had happened. She made no reference to her emotions.

Naftali, his patience already strained by the business of his day cut straight to the bone: "It hurt like hell, didn't it?"

Lilah admitted that it had.

"You're angry, furious," Naftali half-asked, half-declared.

"Yes," Lilah quietly admitted.

Naftali cleared his throat. He waited a few seconds before

speaking. "Let me tell you something," he said, "I'm a dove not because I forget the malice that exists between Arabs and Jews, but despite it. The animosity is real and anybody who pretends that coexistence is going to come about through loving-kindness is a fool. Realism, that's what resolving the conflict is all about."

That was Naftali's message, a man's message. Lilah became aware of something she couldn't name but that he had evidenced since that week they shared together during the New England snowstorm. She saw it several more times during her visit in February, especially but not only at the Knesset or when he spoke to his staff or the press. Naftali had become a master of concision, issuing sound bites while looking at a timer on his wrist. Lilah didn't take to such efficiency and haste. As Naftali summarized in under a minute his experience in dealing with Palestinians and Arabs in general – spurned conciliatory gestures, dead-end negotiations and expressions of sheer prejudice – Lilah found herself tuning him out. She listened though when he said, "There's almost a hundred years of *kasach*, belligerence, between Arabs and Jews and the road to a new day is going to be rough. Don't believe differently."

By the time the phone call was over, Lilah had already decided how she would come to terms with the episode – by not dealing with it at all. She would consign her experience in Jaffa to oblivion. Fatima Abed's path never crossed hers. The events of the past three days never happened. Period.

During the next few days, Lilah worked at her desk by a window that overlooked the sea, cataloging the prints for *Women of the Ports*. The summer heat was waning and the fringes of the sea breeze that trailed into her childhood bedroom, now her workroom, was welcomed.

Lucian had sent her an email: "We are waiting, darling, for the last crop. Your port women beseech you to let them emerge.

We have scheduled galleys for the end of next month," he wrote.

"Not to worry," Lilah replied. Her inhibition about releasing the photos had faded after the contempt she had experienced outside the Abed's house. Still, she was considering adding an *in memoriam,* a gesture of simple respect for the slain woman, and she thought it best to send the photos of her along with the other Israel pictures she was still planning to take. "I will send you the final shots in a week or two, I promise. Just a session or two more," she assured Lucian.

Lilah always aspired to practice his credo, "capture the magic of your subjects. Show us the world in them." Lucian had imparted that approach when she first started studying with him. "If you must be so concerned about some far-off people's misery," he said in 1975 after she had evaded pirates and the turbulent South China Sea to bring back her Boat People collection on Indochinese refugees, "then do it like you have here. Artfulness in the revelation of truth," he exhorted.

She had aspired to do just that ever since.

As she sorted the port images for the forthcoming book, she found them to be everything she had hoped for – stirring, vivid, poignant. There were pictures of women sailors aboard Japanese whalers, herring dealers in Rotterdam, pubescent girls netting shrimp off a wharf in the Ivory Coast, Yucatan cliff divers, Malaysian craftswomen fashioning dug-out canoes, enlisted women aboard an American nuclear submarine and women drying sea sponges on Crete. Lilah arranged the photos according to the sections of the book: Struggle; The Life-Giving Sea; Wrath of Neptune; Serenity; The Endless Expanse; Adaptation; Triumph. The book was virtually complete. It lacked only the Israeli shots.

Lilah had settled on Acre as her next location. It was a port rich in history, now used by fishing boats and pleasure craft.

Acre would also provide an opportunity to see Michal.

When she arrived back at 3 HaGaon Street and was settling in, Lilah half-gasped when she found a note from Michal waiting for her. She recognized the handwriting on the envelope immediately. "Saw your cousin Kobi at a reception several weeks ago and he told me you were returning – for good. What serendipity! Have missed you every day since we got back. Would love to reconnect," Michal wrote.

The note caught Lilah off balance. A lot had happened since they had been friends, the closest of intimates throughout their school years. The year before they were to enter the army Michal broke away from her life, her family, Lilah. She took up with a clique of professed radicals who practiced an inchoate brand of anarchism, free love and general contempt for anything remotely establishmentarian. Michal moved in with some Tel Aviv Svengali and from virtually living in each other's homes and sharing almost everything on each other's plates, Michal suddenly dropped out of Lilah's life entirely. The last Lilah had heard, she left Israel and moved to France.

Over the years, Lilah had heard bits and pieces about Michal, how she had become a respected actress and artist in Paris and though Lilah had been tempted to look her up whenever she passed through that city, she had not.

Lilah wasn't sure if there was still a basis for friendship or if she could endure Michal's personality. The Michal she remembered could be passionate to the point of tempestuousness – though she was always loving, empathic and soulful. Lilah wasn't interested in having any unnecessary commotion in her life, now that she had returned home to rebuild. She resolutely put Michal's letter away in a drawer – for a day.

She fetched the letter the next morning, picked up the phone and dialed the number on Michal's letterhead. The palms of her hands were moist; she felt a tremor in her body, a tightness in her belly. But she took the chance just as Michal had in writing her. When Michal heard who was on the other end of the line, her nervousness was as palpable as Lilah's – at least during the first few minutes of the hour-and-a-half long call.

The conversation flowed, spring water over smooth stones. They reminisced, told each other about their lives over the years, their respective ups and downs. There was much laughter – even girlish giggling.

It was Michal who suggested Acre for Lilah's next round of shooting, a grand idea, Lilah thought. They planned that she would come up mid-week, shoot in the morning and visit in the afternoon, perhaps stay the night.

After she had hung up and thought back on the conversation, there was only one thing that dampened Lilah's elation after her talk with Michal. In all other respects, Michal seemed anything but capricious and impetuous. She sounded stable, moderate and self-possessed. But there was a peculiarity, something troubling she had mentioned though Lilah had not made anything of it while on the phone. She hadn't really absorbed it at the time.

As Lilah sat on her bed and thought back, she wondered what to make of Michal's comment, made in passing and without elaboration that she was married to an Arab man, an Israeli Arab. A Jew and an Arab sharing the same bed? Lilah pondered. Was Michal sleeping with the enemy? Was she still into slumming, just as she had after high school? Lilah flushed at her reaction. Still, she wondered about the integrity of Michal's marriage and the woman who had entered into it. The question hovered in Lilah's mind for a while, but withdrew as sleep came over her. She would see for herself the day after tomorrow.

Dawn was still an hour away when Lilah awoke, though she would have to move quickly if she intended to shoot in Acre in early morning light. She dressed and promptly left the apartment.

The roads were empty. By anyone's standards, it was still early. She sipped the coffee in her thermos and listened to Spanish guitar on the disc player. The mood of her phone call with Michal had stayed with her and she looked forward to seeing her.

Lilah had chosen to travel north along the Coastal Road. The sun had only begun to whiten the pre-dawn sky and the traffic streamed. Thirty minutes out of Tel Aviv she passed Zichron Ya'akov. There, the southern reaches of the Carmel range to her right, the road began to fill with early-morning commuters.

At first, the low rumble didn't arouse Lilah's suspicion, though she did look through her windshield for low-flying aircraft. She had already forgotten the noise when, a minute or two later, she noticed the absence of oncoming traffic on the other side of the highway median: an accident perhaps – maybe a break-down.

Lilah concluded that something was amiss when, a few minutes later, in her rearview mirror, she saw a police car, its emergency lights flashing, rapidly gain on and then pass her. A second one quickly did the same, its siren shrieking.

With the northbound traffic starting to back up, Lilah craned her neck to see what lay ahead. As the car crested a rise in the road, she saw a sea of flashing blue and red lights; from afar she saw that they were surrounding a hulk of some kind belching tall clouds of smoke.

An ambulance suddenly tore past her on the left, weaving between the cars. A little further up the highway she could see that the hulk was a bus. It lay on its side having broken through the median barrier in the southbound direction and now blocked the lanes to the north. All traffic in both directions had stopped – as much from the horror as the obstruction.

After a few minutes of immobility, some of the drivers ahead of Lilah parked on the shoulder of the road. Others turned off their engines, letting the cars stand idle. Lilah put hers in park and turned off the motor as emergency vehicles tore past her and raced to the scene five hundred meters away from where she stood.

Along with other people, Lilah walked toward the commotion. Three hundred meters from it, she stopped and stared in disbelief at the wreckage. The bus lay like a carcass. Police and passersby were boldly trying to dislodge the passengers. Even at this distance, Lilah saw that many of those who had been removed were limp or unmoving. There was an eerie quiet. Only the garbling of police radios and the screams of ambulances arriving and departing intruded on the odd stillness of the woeful scene.

Suddenly, there was the roar of a second explosion and a burst of light. The shock wave threw Lilah hard against a car. She felt a sudden blow and granite-hard pain. Then, as she lay on the hood of the car, she heard a whoosh and what sounded like metallic rain. Some of the people around her screamed as if the precipitation had pierced them.

Lilah slowly rose to her feet and holding her side walked toward her car. Her chest was rising and falling in a short, clipped pace. She came to the realization that this had been an attack. She was momentarily astounded – this could not be happening. The feeling soon turned into revulsion. Finally, she felt the determination rise in her. She reached into the camera bag in her back seat, rummaged around for an old press card, grabbed her Olympia and began shooting.

After vomiting a third time, her stomach acids churning – Lilah couldn't say what would have been better, having had breakfast or not – she was staggered. She had seen human suffering before, but nothing as acutely evil as this. The explosions had left the victims' bodies – of the bus passengers in the first blast, of their rescuers in the second – mockingly contorted. Arms, legs and fingers had been torn away, heads twisted and torsos ripped apart by the force of the explosions. The sounds were no less grotesque: the gravely crunch of shoes and boots on broken glass and shards of metal; savage screams, guttural groans, pathetic pleas for help. An emergency worker who was still standing tried to take command and shouted orders. He slowly realized he was calling out to the fallen: the first responders were now strewn along the pavement and road shoulders. The predators had leveled them with pernicious aforethought.

A smoky haze fueled by the rising heat carried the stench of burnt rubber and catalyzed explosives. A ring of putrid yellow smoke hung overhead. Beneath it, whoever had been and still remained alive after the first blast was now scorched and bloodied by the second.

Lilah took pictures: A little girl, miraculously unscathed, clutched both her doll and a woman, presumably her mother, lying inert on the ground. An old man in a state of shock with metal nails embedded in his neck and cheeks and one perilously close to his eye. These nails, shrapnel, were the metallic rain that had showered with enough force to rattle the chassis of cars a third of a kilometer away.

She photographed determined personnel, newly-arrived and valiant, replacing their stricken colleagues and attending to the victims. This was the Israel Lilah remembered, rising to the challenge. The emergency team acted unhesitatingly, with professional precision. The dead and wounded were evacuated within a quarter of an hour.

Lilah had shot nearly four dozen pictures. She paused for a moment to change lenses and became aware of feeling thirsty, parched. She was heading toward an emergency van to ask for a cup of water when her knees buckled. An alert police officer caught her by the elbow and eased her fall.

Lilah recalled little when she opened her eyes in the hospital corridor. She knew that she was in an emergency room overflowing with wounded. Doctors and nurses attended to patients, some conscious but most not, along the length of the hallway. Lilah spotted a clock. It was past eleven o'clock, hours after the bombing. The hours that had ensued were wrapped in fog.

A harried doctor checked a paper tag pinned to the hospital gown she wore. "There you are," he said, wiping sweat from his face with the sleeve of his exam coat. "Your x-rays are back and the rest of your lab work too," he said as if they had just been having a conversation. "Nothing's broken and the bleeding has stopped. It was absorbed by the muscles of your torso. But you're going to have quite a bruise on the left side of your trunk." He noted something on Lilah's chart and then continued, "We think you collapsed from a combination of dehydration, the extensive bruising and the general trauma. We gave you something potent for the pain when you came in, so you're going to be drowsy for the rest of the day. I'm giving you a prescription for the same drug to get you through the next day or two. I advise you to see your family doctor as soon as you can. Also, drink a lot of fluids – you're still very dehydrated... Nurse..."

The doctor withdrew and an aide came and helped Lilah into a wheelchair. She wheeled Lilah out of the treatment area to a holding space that was relatively quiet.

"Which hospital is this?" Lilah asked. Despite the medicinal haze, her thinking was clearing. She wanted to know what had happened to her and to the others.

"This is the emergency room of Rambam Medical Center in Haifa."

"How many victims were there?" Lilah asked.

"We received forty-three people here. I understand that another thirty or so were taken to other hospitals around the city," the woman said softly.

"How many people were killed?"

"It's up to twenty-seven now. Another ten or so are touch and go. But don't think about that. Let's get you dressed so you can go home."

Lilah felt numb, as if she was hovering somewhere off the ground. This could not be. As she helped Lilah put on her shoes and tucked a sheet around her, the volunteer asked who she could call to pick her up. Naftali was touring constituents in the Arava, the lower Negev. It would take him hours to come, once he was located and contacted. Ido was in the field and even more inaccessible. Lilah felt odd about giving the volunteer Michal's phone number. But who else was there? Lilah found her cell phone in her bag and gave the number to the volunteer. The woman stepped down the hall to make the call.

Lilah had been dozing when a hand on her shoulder gently roused her. She looked up to find Michal, more than 30 years older but utterly familiar. Lilah rose and they embraced long and hard, both of them crying freely.

"Thank you so much for coming," Lilah said once they had stanched the tears.

"Oh, come on," Michal said, waving her hand, "I am just so sorry that you were there. I still can't believe you went through this."

"I'm fine," Lilah said, but then admitted "Michal, it was the most terrible thing. I don't know how to describe it," she said in disbelief. As they waited for the discharge papers, Lilah slowly recounted her recollections in a jagged verbal stream. Michal listened sympathetically, comforting her. "Let me take you home with me to Acre," Michal proposed once Lilah's litany of horrors had slowed. "It's a lot closer than Tel Aviv, and I can look after you there."

Lilah fell silent as she thought. "You don't mind?" she then asked.

Michal's smile was a clear enough reply.

Lilah accepted Michal's arm as they walked to the car. It felt strangely natural to Lilah to be leaning on her old friend at a time like this.

As they were about to get into Michal's car, they were distracted by the sight of an elderly man attacking a young hospital janitor, an Arab, sweeping the sidewalk.

"All of you are terrorists! Murderers of women and children!" screamed the man as he feebly but wildly struck out at the worker. Bystanders pulled the man away from the janitor, though not before he managed to spit in his face.

"Wonderful," Lilah said sarcastically as Michal helped her into the car. "As if that helps things."

"People are angry. This is the bloodiest attack we've had in years," Michal said, her tone even, explanatory. She started the engine and turned on the air conditioner and radio. She backed out of the space and began driving focused, restrained.

"Do they know who is responsible?" Lilah asked.

"Various Palestinian jihadist groups have claimed credit. No one really knows yet. Ever since the talks between Jerusalem and the Palestinians broke down in May, people have been predicting something like this would happen."

As she drove out of the hospital parking lot, the traffic report spoke of heavy delays northbound from Haifa. "It's going to take a while," Michal said gently to Lilah. Close your eyes, dear. Rest."

Lilah already had, having trailed off into deep sleep.

Chapter Four

Lilah had little recollection of arriving at the house by the sea.

Michal had all but carried her from the car, through the wrought-iron gate and garden and into the house. She quickly made up the bed in the guest room, helped Lilah undress and change into a nightgown and then eased her onto the mattress. In her stupor, getting her to drink some fruit juice and swallow a few spoonfuls of yogurt was a challenge. With that accomplished, Michal let Lilah sleep, periodically checking on her throughout the afternoon.

Lilah awoke early that evening, sitting up long enough to have her medicine and a bowl of soup. She checked her cell phone. Naftali had left a stream of worried messages. He knew she had been heading toward Haifa around the time the bombing took place.

Lilah phoned him and, struggling to be coherent, told him that yes, his suspicions were correct. She had been at the site of the Coastal Road attack. It had been dubbed, Michal would later tell her, the Second Coastal Road Massacre, the first having taken place just down the road from the events of that morning. Palestinian terrorists had struck there in 1978: also a bus and also resulting in mass casualties.

"I'm coming to get you and bring you home," Naftali said anxiously. "Where are you exactly?"

Lilah hesitated before replying. What would Naftali make of her saying she was at Michal's home? Would he remember her and if so, for anything other than her radical stage and the scandal she had raised then?

"Where are *you*? "Lilah responded. He answered that he was in a hotel in Beersheva, that his driver had taken his car home for the night but that he would come by taxi to get her.

Lilah consulted with Michal; Naftali wanted to come and take her home.

"Why?" asked Michal. "It will take him at least three, maybe four hours to get here. Why run you both ragged in the middle of the night? You're fine here," she said, "it's our pleasure to take care of you."

Lilah assured Naftali that she was in good hands at Michal's home. "Michal who?" Naftali pressed. Lilah groggily elaborated. Naftali was confused – the relationship with the Michal he had known had long ago ceased to exist – though by the end of the call, his recollection of their close friendship began to come back to him, easing his concerns and he relented. Lilah hung up, mumbled a few words of relief to Michal and turned over in bed, depleted.

Later, after nightfall, Michal sat on the couch in the darkened living room waiting for the start of the television news. Her husband, Issam, had not yet returned home. She was anxious, worried about reprisals against Arabs. The orange glow of her cigarette repeatedly rose to her lips and she nursed a glass of wine, bracing herself for the ugly scenes she expected on the newscast.

In the twilight, as she tucked herself under an afghan in the receding heat, Michal gazed at the television screen waiting for the start of the evening news. She watched irritably as an array of television advertisements were screened, flashy productions that had cost a fortune to produce. They paid homage to the country's biggest companies and the offerings they purveyed, stepping stones to the "good life" being the subliminal message. Michal thought it sad how materialistic the culture had become in a society where the gap between rich and poor – no, rich and everyone else was growing daily. Michal yearned for the simpler Israel she had known growing up when people meant more than things. When had it slipped away? Who had withdrawn it?

The newest fare the television offered was the government's

infomercials presented by one of the Nationalist's darlings, a full-faced, wide-girthed apparatchik whose career had been spent as the head of minor ministries where he had concocted various schemes that served the Nationalist agenda. The infomercials were his baby and he was their host. Here he was, smiling broadly, heavily made up, explaining how the government's proposal to deregulate the building and construction industries would energize the economy and surely, surely provide more jobs. That no one but the affluent had money to buy new housing was never mentioned. That the new construction was targeted to be built on the country's shrinking beachfront and former nature reserves was never addressed by the minister. His pearly smile, iconic of the government's most public huckster, repulsed Michal. She endured it though as she waited for the impending newscast.

The newscast began with the anchorman grimly narrating the footage. Sixty-three people, among them nineteen children, had been killed – bus passengers, rescue workers and police. Well over one hundred people were injured by the two explosions – the largest number of casualties of a single terrorist attack in Israel's recent years. The first blast had demolished the bus and decimated its passengers. The second charge propelled long nails in all directions and was, as one police sapper described it, "the proverbial icing on the cake." The terrorists had succeeded in maximizing the number of dead and maimed.

The pictures from the blast site, the life-and-death dramas in hospital emergency rooms and the burials hastened to take place before the Sabbath were difficult to watch. Michal made liberal use of the box of tissues on the coffee table. She removed a bottle of *arak* from a cabinet in the kitchen and poured herself a glass.

The authorities had quickly arrested seven members of a terrorist cell who readily confessed. The self-described "commander" of the cell, filmed as she was led under heavy guard to a detention center was a woman in a long black dress and *hijab*. Only her steely eyes could be seen. As she was being placed into a security vehicle, she brazenly shouted in English: "As is Allah's will, the Palestinian people have avenged the martyrdom of our sister Fatima Abed. Death to the Zionists! Palestine for the Palestinians!"

The government responded to the attack with an iron fist. Curfews and closures were immediately imposed throughout the disputed territories and all points of entry for Palestinians into Israel were closed. Within hours of the arrests, the homes of the terrorists were razed. The village near Nablus from which most members of the cell came was searched from house to house by soldiers who were clearly not in a forgiving mood. All roads to Nablus were shut down "until further notice" by the Israel Defense Forces troops.

Israelis interviewed at random on streets throughout the country expressed a combination of grief and fury. Not a few cited the long-standing norm of Middle Eastern retribution: Someone, presumably the population from which the terrorists had come would have to pay the "price tag," as the more extreme West Bank settlers ghoulishly demanded vengeance. One settlement leader called for immediate payment in the form of the summary execution of the terrorists in custody.

Right-wing politicians were quick to pick up on the public's outrage. Dr. Eliezer Porat, the Nationalist Party leader with whom Naftali had butted horns the previous Friday night in Abu Ghosh, said that the government should consider military retaliation against Syria, which he claimed had trained and bankrolled the terrorists. Another parliamentarian from his party, locked in a power struggle with Porat, called for the breaking of all ties with the Palestinian Authority and for the abrogation of the peace agreements with Egypt and Jordan. The absence of a reason for doing so did not deter him from trying to outflank Porat on the Right. The Yesha council of West

Bank settlers announced that their response to the attack would be the establishment of five new settlements that would form a ring around Hebron.

There had been even uglier responses. Members of Rabbi Yehezkel Epstein's "Hebrew Fighters Association" activated unemployed thugs and other malcontents to rampage in East Jerusalem. Several Arabs in the Old City bazaar were injured by the hooligans, who vandalized shops, overturned pushcarts and threatened merchants. "We must gouge out the eyes of Amalek," declared Epstein at the height of the riot, a reference to the hostile tribe that attacked the Children of Israel in the desert. "We must eradicate their presence from our midst."

The cold-blooded threats were still hanging in the air when Michal heard Issam unlock the front door.

Lilah passed the night in deep slumber. When she awoke, her side still ached though the pain was less insistent. She got up and steadied herself and walked out of the guest room down the short corridor toward the living room. There, the glare of the morning light that shimmered off the sea through the large window blinded her. She followed the sounds of people talking on the terrace.

"Good morning," Michal said welcomingly as Lilah shuffled onto the veranda. She rose quickly to guide Lilah. "How are you feeling?" she asked.

"Better, I think." Lilah replied tentatively. She raised her hand to shield her eyes from the sun while clutching her side: She hobbled from the pain.

Michal led her across the veranda. Someone, a man, stood up and eased Lilah into a chair next to a table under the pergola. Once seated, Lilah turned her head and looked at the dark-skinned man tucking a cushion behind her back.

"Lilah Kedem, meet Issam Halaby, my husband," Michal said proudly.

"I've heard many wonderful things about you," he said with a warm smile, placing his hand softly on Lilah's arm. "I've looked forward to meeting you for a long time," he said. His voice was velvety, thought Lilah, welcoming.

"Thank you," she replied, trying to smile, her voice unexpectedly raspy and dry.

Issam stood over Lilah, his hands on his hips, his eyes peering clinically through rimless eyeglasses. "How did you sleep?" he asked, his tone inquiring and professional.

"Well, I don't think I woke up at all," she answered, looking around the veranda, trying to orient herself to the surroundings.

"Good, I'm glad. Sleep and rest will help you heal," he said. "I'll leave the two of you to rediscover yourselves while I put together some brunch," he added and withdrew, leaving the two women alone to converse.

Michal poured a glass of orange juice and handed it to Lilah. She took it and drank thirstily. Michal refilled it.

"I hardly remember coming here yesterday," Lilah said.

"You were barely conscious," Michal explained. "You really had us worried. You seem much better now," she said, smiling in the same affirming way Lilah remembered from when they were growing up. That look had always been a kind of gift, encouraging and strengthening Lilah's self-confidence when she was an adolescent.

"I feel better," Lilah said as she stared out at the sea. She sipped at the juice. "This is one glorious view you have here."

"Yes, and it is so peaceful out here," Michal said as she rose and tilted the table umbrella to shield Lilah from the glare and heat.

The conversation lulled. A clock ticked. The waves eased onto, then retracted from the shore. Lilah felt awkward. The company and the surroundings were so new and unexpected, an abrupt departure from the post-return routine she had been trying to establish. Yet there was something comforting and curious about being here in the presence of someone who had once been so dear to her but who she now had to relearn.

A large wall hanging intrigued her. "Who painted that?" Lilah asked. "It's really lovely."

"Thank you," Michal said, "I did," she said matter-of-factly.

"You did? I'm impressed," Lilah said. She leaned forward to get a closer look. But she did so too quickly, and a jolt of pain shot through her side.

"Slowly, now," said Michal. She got up and rearranged the pillow behind Lilah. "You last took medication eight hours ago. Maybe you need more now?"

"I think I do, but whatever I was taking seems to be too strong."

"Issam must have something he could give you. I'll ask him," Michal said. She explained that Issam was a doctor.

Michal went into the kitchen to speak to her husband, and Lilah sat back in the chaise lounge. She closed her eyes. It helped to be soaking up the sun's warmth and inhaling the smell of the sea while waiting for the pain to ease. Issam came out of the kitchen a few minutes later carrying a large tray, intricately crafted with Arabesque motifs. It was crammed with plates of salads, cheeses and omelets.

"Now tell me," Issam asked Lilah, as he delicately wrapped his hand around her wrist while looking at his watch, "on a scale of one to ten, how much pain are you feeling?"

"To be honest, my entire body really hurts. Is seven too high?"

"No, but that suggests that you're in quite a bit of discomfort," Issam said, his tone one of concern. "I had a look at that bruise on your side last night. I would think that you might be feeling a great deal of pain. I can give you something less dummying than the medication you are taking now – if you're willing to have an injection – and it will work a lot faster than a pill."

Lilah said that was fine, she wouldn't mind an injection and Issam headed downstairs to his clinic. Michal put a wicker tray on Lilah's lap and served her. "Please start eating," she said. "You haven't really had much of anything since the attack." Lilah nodded and took a few bites of the omelet and the salads. She was hungrier than she had realized.

"I hope you don't mind that we took a look at your side while you were sleeping last night. Issam was really quite concerned. He wanted to make sure there were no signs of further bleeding," Michal said.

"No, that's fine. Thanks," Lilah said, reaching for a piece of pita. She asked what kind of a doctor Issam was.

"He's a cardiovascular surgeon. He works at two of the hospitals in Haifa but he also practices general medicine a day or two a week circulating between a few villages in the Galilee."

Michal also began eating. The scene was placid, sea and sun and food. Two youngsters crossed the beach in front of the house and waved to Michal. She waved back, exchanging a few words in Arabic with them. "Kids from the neighborhood," she said to Lilah.

It grew quiet again. Lilah felt less out of place. The rise and fall of the waves and the squawking of the seabirds lulled her, and the warm sunlight and the caressing wind were blissful.

Lilah finished eating and lay back on the chaise lounge. "How long have you and Issam been married?" she asked.

"Fifteen years."

"You met here in Israel?"

"No, in Paris. I had been living and working there, and he was completing a fellowship."

"Do you have any children?"

"I had a hysterectomy many years ago, after a car accident, before he and I met," Michal answered matter-of-factly.

Issam returned. "Here we are," he said, and he proceeded to

rub a moist cotton swab against Lilah's upper arm. His hands, covered in thick, dark tufts of hair, were smooth and steady. Lilah looked out at the sea, trying to focus on a sailboat. "That's it," he said. "I hope it didn't hurt too much."

"I didn't feel it at all," Lilah replied. "You have a soft touch. What does it take to become a regular patient of yours?"

"Only need," he said, and sat down to eat his breakfast.

Lilah lay comfortably back against the cushion. Michal was reposed, her eyes closed and facing the sun as the wind flagged her long, loose skirt. Issam ate slowly, his motions deliberate and frugal.

It seemed so natural, Lilah thought. It was as though the three of them spent every Saturday this way. But the welcome she felt was based on a friendship that went back forty years. The last thirty years, in which she and Michal had been out of touch, were a blank. There were questions to be asked, pasts to catch up on.

"Do you still paint?" Lilah asked Michal.

"Yes, and I also sculpt in stone. I'll take you down to my studio when you're up to it."

Just then a glancing, almost mischievous smile crossed Issam's face. "Speaking of art, well, Michal probably hasn't told you yet," he said, as he spread some jam on a thick slab of bread, "but we own a number of your photographs."

"What?" Lilah said, surprised.

"Yes we do," said Issam as he took a full bite and chewed. He nodded affirmatively, drank from his glass of lemonade, raised a napkin and dabbed his lips. He continued. "We took an instant liking to your work."

"Issam bought our first Lilah Kedem without even knowing who the photographer was." Michal added. "Do you remember a lecture you gave in the late spring of 1997 at the *Haute Ecole de la Photographie* in Paris?" The words, in French curled off Michal's lips. Lilah realized there was an entire dimension to

Michal that she did not know.

She remembered being in Paris in the spring of 1997.

"I had the pleasure of attending your talk that evening and purchased one of the works right then and there," Issam continued. "And I brought Michal back to the exhibition that weekend. I had no idea she knew who you were. So this may be the first time you two have seen each other in three decades, but I had the pleasure of seeing you just a little bit more recently."

"I'm glad to hear that someone got something out of that lecture," Lilah said. She yawned; her eyelids suddenly felt heavy.

"You, my dear, are ready for another round of bed rest," Michal commanded, and she took Lilah by the arm and led her off the veranda. The thing you need most for your recovery is sleep. Isn't that right, Dr. Halaby?"

"That's correct," he said, as he began to stack the dishes. "You are very lucky to have escaped a terrible fate yesterday."

"I know, I know," Lilah agreed as Michal led her back to the guestroom bedroom.

It was late afternoon when Lilah next awoke. She felt rested, safe and protected. She stayed in bed for a time, listening to the wind chimes in the soft breeze that filtered in through the windows. The shades had been drawn two-thirds high; presumably Michal had been in to check on her. Lilah scanned the room. The shelves were filled with books in French, Arabic, Hebrew and English. Several of Michal's paintings were mounted on the walls, as were several photographs – including one that Lilah had taken of two *campesinos* in the Yucatan.

The surf whispered as it rose and fell. Lilah sat on the edge of the bed. The pain was much milder and her head clearer. For a moment, as she sat with her feet dangling, she felt as if the clock had been turned back decades and she was back sitting on the youth bed in her room at 3 HaGaon Street listening as the sea inhaled, then exhaled, then inhaled again. She had felt completely whole then, at peace. She felt the same way now, in Michal's house.

Lilah wanted a bath. She went into the bathroom and filled the tub. The shades were up and sunlight poured onto the beige ceramic floor and tiled walls. She slowly pulled off her nightgown. She was unprepared to see the large purplish blotch on her side. Her mind reeled back to the terrorist attack. She felt light-headed, then inhaled deeply and sighed.

Lilah ran the bath and settled into the warm water. Tension seemed to flow away and with her eyes closed, her thoughts turned to Issam. In her mind's eye, he was tall and well-built and stood in a pose at once authoritative and subdued. His face was broad and compassionate.

He was so vibrant, so magnetic and full of life. Lilah liked him. She liked him very much. But at the same time she was skeptical of her kindly feelings for him, his being an Arab. Lilah was troubled by her thoughts. Weeds of prejudice that she regretted. Politically incorrect. An attitude that had to be excised. But then, who had been the attackers that morning if not our generational adversary, the "cousins," sons and daughters of Ishmael? She could not disregard those facts.

Lilah thought of the turns that her life had taken. She thought of the trips she had made to the Ecole in Paris, and from there a three-month trip to Francophone Africa where she had shot a collection on marketplaces. She was delighted that her work had admirers she had not even been aware of. It pleased her that her work was displayed in the homes of people like Michal and Issam.

She stayed in the bath until the water cooled. She stepped slowly out of the tub to avoid a bolt of pain which came, nonetheless, when she bent over slightly to dry her calves. For a moment, it was overpowering and she nearly fell. Lilah lowered herself onto the edge of the tub and waited for the pain to pass.

When it did, she stood, wrapped herself in the towel and shuffled out of the bathroom.

Beasts, she thought to herself, shaking her head in anger, thinking about the attack and the attackers. Animals without souls in human guise.

She had intended to wear her own clothes, the ones she wore the day of the bombing. Michal had laundered and ironed them. They smelled fresh and clean and were folded on the bureau. But they repelled her now, as if they had somehow been infected in the attack by a pathogen. Lilah felt like burning them.

It seemed that Michal had anticipated that. She had placed a pair of slacks and a blouse, too small for her but right for Lilah, out on the dresser. Lilah was glad to have the choice, grateful for Michal's thoughtfulness.

The big discolored blotch on her belly and side made her feel washed out, so she found some blush tucked away deep in her purse and used it on her high cheeks. She took out an old mascara wand and drew out her lashes. She smoothed her lips with gloss and brushed out her hair in full strokes.

Finally, she felt more or less ready to face the world, ready for a proper evening with Michal and Issam. She opened the door of the guestroom and walked down the hall toward the living room.

The sound of voices – more than just Michal's and Issam's – wafted out of the room and Lilah stopped in the hallway to listen. She heard a hushed male voice reciting verses in Arabic. Lilah was taken aback. Her heart sank. She felt fearful, suspicious. What were Michal and Issam about? After pausing, the voice continued in the same cadence, but this time, the words were in Hebrew.

Poetry, Lilah realized.

She was still standing in the dark listening when Michal nearly tripped over her. Startled they both gasped and grabbed one another in surprise.

"You scared me!" Lilah exclaimed.

"And you frightened the wits out of me," Michal replied. "I was just going in to check on you."

"I'm sorry."

"That's okay, silly. What are you doing, standing out here like a little girl?" Michal teased. "How do you feel?"

"Better. I had a lovely bath."

"Did you sleep well?"

"Very."

"The pain?"

"I'm sore, but definitely better."

"You must be starved," Michal declared. "Come on, let's get you some food."

They circumvented the living room and walked into the kitchen. Issam was leaning against the frame of the other door leading to the living room, listening to the voices that stirred there. He spied them and smiled broadly, then turned his attention again to the others.

It was a large kitchen with a broad window that overlooked the front yard. A stove was built into a U-shaped counter and a table of crafted wood stood against the far wall. Cooking utensils and pots hung from a wooden lattice that was suspended from the ceiling. The walls were made of mortared stone.

"There's some chicken stew. It's very good, and not too spicy. Can I serve you some on rice?" Michal asked.

"Sure, but I don't want you getting tied up in here. You have guests. I can serve myself," Lilah said firmly.

"They'll entertain themselves," said Michal, lighting a flame on the stove beneath a clay pot. "Go ahead, sit down."

"It sounds like there's quite a crowd out there," Lilah half observed, half asked after she had sat down at the table. She looked up at Michal and thought of Michal's mother, the resemblance undeniable, and the many times as a child and teen she had sat in the kitchen at Michal's house.

"There're about fifteen people here. You'll meet them soon. I've told them about you."

"Friends?"

"Some are. Others are people we know more casually. Issam and I are part of a literary circle, Arabs and Jews. We get together every so often at each other's homes. People read their poems or stories or journal entries, and we discuss them. Mostly it's about Arab-Jewish coexistence."

"When did you start writing?" Lilah asked.

"I don't. Issam's the writer. Poetry. He's very good I think, although I don't pretend to be objective," Michal said, as she stirred the pot.

"He's a man of many interests," Lilah said. "A very special person it seems."

"Yes, he is," Michal agreed, smiling demurely.

The sound of Issam's voice filtered in from the other room. It rose with passion as he recited in Arabic, then in Hebrew.

Michal listened to the words, mouthing them silently. "That's 'My Father's Fields,'" she said. "It's my favorite."

Issam's speech tapered off, his words hanging in the air. "Does he write in Hebrew or Arabic?" Lilah asked.

"Both. It depends on what he is writing about, and on his mood."

"How's your Arabic?"

"Eh," she answered, "I never really got into it. I am much more comfortable in Hebrew or French," Michal said, stirring the stew. "When we talk to each other, we speak polyglot, all three languages."

Lilah was curious: "How did the two of you meet?"

Michal seemed almost to expect the question – and to welcome it. "Well, it's a syrupy, romantic tale. We met on a cruise on the Aegean. A long time ago – or so it seems."

"Love at first sight?"

"To tell you the truth, no," Michal said girlishly. "At first I thought he was a bit stuffy – too intellectual. He also told me he was from Israel, and the last man I wanted to get involved with was an Israeli. Believe it or not, it took several days until I realized he was an Arab. He grew up around Jews and his Hebrew is so good that there was no way I would have ever guessed he wasn't Jewish." Michal paused, placed salad into a serving bowl, handed it to Lilah, then continued.

"We took a few walks together on the ship. I was there with a former lover; we had gone on the cruise to try to salvage our pretty-much dead relationship. Toward the end of the trip, Issam and I spent a morning together in Corfu. I began to find him very charming, but decided that it wasn't the right time for me to get involved. When the cruise was over, we said goodbye and that was it – or so I thought.

"About a month later, in Paris, at an acting class that I was giving – I was on stage demonstrating to the class how a character from a Molière play should be presented. I remember really hamming it up, the class was in stitches – I stepped off the stage and headed toward my seat when who do I see sitting in the back row but Issam. He can be very determined and persistent," Michal said, as she ladled the stew onto the plate and placed it on the table in front of Lilah. She then sat down next to her. "One thing led to another, and within a couple of months, we were renting an apartment together."

"Romantic," Lilah said, between bites. "Are you happy?" she pried.

"With him, very."

"Is there a caveat?"

Michal thought for a minute. "There is no caveat. I'm very happy and proud to be with Issam and with our life together. I suppose I never expected to be an Israeli again. I am still readjusting to that," she said.

"I've got to admit that I was surprised to hear that you had come back to Israel. I mean, as I recall, you didn't exactly leave feeling enamored with this society."

"No, I sure didn't leave here with good feelings. But over the years, I realized that my radicalism had more to do with my personal evolution than with politics. But by then I had this very fulfilling, very comfortable life in Paris, and after my parents passed away, I had no real impetus to return."

"Why did you?"

"Issam wanted to. He pretty much insisted. He was homesick, not in a sullen sort of way, but he really wanted to be here – and it was contagious." Michal rinsed her hands at the sink, then sat next to Lilah at the table.

"Through my work, I became very friendly with some Israelis living in Paris. I started reading Israeli papers and speaking Hebrew again. I even got involved in a synagogue."

"You what?" Lilah was incredulous. This was hardly the Michal she had known.

"Yes, though not out of any religious convictions. I just felt like identifying. The hypocrisy of the European Left really upset me – it still does. I was still unhappy with the government's policies, but at the same time I felt that Israel was the home of my people and that we deserve a place under the sun. Issam, as it turned out, agreed."

Michal poured lemonade for Lilah and herself. "We came for a visit in the summer of 1990. I hadn't been back for nearly sixteen years. I guess I began to fall in love with this place again. Issam went through some similar things, too, though he was appalled by attitudes toward the Arabs living here and in the Territories. Anyhow, we went back to Paris, as planned. I definitely had to work through my own personal history, and Issam had his issues too. His family has lived here for generations. In fact, this house – at least the back rooms – was built by his great-grandfather almost a century ago. Issam was born and raised here, and went to the Reali high school in Haifa. Then he went to medical school at Hebrew University in

Jerusalem. So he was always surrounded by Jewish friends and Jewish teachers, and was very much at home with the culture.

"Things were complicated for him though. He had never felt completely comfortable with Israeli society because, well, the society never seemed terribly comfortable that he was an Arab. He was caught in the middle of this conflict between his country, Israel, and his people, the Palestinians. So after his residency, he applied for a long fellowship in Paris and ended up staying there afterwards." Michal abruptly stopped talking. "Listen to me drone on," she said, embarrassed.

"No, go on, please" Lilah said. "I really want to learn what life was like for you all these years."

"Alright then," said Michal and continued.

"We tried to put Israel out of our minds and resumed our very full lives in France until, well, I don't know if you remember, or even noticed. There was an incident, what we call in Hebrew a *lynch* in October, 2000 in Ramallah, two Israeli army reservists in the West Bank. Do you know what I'm referring to?"

Lilah realized that she didn't. "There were so many awful incidents, I blocked most of them out."

These two guys were doing their reserve duty, took a wrong turn and entered Ramallah, where Arafat had the headquarters of the Palestinian Authority. They were taken to a police station and a crowd, the *shabbab*, a bunch of pent-up no-goods went down to the station, took control of it and tortured and killed the Israelis. They threw their bodies out a window to be mutilated by the cheering crowd. There's a video of the whole incident. You can watch the butchery on YouTube," Michal said. She paused, and then took a deep breath. "One of the murdered guys," she said dolorously, "was the son of friends of my parents. He was married with kids," she said, shaking her head.

"It was then that Issam and I reached the conclusion that

Jews and Arabs were going to have to learn to live peacefully with one another and that the best place for us to contribute to that was right here. We came for another visit. Issam looked into renewing his Israeli medical license while trying to convince the security establishment that he didn't pose a security threat. They gave us a rough time – as you can imagine, a mixed Arab-Jewish couple of progressive outlook wasn't exactly their cup of tea – but said they would consider Issam's request for his medical license on professional grounds. He had great recommendations from professors and colleagues who knew him at the university in Jerusalem. I got in touch with some theater troupes here and made contacts. We began to have work done on this house.

"We went back to Paris and six months and several appeals later, Issam got his Israeli medical license back. We renewed our papers at the consulate in Paris, sold our apartment and our country house there and moved back here."

"There you are. We've been missing you," Issam said to Michal as he walked into the kitchen.

"I was getting Lilah some dinner and giving her a rundown on our lives," she said.

Issam crossed the room toward Lilah. "And how are you feeling?" he asked.

"Better. I slept well, had a lovely bath, ate a terrific dinner and am catching up on Michal's – and your – last few decades. What could be better?"

"Very good. Very nice, and how is your pain?"

"Well, to tell you the truth…"

He went down to the clinic to prepare a syringe.

Michal put a cake on a serving dish. "I guess it's time that I started acting like a hostess," she said, gathering the dessert forks and napkins. "Come on, Lilah," she said. "Let's see what you think of these people."

Moonlight poured onto the sea, the darkness paler for it. In the nocturnal blue, the terrace looked different to Lilah than it had that morning. The waves crashing a hundred meters away distorted the sound of voices in conversation. Lilah was disoriented, and her side began to throb. She felt the fatigue beginning to return and with it growing discomfiture.

A woman in her late twenties, her hair cropped short, wearing a sleeveless top revealing a peacock and snake tattooed on her upper arm was reciting Hebrew verse from a notebook she held tentatively in her hand. The poem spoke of hungry birds and sated birds. The woman's voice was gruff, combative.

Lilah considered the image: hungry birds, sated birds. She imagined scavengers swooping down on the site of the terrorist attack, pecking at the flesh of lifeless corpses and tormenting the little girl who was clutching her dead mother and the doll. Lilah felt a tightening in her throat, her breath growing shallow, her muscles felt as if they were being wrung.

Issam walked onto the veranda and slid into a chair next to Lilah, in the dark shadow under the eaves of the roof. He had something in his hand. The moonlight glinted sharply off the needle and Lilah instinctively pulled herself away. Pain shot through her body like lightning. At that moment, she glanced at Issam and was taken aback; he seemed swarthier than before. Her mind toyed with her perceptions and she thought of the frenzied mob mutilating the reservists, "No, don't," she cried out in alarm as Issam's hand took her arm.

It drew everyone's attention.

"I'm sorry," Lilah muttered apologetically. She was mortified, certain that the others had seen through her, the stereotyped drama that had played out in her head.

Michal rushed over, "Lilah?" she asked anxiously.

"I'm okay. I had some pain," said Lilah. "I turned my body the wrong way and was overwhelmed for a moment."

Issam approached cautiously, looking at Lilah's eyes. She nodded and he administered the painkiller.

"Everyone, I'd like you to meet my dear friend of many, many years, Lilah Kedem," Michal said once Lilah had recovered.

"We heard that you were wounded in the attack on the Coastal Road yesterday," a pleasant-looking man said to Lilah. "I'm so sorry," he sympathized. Michal handed him a plate with a slice of cake. Lilah was jolted by the sight of him taking the plate in the metallic hooks of prosthetic arms. Later, Michal told her that the man had lost his forearms in a tank battle along the Syrian border during the first week of the 1973 war.

"I'm sure it was ghastly," commented an elderly man. He seemed to be waiting for Lilah to expound on the experience.

"It was an absolute horror. Barbarism, premeditated Arab terror," Lilah said. She had been thinking of the man with the prosthetics. Her heart was weeping. Too many emotions swirled in her at once.

The woman who had been reciting *Hungry Birds, Sated Birds* looked pointedly at Lilah. "While one can understand your being upset, Ms. Kedem," she said in rebuke, "the act was undertaken by desperate people trying to bring the plight of their nation the attention it so deserves."

Lilah saw red. "Killing innocent people doesn't justify any ends," she snapped.

There was a harsh silence. Charged, conflicting emotions clashed in the air hanging there clumsily for a minute or more. They were a reminder, a symbol of a stalemate, intolerable and begging change.

The sound of the waves trailed in from the sea. The steadiness of the transcendent rhythm was sobering. It dampened the passions.

Issam ventured to speak in the uneasy quiet. "I wonder what you think of this," he said, as he put on a pair of eyeglasses and calmly searched through a sheaf of papers that were on the buffet near to where he had been sitting. He found the sheet he was looking for, and read in Hebrew:

Father,
Son of man needs to know
what humanity there is
lifting a stone against another
who speaks a different tongue,
and, for that,
must be smitten.

This land is ample, kind enough,
both brothers can
drink from the same fountain,
righteous in the sharing.

Is there no sky mural you might place
Over the Lawgiver's land
The Prophet's furthest, but closest to you
that might guide us
to share
water?

We implore,
the stones are heavy and
an evil wind blows here.
Make us warm.

The poem acted as a balm; it eased the soreness in the air after the clash between Lilah and the poet of *Hungry Birds, Sated Birds*. The conversation took a turn. More poetry was read. Gradually, spirits lifted.

The evening ended. The gatherers dispersed. Lilah went to bed.

Lilah had already settled into a deep sleep when one of the last guests to leave returned to the house. The man was agitated. He had just started his car when a news bulletin came across the radio.

Something terrible had taken place. On the road between Jerusalem and Ramallah, at the refugee camp called Al-Bakr, something awful had transpired.

Chapter Five

A B-area camp, Al-Bakr, was under the joint control – and suffered the parallel neglect – of both the Israeli military and the Palestinian Authority. With an official population of 273, Al-Bakr so closely abutted Highway 443 that as a running joke had it, the highway's maintenance crew was the closest the settlement had to municipal services. Wedged between Palestinian East Jerusalem and Ramallah on pastureland demarked by two hills, the Palestinian Authority overlooked Al-Bakr. There was little by way of taxes to collect there and it had no advocates. Until the attack on the village that night, the Israeli military had found no reason to bother with it either. It was docile and had caused no trouble. For all concerned then, Al-Bakr was a raggedy patch of misery fated to be forgotten.

Al-Bakr came into being in April 1948 when Arab residents of the area known as the "Castel," a contested high point between Jerusalem and Tel Aviv quit their homes in the ruins of a Crusaders fort atop Tel Tzuba. Jewish forces were battling the Arab Legion for control of the locale. The Jordanians had used the heights to cut off supplies being sent to Jewish Jerusalem from the north. The Jewish fighters sought to break the siege.

In advance of the anticipated battle, the Arab inhabitants fled. They settled for the night at a place known as Al-Bakr, a three-hour walk eastward and north of Jerusalem. It was an uninhabited pasture with three *shomerot*, small stone structures that farmers of antiquity erected so that watchmen could guard against the pilfering of crops and in which shepherds could take shelter while tending their herds.

In April 1948, Abed al-Kadr al-Husseini, the commander of Arab forces in the greater Jerusalem area attempted to consolidate his hold on the Castel after learning that the Jewish underground forces were planning to wrest it from his control.

He summoned every able-bodied Arab male in the region to join the fight, and the fathers and sons of the group that had encamped at Al-Bakr heeded the call. They left their women and children in the care of their elders until the Jewish forces were routed and they could return.

The Jews, however, took the mount. There had been heavy casualties including many of the fighters of the Al-Bakr group. And so, when five weeks later Israel declared its independence, the population – mainly women, the elderly and children – waiting at Al-Bakr to return to the Castel found themselves on the Jordanian side of the armistice line, subjects without suffrage of the Hashemite Kingdom. Al-Bakr was designated a refugee camp sustained by alms from Amman, later by allocations received from the United Nations Relief and Works Agency and whatever wages the populace garnered as day laborers on either side of the ceasefire line. The inhabitants also grew cucumbers, peppers and tomatoes for their own consumption on the ten acres of arable land triangulated by the shomerot structures. They lived from hand to mouth.

What had developed on the site was something between a migrant camp and town. Along the three badly paved streets, thirty-five ramshackle dwellings had been erected. There was an elementary school run by UNWRA, a mosque paid for by a Turkish charity and a community center maintained by donations from Sweden. There was a small grocery and a woman's sewing circle that sold embroidered cloth.

That was all, at the end of the first decade of the 21st century, that constituted Al-Bakr's resume.

Entry to the village was off Highway 443, the Israeli road built in the 1980s as an alternative route between Jerusalem and Modi'in. From a Palestinian point of view, the road links the villages along its length to the city of Ramallah, the headquarters of the Palestinian Authority and the relative metropolis that serves as an alternative to Jewish Jerusalem for commerce, healthcare and other services.

Following the murder of Israelis by snipers along the highway in 2002 and other havoc that troubled the road, the Israel Defense Forces closed access to 443 from the roads leading from Al-Bakr and neighboring Palestinian villages. Large cement blocks were placed at the entrances of these roads to prevent the passage of vehicles.

The cement blocks kept Palestinian cars and trucks from accessing 443. It did not, however, keep out intruders intending to enter the villages, including determined individuals riding motorcycles. It was apparently in this way that the perpetrators had entered Al-Bakr and engineered the devastation that ensued.

The much-awaited match between HaPoel Tel Aviv and Sparta Prague was being televised that evening and although Beitar Jerusalem was the home team, the rise of the Tel Aviv Red Devils from years of oblivion was being heralded even in the capital. With things looking good for the Israeli team, there was much anticipation among those gathered at Eli's sister Dinah's home. She lived in Baka, an incongruous Jewish neighborhood composed of nondescript apartment blocks inhabited by families of modest means interspersed among villas, formerly inhabited by well-to-do Arabs who ran from the city during Israel's War of Independence and which are today the upscale abodes of Jewish professionals and academics. The unused tracks from the old railroad station to Baka abut streets named for the Twelve Tribes of ancient Israel set out in herringbone fashion. Under the canopy of trees, residents go about their business with a blasé calm that has settled like low clouds along this seam between Jewish and Arab Jerusalem.

Eli had promised Lior, his nephew, that he would come to spend the day with him and stay for the big match.

The second period had just started when Eli's cell phone rang; the display showed it was a government number. Eli lifted Lior off his lap and gently set him down on the couch. He went into the master bedroom and took the call.

The duty officer at the Prime Minister's Office said only that there was a situation developing and that Amos had asked Eli to be located and that he stay available in case he was needed. Eli assured the caller that he would.

A second call fifteen minutes later directed him to proceed to Al-Bakr as soon as possible.

"You always have to leave whenever we're having fun," cried Lior.

"How can you go now?" exclaimed one of the guests crammed into Dinah's living room amid tumblers of black coffee, ashtrays full of sunflower and pumpkin seeds and cans of Goldstar Beer, "we're about to give the Europeans an enema they will never forget."

"It's a client, Ezra, a big account," Eli said. No one asked him for details, as they knew that he would provide none. Eli stepped past those assembled to retrieve his wallet and keys and to kiss Lior goodbye. The boy was sulking, his arms crossed across his chest. "Come on, guy," Eli said as he scooped up Lior and lifted him high, "We can't spend all our fun in one day." Lior finally accepted a kiss and Eli left the apartment.

Eli raced toward Al-Bakr. It took him eighteen minutes to drive from Baka to the Kalandia check post. Once he got there, he found that entry to Route 443 was blocked off. "Security and emergency vehicles only," the young woman, a Border Police officer, said nervously, clutching her M-16.

Eli identified himself and was allowed to travel the road.

Five kilometers later, Route 443, packed with military and emergency service vehicles, converged in the darkness as if drawn there by a magnet. Along the shoulder, ambulances bearing both the Red Star of David and the Red Crescent were parked at angles, jostling for position for ease of entry and departure.

Eli climbed the embankment from the highway as a steady stream of men in uniform, Israeli and Palestinian, took up stretchers carrying the injured from further in the woods. In the distance, Eli saw bright yellow and orange light –flames burning in the village center.

A squad from the Engineering Corps had entered the woods on foot and laid out a string of high-intensity lamps. Suddenly, light flooded a footpath. "Good," grunted an officer, "widen it enough for the evacuation vehicles." Like clockwork, the engineers began clearing foliage and deployed low explosives that reduced large stones to gravel with only the sound of a quiet "whoof, whoof, whoof."

Eli could smell the burning even at a distance. The stench grew stronger as he approached the ebbing flames. At the junction where the three streets of Al-Bakr met, Eli saw the houses that lined them in various states of ruin. He was staggered by the extent of the damage. Some of the structures were completely collapsed, some partially; almost all had been touched in some way. There was the smell of chemicals, explosives Eli recognized, that evoked grim memories of his military service in southern Lebanon.

Eli's handset squawked loudly. "I'm coming by chopper," Amos hollered, the rest of his sentence squelched indecipherably by the static. "Landing soon" was all that Eli could make out.

Eli walked through the camp disbelieving what lay before him. It was as if a firestorm had roared through the settlement. Inhabitants of the village, men, women and children had been shepherded by the police to higher ground next to one of the shomerot. so that the rescue teams could search for victims in the rubble that had been their homes. Two platoons, one of Israeli Border Police and the other composed of troops of the

Palestinian Forces, stood awkwardly, idly, on either side of the survivors on the slope. They mirrored each other, gawky stick figures veiled in acrid smoke and assembled without purpose. These impoverished souls who had just lost all that they owned did not need to be guarded and it was too late to protect them. How forlorn they seemed, like forsaken orphans, thought Eli. He looked on soberly as a military doctor ordered his troops to erect a second tent next to the one that served as a triage station. The second was needed as a makeshift morgue.

Officers were debating whether to set an inner perimeter of buildings on fire in an effort to halt the advance of flames that, like a river of lava, was flowing through the flimsy houses in its path and consuming them. Unless fire retardant arrived soon, even more would be lost to the flames. To make matters worse, and for reasons no one could explain, water pressure in the camp had dropped to a trickle.

Where the flames had been extinguished, rescue and disaster relief units had begun pulling away debris to expose victims. Troops, Israeli and Palestinian, were digging with shovels and their bare hands to reach those trapped in the rubble. Eli gazed in disbelief at the shambles, a community laid to waste.

As he stood facing the devastation, Eli tried to block out the cries and moans of the wounded. The scene evoked in him a sinking feeling, the feeling he had felt on the night that he, his sister and their father had fled Benghazi and his mother was caught behind. Here, seeing the devastation at Al-Bakr, he had been punctured again. It was wrenching, horrific.

An air force helicopter landed on the loading dock of the vegetable packing station. Amos was the first to get off. Short and barrel-chested, sixty years old with buzz-cut hair, he walked with a deliberate gait. He was an experienced veteran of many, many wars.

Their greeting was comradely but brief; Amos wasted no time. He started by handing Eli a sheet of paper, a "communiqué" received by police at 20:40. Eli read the text by the light of the helicopter's landing gear:

> *A Sons of Gideon commando unit, in retaliation for the Coastal Road bus bombing, executed a successful operation on the den of terror at Al-Bakr this evening. A large number of the children of Amalek were destroyed.*
>
> *The Sons of Gideon will escalate its scorched-earth program to drive out the Arabs not only from Judea and Samaria but from all areas of the Homeland. We will deal severely with any traitors, Jews, attempting to interfere with our work.*
>
> *Sons of Gideon*

Eli looked up at Amos and nodded his understanding. The reason he had been summoned to Al-Bakr was abundantly clear.

Eli and Amos walked through the camp and surveyed the juxtaposition of blood and fire to which Al-Bakr had been subject that fervid night. In the days since the Coastal Road attack, Eli had been expecting a new turn in the vengeance cycle. Security strategists had begun to think that none would come, that whoever had killed Fatima Abed was a sole aberrant who had taken on the name Sons of Gideon in self-aggrandizement. Eli was not convinced; he counseled caution. Now, with Al-Bakr in ruins, it was clear that the Sons of Gideon had emerged once again. Eli, though found little comfort in such vindication. The perpetrators had not been satisfied with just Fatima Abed's murder. They were engaged, it seemed, in a more ambitious pursuit.

"Where do we begin?" Amos asked. And then, as if in reply, the walls of a house they were about to enter collapsed loudly, striking a neighboring house and bringing it down as well.

"We've got to start reading this place, figuring out what happened here," Amos said, sobered and grave.

Amos wanted a briefing and sent for the officer in command. The commander was occupied, busy supervising the extraction of a child from under the remains of his family's house. The officer through an aide asked Amos and Eli to wait in the schoolhouse, that he would come as soon as he could. They were led to the building, scorched but still standing. They waited until lanterns could be brought and lit. The bombing had left the building, in fact all of Al-Bakr, without electricity.

When Superintendent Yehoshua Eliav of the Border Police crossed the threshold and entered the school, he was dripping with sweat, his uniform was soiled and his hands and forearms were lacerated. He had joined his troops in clearing away debris and removing victims. As the highest-ranking officer to arrive on the scene after the incident was first reported, it was he who took command, initiated the rescue efforts and summoned the other forces.

Eliav leaned against a column, exhausted. An aide handed him a bottle of water. He drank it slowly, his brow knitted in worry and thought. In a voice hoarse from smoke and shouting, he solemnly described the devastation. The number of fatalities was up to thirty-seven with no letup in sight. A junior officer who had joined them corrected the commander. The number was now thirty-nine. "There are over one hundred and twenty injured. The dead and most severely injured were in the structures directly struck by the missiles."

"What missiles?" Amos demanded. "Missiles imply that the attack came from outside the camp."

"That's correct. Our initial assessments point to projectiles fired from outside the camp perimeter but at close range, perhaps no further than the woods between the camp and the highway. We're combing the area now for evidence, although in the darkness it will be difficult to find the remains of the launch pads."

He continued. "The devices were fired with great precision and several were calibrated to strike clusters of half-buried explosives – we found a box full of material that hadn't gone off on the grounds of the community center. The canine unit has located the probable central cache, in the center of the camp, at the intersection of the cross streets. These fellows were very well informed. They knew exactly where and how to hit."

Eliav described his deployment of forces, coordination with the army's medical and engineering corps, the dispersal of earthmovers and cranes that had been ordered to the scene and his discussion with a Palestinian commander who had just arrived from Ramallah.

Amos asked about crowd control.

"That's been the least of our problems," said Eliav. "It's barely been two hours since the incident, and I've concentrated all my personnel and resources on rescue and evacuation. I had local troublemakers anywhere within five kilometers of here rounded up shortly after we moved in. Since then, everyone – residents, soldiers and police, both Israeli and Palestinian Authority – have been busy digging people out."

Eliav grew pensive. His brow knitted as he reckoned and his tone changed, growing tougher, gruff as he spoke.

"The electricity and telephone lines had been deliberately cut just before the attack and the water mains were damaged by precision explosions. The camp is now without water," he said, his voice coarse and cracking. "Soon, when the news gets out, we'll have trouble. You can expect a reaction, not from these poor people but from elsewhere in Judea and Samaria. There will be problems throughout the country," he warned. "We should prepare for contingencies."

In the quiet and darkness, lanterns casting their shadow looming large against the wall, Amos glanced at Eli, then turned and looked level-eyed at Eliav, an officer who had spent his career containing violence on the West Bank. Amos asked plainly, directly – the deployment of scarce resources and the object of their focus depended on the right answer – "What's your gut reaction? Who are the savages behind this – Jews or Arabs?"

"Look," began Eliav, "I would prefer to think that these were terrorists linked to Hamas or the jihadists acting for whatever demented reasons they might have. The thought of this having been done by Jews sickens me. This was an exceptional operation. It was not an honor slaying or the settling of accounts between clans or a show of one-upmanship between factions, but a well-planned, systematic, meticulously executed operation. Its objective was not just to rough up one or two Arabs. The intent here was a massacre."

He stopped for a moment before continuing. "This came in under our radar. We know very well when something is going on in the mosques or in the Palestinian streets. I understand that the communiqué reached headquarters within minutes of the attack. You asked me and I'll tell you what I think. Whoever the Sons of Gideon are, it's a good bet that they were behind this. Focus your investigation on them."

The briefing ended. Eliav was being pulled in five different directions, each of them urgent. Amos saw no reason to remain at Al-Bakr; he had seen enough. Everything that could be done was being attended to, and he was due back to brief the Prime Minister on the situation. What most concerned Amos now was preparing for contingencies of the kind Eliav predicted. Clearly, there would be ramifications to what had happened at the camp that night.

Eli texted his men to come to Al-Bakr. They would come as soon as they could but it would take time, each from wherever they were, at home or on assignment. As he waited for them to arrive, Eli continued to circulate among the rescue teams. He stuck to the shadows, consulting with the officers but standing clear of their men. He lent a hand where he could, though his mission was clear: find the beasts that had perpetrated this carnage.

There was poignancy, Eli thought, as he watched the Israeli forces in green fatigues working arm in arm with the black uniformed Palestinian police to free survivors. Between the rudimentary Arabic of the Jewish troops and the laborer's Hebrew spoken by some of the Palestinians, the Jews and Arab rescuers, formally adversaries, cooperated, collaborated without hesitation. As he waited in his car for his team to come and scour the remains of Al-Bakr, Eli wondered: Why did it have to come to this?

Later, in the late-night darkness as Eli and his team inspected the remains of the conflagration, he found it all maddening: the gall of the Gideons, their audacity and bloodlust. Eli's eyes prowled the scene, looking, searching for something evidential, a mark or token the Sons of Gideon had left, something forgotten, a slip-up that could lead him to them. He walked slowly, methodically around the fringes, circling and peering into the eyes of the villagers, probing for artifacts, pieces of the Gideons' material culture. His ears were attuned for a whisper or the sound of movement. He strained to catch even the faintest whiff of a clue.

Come on Gideons, talk to me.

Eli took stock as he walked. These guys were not vandals – they were planners, cerebral in their approach. This was an important trait to note as Eli began composing a profile of the Gideons. They were different from the hilltop youth, the wild gangs in the more feral settlements where they relished rock-throwing, graffiti-writing, and uprooting olive trees belonging to their Palestinian neighbors. Nor did the Gideons conform to the second category of extremists Eli had profiled, the "viscerals," a term he had coined for the slashers and stabbers, the extremists who acted out of a deep guttural pathology and struck randomly at any available Arab who came their way in the back alleys of Jerusalem or in isolated spots on West Bank roads. No, the Sons of Gideon were a different breed, wily foxes, calculating how and when they would pounce on and disembowel their prey.

ೞ ❖ ಬ

Lilah woke up feeling markedly refreshed. She had gotten seven hours of solid sleep. She rose haltingly from her bed but then, feeling her movements less constrained by pain, she took a shower and dressed.

When she heard the voices, Michal's and others' in the living room, she was confused. The literary group had long ago broken up, before she went to bed. She heard the television blaring loudly in the background and wondered what it was doing on at this hour.

When she entered the living room and saw Michal, it was clear that her friend hadn't slept that night. Michal's eyes were bloodshot, her face puffy and she was dressed in the same clothes she had had on the previous evening. The room was smoky from cigarettes. There were coffee and tea mugs everywhere.

Michal walked toward Lilah. Her carriage was crooked, carrying the weight of a sleepless night.

"What's happened?" asked Lilah.

Before Michal could answer, the television announcer's voice rose in volume. A spokesman was about to give the government's first official statement on what had occurred at Al-Bakr. At the podium, graced with the state's emblem, the cabinet secretary appeared. He looked exhausted as he made his statement, first in Hebrew and then in English for the benefit of the foreign press assembled in full complement in Jerusalem.

He recounted the details. The number of dead had risen to fifty-three with one hundred thirty-five injured. Nearly half of the wounded were hospitalized, primarily in Israeli hospitals. Most of the homes in the camp had been destroyed and the Palestinian Authority was arranging for the survivors to move into temporary quarters elsewhere under their jurisdiction.

The spokesman stated that the shadowy, self-styled "Sons of Gideon" who had taken responsibility for a murder in Jaffa late that June had credibly taken credit for this attack. The security authorities were considering all possibilities including the involvement of neighboring states, jihadist groups or criminal organizations in instigating, supporting or executing the attack. Initial indications, however, pointed to the Gideons.

On behalf of the Prime Minister and the cabinet, the spokesman extended the sympathy of the government of Israel to the survivors and to the families of the victims. The spokesman took no questions from the press but promised updates throughout the day.

The consensus of the commentators and pundits, academics and retired military men gathered around the table in the television studio was that the tepid statement represented the government's characteristic inertia in dealing with such affairs. Hardliners in the cabinet were undoubtedly going to blame the attack on Damascus, part of the ongoing tensions between Syria and Israel. They condemned as "handwringing" the concerns of the foreign affairs and public diplomacy ministers regarding the international fallout that had already begun in the aftermath of the attack. The ministers from the religious parties said it was patently absurd that Jews were involved in such an affair and claimed that any assertion that this was the case would only encourage anti-Semites. As always, the Prime Minister, as front man for the Nationalist Party executive committee, counseled prudence and an understated response to the Al-Bakr attack pending developments – which in his parlance meant taking no action unless and until the cabinet was compelled to do so by outside pressure.

During the long night, shortly after news about Al-Bakr began filtering out, neighbors, friends and others from throughout the Jewish towns and Arab communities in the Western Galilee had convened at Michal and Issam's house. The Halaby home was viewed as a safe house by people who wanted to heal the rift between Jews and Arabs in the aftermath of the Acre riots of October 2008. Back then, Arab and Jewish ruffians brawled after one of the former set off a tinderbox of latent antagonism by driving into a Jewish neighborhood during Yom Kippur. While Lilah slept, the bridge builders had congregated in Michal and Issam's living room seeking consolation in the company of like-minded people.

By ten that morning, the last of the visitors had left and Michal and Lilah were alone. Michal said she was exhausted by the loop of news reports, interviews, background pieces and commentary relating to Al-Bakr that was being broadcast. What had transpired was known. Only the identity of the Sons of Gideon remained to be uncovered.

"There's only so much of this I can stand," Michal said to Lilah as she switched off the television. The house seemed to exhale in respite after she did so.

"You know," Lilah said as they began retrieving coffee mugs scattered throughout the living room. "Since I've gotten back, I feel like I'm standing inside a ringing bell."

"That's about the way I've been feeling, although it feels like it's been ringing forever," Michal said. She stood in the archway between the living room and dining room, positioned in front of the large picture window. She was silhouetted in the bright light against the backdrop of the sea and the sky, their tranquil hues a sharp contrast to the mood of the day.

"When's it going to end?" Lilah asked.

"I wish I knew," Michal replied.

Lilah felt an urge to speak, but relented. Michal seemed ready to totter from sleeplessness. "Go to bed," Lilah said gently to her. "I'll finish up here."

Michal gratefully headed to her bedroom. Lilah did a good bit of the cleaning up until her side grew too sore to continue. Naftali was on her mind. They hadn't really spoken since she had arrived in Acre after the Coastal Road attack as Lilah had been sleeping off the pain and medication. She was about to dial him on her cellphone when he anticipated her, calling on the house line. He was relieved to hear her voice but had little time to talk as he was on the way to a special Knesset session convened in the aftermath of the Al-Bakr incident. He told her how worried he and Ido had been and that Ido had been calling him at all hours from his phone in the field, worried about his mother. "Tell him he can come and see me soon at home. Tell him I'm almost ready to come back to Tel Aviv. I miss the plants," she joked, speaking with more vigor than she had since being struck down on the Coastal Road. Naftali said he would get the message to Ido and that now that she felt up to it, he would come to pick her up and bring her home. Lilah was sure that Naftali was sincere but whether he could take the time to drive up from Jerusalem depended, Lilah knew, on developments.

Before they hung up, Lilah asked Naftali how he was. She was asking with no particular reference to Al-Bakr.

"How do I feel?" he repeated, "since Al-Bakr? Well, somebody wrote a play – *Cat on a Hot Tin Roof*. I have no idea what the play is about, but that's the way I've been feeling for the last eleven hours, like I'm walking on coals."

He had to hang up; an aide was tugging at his elbow. He promised that he would come the next day to pick her up and bring her back to 3 HaGaon Street, "barring complications," they agreed.

Lilah was glad to be feeling so much better. A breeze had

picked up off the sea and entered the open windows along with the treble warbling of a bird. She was pleased for the company. All the years she had lived abroad, she had always been grateful for the soothing sounds of nature. These had made her feel less alone, less solitary an interloper in the many places she had ventured.

It had been five days since she had looked at her email and in the nook off the kitchen where Michal kept her computer, Lilah logged into her account and took stock of the scores of messages that had accumulated. She opened the latest arrival, an email time-stamped at 11:16 that morning. It was from the Herzliya Sinfonietta. She had forgotten that she had a ticket to watch them perform a Prokofiev concert that evening. But even if she had been well enough, there would have been no performance to attend. "Due to the great tragedy that has befallen the people of Al-Bakr and in light of the events that preceded it, we, the musicians of the Sinfonietta do not feel that we can perform as scheduled this evening. We grieve for the dead and injured. We are deeply concerned for the future of our society...."

A similar message was contained in *The Arts Community Circular* advising members that events scheduled for the next three days would be rescheduled "in honor of the dead and injured of the Coastal Road Massacre and Al-Bakr. We advise members to use this period to search their souls. Israel is on fire...." The newsletter of the neighborhood association where 3 HaGaon Street was located in northwestern Tel Aviv sent out a message informing readers that contributions of canned and packaged food and clothing on behalf of the people of Al-Bakr could be made at the community center.

As Lilah tried to digest what had happened at Al-Bakr, she found some comfort in these expressions of sorrow and dismay, the desire to help, the reaching out. Civil voices in uncivil times.

She opened emails and discovered that people were worried about her. Messages of concern had arrived from good friends in Sydney, a former student in Nairobi, a curator who had exhibited her work in Strasbourg. "I can't imagine you in the middle of all that rancor," wrote a colleague from Singapore. "We have no concept of what it's like to live with so much violence. But we do know you, Lilah, and your soul is certainly getting a bruising. We are worried. Write please or call us at any hour. Please do let us know that all is well with you."

It was nearly three when Lilah finished answering the emails. She sent brief messages to those who had written her, meant to ease their minds and assure them that she was safe. She decided not to reveal that she had been present at the Coastal Road attack. She needed some time, wanted some perspective before deciding if she wanted others to know the horror of what she had witnessed. She would decide later how, if at all, to use the photos she had shot that morning.

Lilah couldn't be perfunctory with Lucian. He had sent three email messages and, Lilah discovered on her cell phone log, had called twice, leaving messages dizzy with worry. "If I do not hear from you by today," he wrote in a late-night message, his time, sent several hours earlier, "I shall book a ticket and upon finding you (may it be so), I will set about scolding you for giving us such a fright. I mean, really Lilah. Write or call forthwith, please!"

Lilah could hear his booming voice in the text and imagined his face purple with worry and frustration. She sat across the computer monitor and wrote cathartically to him:

Lucian,

I am ever so sorry that I have been out of touch these past few days. These have been among the worst days of my life and also among the most compelling.

As you feared, all this turmoil in Israel has directly touched me. I was present and became a victim of the terrorist bombing on the Coastal Road. No doubt you have heard about it.

After that experience and now after learning about last night's tragedy, I feel even surer that my coming home was right for me. I feel strongly that I am needed here – although I don't yet know how.

Taking part in the healing will, I believe, help me recover from the demons of my past. Something must change deeply in this land and while I don't yet understand it all, I know that I must help. I do not know when we will recover. But I know my people, and we will.

I promise to write regularly, short messages maybe, but I'll keep you informed. The photos from Jaffa will be couriered to you in the next few days – I promise. Once they arrive, don't wait for photos from other Israeli ports as I don't know when I can get to them. Go ahead and put the book to bed.

I promise to take care of myself. I'll call you soon.

Lilah

By the time she had finished, the sun had begun to drop into the sea and daylight was waning. Lilah felt tired, went to the guestroom and tumbled into deep sleep.

It was dark when Lilah awoke, nearly eight according to the clock on the nightstand. The smell of pasta sauce, richly-spiced, filtered into her room. Lilah tidied herself up and headed for the kitchen where she found Michal busy preparing dinner.

"You look like you've returned to the living," said Lilah as she walked over to Michal by the stove and placed her arm around her. "Feeling better?"

"I feel like I slept for a week," Michal said as she sipped from a glass of wine. There was the sound of music playing low, Aaron Copland off the sound system in the living room.

Lilah made salad while Michal tended to the sauce and pasta. They set the table for three. Issam had called to say he was on his way back from the hospital in Petach Tikva and would be home soon. He had left for Beilinson before dawn when a colleague phoned and told him that the emergency room at the hospital was overflowing with wounded from Al-Bakr. As an Arabic-speaker and surgeon, his assistance would be welcomed.

A short time later, Michal heard his car pull up. She rushed to the front door, opened it and hugged her husband close to her. He quickly conjured up a smile, albeit a sad one and entered the house. He looked exhausted, as if he had been pummeled.

Issam slouched formlessly in a kitchen chair. "Can't describe it," he said when Michal asked how things had gone at the hospital. He wanted to know what the latest developments were.

Michal and Lilah began to tell him in telegraphic recitation. All the residents of Al-Bakr had been accounted for. A massive manhunt was on for the attackers on both sides of the Green Line.

Then, in more detail, they related that Prof. Shmuel Lustinger, Israel's aged president, a child of the Holocaust, a dedicated humanist often at odds with the Nationalist government, had furiously condemned the attack. Despite the government's caution against him doing so, he had visited the Israeli Arab city of Uhm al-Fahm, an epicenter of solidarity with the Palestinians, and expressed his sympathy for the victims and his determination that the well-being of both Jews and Arabs would be guaranteed without distinction by the State, its institutions and forces. While the Nationalist press had issued a statement indirectly criticizing the visit as "liable to be misunderstood by our enemies," one of their own, the Speaker of the Knesset, a moderate who increasingly dissented from the Nationalist party platform, expressed support for the president's mission. Condemnations of the attack were also made by the president of the Supreme Court, the state comptroller and the army chief of staff.

The events at Al-Bakr had shaken, if only briefly, a significant part of the Israeli public from "our gelatinous condition," as one progressive news commentator described it. There had been a spontaneous outpouring from the public. The aid agencies had been flooded with contributions to a special fund dedicated to the rehabilitation of Al-Bakr's victims. The press noted that public assemblies to commemorate the victims of both the Coastal Road and Al-Bakr attacks had been scheduled by citizen groups in Carmiel, Raanana, Mevasseret Tzion, Ashdod and Omer.

But as another analyst noted on the evening news, the assault on Al-Bakr was "a cluster bomb that had hurled bomblets throughout Israel and the Palestinian territories." After the police arrested the spiritual leader of the Jewish extremists, Rabbi Yehezkel Epstein, on charges of incitement after he praised the Sons of Gideon, right-wing Jewish activists confronted stone-throwing Palestinian protestors in Silwan and Issawiya. So frenzied grew the fighting that the seasoned Border Police units on the scene had to call for reinforcements to quell the unrest. There was rioting in Arab East Jerusalem and heightened tension in the mixed Jewish-Arab cities and neighborhoods – Jaffa, Lod and Acre. Contacts on both sides were being pursued by the local authorities to keep the cauldrons from boiling over.

In Israeli Arab towns, youth had taken to the streets chanting nationalist slogans, raising Palestinian flags and, in at least two cases, "Death to the Jews" was reportedly heard. Arab community leaders noted that the recent events were trying the patience of their constituents. A strike of all municipal authorities in the minority sector was declared. Members of the Knesset from the radical Arab lists were spewing anti-Israel rhetoric any place they were given a forum.

Journalists in the West Bank reported that Palestinian demonstrators were burning tires and hurling rocks and firebombs at Israeli soldiers and civilians throughout Area C, those parts of the territory under Israeli control. Palestinian forces were having a hard time maintaining order elsewhere in Judea and Samaria and the Israeli military advisedly kept a low profile there.

Such was the news of the day, Michal and Lilah recounted.

The conversation drifted to other subjects. Issam revived slowly over dinner and once they had finished eating, Michal, Lilah and he lingered at the table. They spoke softly and in the gray tones of hurt and worry. Issam told snippets of what he had seen and done at the hospital the day – survivors fighting for their lives, breaking the news of death or permanent injury to relatives who had themselves been battered by what had been done at Al-Bakr. There had been some affirming moments as well, Issam related: The spirit of cooperation among the medical staff, both Jews and Arabs, the professional regard he had been accorded, advising families that two patients who had been believed to be mortally wounded had come around.

The subject of the Coastal Road attack came up and it was apparent that the time had come for Lilah to talk about it. "Don't leave it within," said Issam, looking enormously tired but anxious to have Lilah rid herself of the trauma. "Come now," he said soothingly, "You must share it. It will be worse if you don't."

Lilah, slowly at first but then in a flurry spoke about the experience. It had been as if she had seen "blood leaking from a yellow sky." she said with disgust, her eyes teary yet incensed.

Lilah told them about how the murder of Fatima Abed had

touched her personally. She related how she had found her an extraordinary subject to photograph, a port woman whose bearing suggested the timelessness of the sea. When she saw the splendor of the woman's image peering up at her in the developing tray of her darkroom, she had no premonition about what she would find on the front page of the newspaper the next morning.

Lilah told Issam and Michal about how earnestly she had wanted to reach out to the victim's family, a simple human gesture. She bitterly related her shock, then outrage when Fatima Abed's widower rejected her gesture in a hateful rebuff, "being a Jew had never been as stinging for me as it was that afternoon," she expressed.

"That there is bad blood between Arabs and Jews is news for you?" Michal asked.

As the evening grew late and the subject of Al-Bakr resurfaced, Lilah said of the Sons of Gideon: "I never expected I would see such evil here. Where did these monsters come from? Did they really crop up among us? I don't know how anyone calling himself a Jew could be involved in anything like this," she said.

"No people, not Jews and not Arabs – no one – is immune from this blind hatred for the other," Issam said resolutely. "Such fanaticism feeds on social, economic, psychological conditions, what the philosophers call alienation," he averred, his voice rising. Of this, he was absolutely sure. He cleared his throat, changed his tone and continued.

"When you have so many people disappointed – the economy, the growing conservatism, the breakdown in the educational system, the extremism – and worried about whether their children have a future in this kind of environment, all the tension, all the pressure – produces discontent. When faced with all this, people crave the known, they want the familiar. And the youth? What kind of role models do they have? The corrupt politicians? The super-rich? The idiots on the celebrity shows? The demagogues, whether they are Arabs or Jews, feed on the alienation. These conditions make it easy for the fanatics to make pay dirt of hatred, especially of the other, the stranger."

Issam continued, his voice tinged with resentment. "The religion I was raised in, Islam, which has so much good, has been hijacked by the simple-minded, the cynics, maniacs, murderers, thugs and people who cling to the worst possible reading of the sources. I hope that the Jewish people can stop the takeover of their heritage by the same kind of people – they exist in every group," he said, his words streaming out from deep within him as if he had been wanting to release them for a long, long time.

He took several long breaths. Neither Michal nor Lilah sought to disrupt his soliloquy.

"All people, in this country of ours, both Arabs and Jews, Druze, everybody must fight against the extremist elements or there will be total contamination of the society. The Nationalists lull the majority to sleep promising the good life, but what they are really committed to is keeping things as they are, guarding the interests of the wealthy, and if that means tolerating the extremists, they tolerate the extremists inside the government and out. Things must change, and those of us, whatever community we come from, have to join together. We must find leaders to lead the biggest part of us forward," Issam said in beautiful, eloquent Hebrew. "I believe that most of the inhabitants of Israel, most Jews and most Arabs, want peace here. We have to go and find a way to make that happen."

The moment lingered, then dissipated slowly. "I am tired," Issam said as he rose heavily from the chair. "I should get some rest, sleep for a few hours before I head back to Petach Tikva."

"You're going back?" Michal said, at first alarmed, but then stopping herself. "Alright, I understand," she said, "go ahead.

Go to bed, love."

"I think I'll lie down on the back porch. I could use the sea air."

He left the room. Michal brought him a pillow and blanket. He was asleep before she returned.

"He's quite a man," Lilah said as they gathered up the dishes. "He's cut from some special fabric. He's not just smart, he's wise."

"That he is," agreed Michal, "and there's a shortage of that everywhere, it seems."

After they had done the dishes, Lilah asked to see Michal's work and followed her downstairs to the studio. When Michal turned on the various lamps, the large room seemed to burst with sculptures and paintings, an indoor garden rich in form and alive with color. Lilah walked slowly past the paintings mounted on the walls. They seemed to meld into a fantastical landscape of creatures tame and wild blithely intermingled. The sculptures, nearly life-sized statutes chiseled out of wood, depicted men and women in embrace: couples lying in repose, standing, or seated as if on the shore and staring out at the sea.

"I can't tell you how impressed I am by all this," Lilah said, her voice subdued as she concluded her walk past the paintings and sculptures. "You find harmony in subjects that seem so different," she added as the two sat on a futon couch in a corner of the room.

They spoke about each other's art, about books and movies, likes and dislikes. There was the comfort of deep familiarity. It was as though they had not spent all those years apart. Lilah softly studied the artist, the closest friend she had had during her growing years. Michal was a weightier, more rotund version of what she had been and the ringlets of her hair had now whitened. Still, the beauty of her youth remained etched on Michal's face. Her lips, gently reaching into a small web of wrinkles on her cheeks, were still lusciously full. Her celestial blue eyes were as Lilah remembered once describing them in a birthday card, "windows to a soul as broad and bright as a sun-filled day."

There had been a pause in their conversation when Michal remarked to Lilah, "It's ironic, isn't it, that in the middle of all this craziness, our lives have crossed again." She then said. "Some people would call it karma. I suppose I was just destined to find you again."

"And I was fated to find you," Lilah concurred.

Michal grew wistful. "You've never stopped growing, have you, Lilah?" she asked.

Lilah thought about a proper reply. "I guess not – in most respects," she replied.

"Most?"

"Well, I've lived many of my dreams but," she paused, "I became too estranged from this place. Ido and Naftali suffered from my going back and forth and dragging them halfway around the world," she lamented. She paused, looking off to some melancholy place and then said, "I've become a stranger here – Israel has become unfamiliar to me. Terrorism, fundamentalists, explosions, bullets – they were always there in the background but they never got this close to me." She paused again. "Well, with the exception of Yonatan," she said, her voice dipping, sorrowful.

"I was born in this country. I was brought up speaking Hebrew," she continued. "The food, the tastes and smells – all of it is familiar, but it isn't the place I knew when growing up. It's like the line from one of Shlomo Artzi's songs, 'Once I was part of the landscape. Now I am a visitor,'" she said, and then stopped again in self-reflection.

She continued her voice stronger. "One of us, Israel or me, is an imposter. And I am pretty sure that the guardians of the State, the politicians and the gatekeepers of religion – they're the imposters. Those powers make a mockery of what Israel is meant to be. They corrupt the dream," she said resolutely.

"What should Israel be?" Michal gently probed.

"This is supposed to be the homeland of the Jews, but nobody said that has to be about lording over other people. Okay, the Arabs haven't exactly been welcoming us back home, and their lack of understanding as to why we need our home and that this is the only place where that home could be has been responsible for a lot of the bloodshed. But our heritage is about the vision of the prophets, social justice, what our parents raised us on. The society – or at least parts of it – has changed. A tolerant society, a cooperative society – where did the dream go? It's as if it has been hidden away somewhere."

"People change, why shouldn't societies?" asked Michal.

"This violence, wave after wave – it has got to stop. Both they and we have to put the past behind us and build a common future. And the 'they' and the 'us' isn't just across the Arab-Jewish line. I see new battle lines being drawn here, especially among ourselves. New fracture lines with the privileged on one side and the rest on the other. Other societies, wealthy without external threats, can afford that kind of stupidity. But here, in Israel, it will tear us apart."

"There's violence of one sort or another everywhere, and there's a lot less here than in other places," said Michal as she rose.

"Wait a minute," Lilah smiled, "is that Michal talking? You used to expect so much from Israel, and it was always me who tried to give you a sense of balance."

"Look, of course I think there's a great deal wrong here. My personal life hasn't been very sedate this past week, you being injured in the bus bombing and my husband's cousins being massacred at Al-Bakr. I very much want things to change. But change isn't going to happen if we have an unbalanced view of reality. If we are willing to be realistic, things can change."

"You think it's possible?" Lilah asked, "I'm beginning to wonder."

"The difference between the Michal of today and the person I was a generation ago is that I've become an optimist. I believe that change is part of everything that lives. That doesn't mean that you have to wait passively for things to get better. People have got to make that happen."

Michal stood and smiled. She seemed a beacon of hope and confidence. It was her pose, the one Lilah remembered seeing when she was a little girl, the way her mother – all the mothers stood in the 1960s when they and the young State were one.

There was hope, Lilah concluded after she went to bed and heard the wind chimes in the sea breeze. There was hope if one went out and turned it into something real. That was the lesson that the young Israel had taught her children.

Chapter Six

The prime minister's spokesman convened his second press conference in as many days, the attack on Al-Bakr being the subject of both.

Exhausted and haggard, the spokesman addressed the dozens of journalists gathered in an auditorium at the premier's new complex in the center of the capital. Among those attending were foreign correspondents who had descended on Israel like a flock of voracious ravens eager to probe the remains of Al-Bakr.

The spokesman, Ambassador León Ephrati, a senior diplomat in Israel's Foreign Service had been hurriedly seconded to the Prime Minister's office when the swell of indignation from abroad over what had happened at Al-Bakr began to be felt there. Ambassador Ephrati was well-known for his integrity both in and outside of the country. He was above politics and, like Eli Zedek, was a servant of the State and not of the particular government in power. He was no trumpet boy for the Nationalist Party, which is exactly the reason the Prime Minister had tapped him to face the nation and the world.

Amb. Ephrati was no longer a youngster. He slowly climbed the steps to the podium with a sheaf of papers in his hand. His tie was loosened, his collar open. A cultivated man, his gray goatee and hair were well-groomed. But as he assumed his place behind the podium, he looked troubled and worn and aged.

He was equipped with two narratives, one in English and another in Hebrew. He began with the former, which was geared for international consumption and was comprised of little more than the known facts and a restatement of the government's commitment to bringing the attackers to justice. He took no questions from the foreign press representatives. That, of course, raised their hackles, but was of little concern to the ambassador at the moment.

He then pulled out a second sheet, the one in Hebrew, from the batch he clutched in his hand. It carried the text pertaining to the primary purpose of the convocation: addressing the Israeli public through the domestic media to convey a message that the premier's security advisor, Amos, felt was urgent.

Speaking directly to the country's citizens, León Ephrati's brief remarks were conspicuous by their candor, something even those who did not comprehend the ancient tongue in which he spoke could doubtlessly detect from his tone. He began by reading directly from the prepared text.

"The attack at Al-Bakr not only resulted in the murder and injury of innocent victims and the loss of their homes, it was also a crime that has inflicted enormous damage on the State. In the absence of evidence concerning the identity of the perpetrators, the public is asked to bring to the attention of the security forces any and all information that might lead to a break in this investigation. Please scour your memories," he implored. "What has happened will detract from Israel's standing in the international arena."

Ephrati's words trailed off. The ambassador paused for a moment, his head bent slightly to the side as he pondered something deeply felt. After a few moments, he looked directly into the camera and rather than continue reading from the written text, he spoke extemporaneously. "Citizens of Israel," he began somberly, "this it is not our way. We do not shed the blood of innocent people. This evil must be stopped and its orchestrators brought to justice. Please, please, if you have any information that can help stop these raging criminals, in heaven's name, let the authorities know." He paused again and as potently as could be said, stated, "We have come too far, survived so much. We have returned and renewed ourselves in this land. Now we must fight this malevolence before we are drowned by it."

His words hung in the air, even after the pecking on the reporter's laptops and the scribbling on notepads had ceased. Amb. Ephrati took only a few questions from the Israeli journalists, then stopped. Releasing further details of the investigation could compromise it, he cautioned. For now, the domestic press lent him their credence. His plea ran on every newscast throughout the next day.

Amos had insisted on the news briefing as a result of an unfolding not directly related to the Al-Bakr massacre, but one which coincided with it. At about the same time that the Sons of Gideon had set out from their lairs to set Al-Bakr on fire, military intelligence detected a surge in Syrian military activity in that country's southwestern region, in an area abutting Israel. An armored division of the Syrian army had been assembled in offensive formation and satellite photos of bases elsewhere in that country confirmed the presence of missiles that had not been previously detected. To make things worse, an influential Hezbollah imam had issued a *fatwa* directing his followers to avenge the faithful killed at Al-Bakr with actions "beyond the border."

The army leadership was much alarmed by these developments and the Chief of Staff ordered all available resources mobilized to the north. The Defense Minister placed the Israel Defense Forces on full alert while a flurry of diplomatic activity was being undertaken in capitals around the world to seek clarification from the Syrians concerning their intentions.

On the home front, the events at Al-Bakr had spawned rioting in the Territories and in Israel proper, and the Israel Police along with the Shin Bet, were consumed with trying to contain the fury.

With every security resource suddenly occupied, Eli and his small team would have to carry the entire weight of the Al-Bakr investigation alone. Amos did not relish leaving them so deprived and decided to turn to the country's reserve forces, the public, for help. Specifically, he hoped that by appealing directly to the Israeli citizens, someone might offer leads that could help identify the Gideons – before they acted again. He approached the Premier, strongly advocated the measure and received his approval. Ephrati was drafted to make the appeal and the press conference was quickly assembled.

Eli and his men were too busy to appreciate how forlorn the situation had left them. They had already begun to confront the challenges the Gideons had left in their wake.

Al-Bakr had given up very little by way of forensics that could shed light on who had been responsible for razing it. "These guys cleaned up better than five hundred Jewish mothers before Passover," said one of the members of Eli's team after they had inventoried the evidence that had survived the inferno at Al-Bakr. "They didn't bother leaving a business card," said another agent at the post-mortem Eli and his staff conducted twenty-four hours after the attack at the still smoldering ruins. "Fancy work," said one of his other men, "these guys aren't like anything we've seen before."

Eli had remained at Al-Bakr throughout the night, long after the casualties had been evacuated and the fires put out. He lingered because he wanted to see how the village, or what remained of it, looked in daylight. He was interested in the rhythm of the place, in the traffic flows on the highway and in any detail that could provide insight into how this outrage had been perpetrated.

Eli left and drove to his apartment to shave, shower and change clothes. Haunted by what had been left behind at Al-Bakr, he went to his office, sat at his computer and fired off directives, issued requisition orders and filed requests to judges for wiretaps and administrative detentions aimed at far-right-wing activists on his watch list. He then pored over the printout of the information his assistant had assembled from various government databases employing a single keyword: "Al-Bakr."

Later, disoriented after awakening in his desk chair from a few hours of dead sleep, Eli considered whether Al-Bakr might have only been something that he had dreamt, a nightmare. It was improbable, he reasoned, that a group of Jews, hell-bent or not, could have concealed powerful explosives in the heart of a densely-populated Palestinian settlement, then ignite them with meticulous accuracy such that thirty homes were destroyed and dozens of people killed and wounded. It was a huge crime by Israeli standards, a deliriously bold undertaking that was boggling in its conception and implementation.

Then again, the country was still reeling from what a band of Palestinian militants had pulled off on the Coastal Road the week before. The price in lost lives and trauma that had resulted from that attack had been heavier still. If the Palestinians could pull off such an atrocity, why couldn't a group of Jews of similar temperament and intent?

Eli glanced down and saw his field notes. They were soiled, as he had written them with hands that had been picking through the burnt-out remains of refugee homes. The devastation he had seen at Al-Bakr came hurtling back to him with harrowing clarity. If he had any doubts about what he had seen, there was plenty of evidence to dispel them. The unthinkable had taken place.

By noon, Eli had composed the profile of the Gideons he would distribute among the security services. After he completed the document, he sat back and contemplated the facts he had noted and reread the communiqués the Gideons had sent relating to the Abed murder and Al-Bakr. There was something about the assailants that irked him. Something not conveyed in the spare facts, a certain hollowness of spirit, something alien and cold and detached. Eli recalled what a member of his team had said at Al-Bakr at their summary discussion the previous night: "These guys aren't like anything we've seen before," and wondered who they could be.

That question would drive him relentlessly these coming months.

Eli dove into his work totally resolved that he would track down the Gideons, to the last man.

ೞ ❖ ಜು

The Knesset session on Al-Bakr had gone on into the wee hours and in its wake, Naftali had considerable follow-up to attend to at his office the next morning. He called Lilah at nine and said he hoped to pick her up in Acre at about one that afternoon. He phoned again at three, still in Jerusalem but believed that he would be able to reach Michal's home by six-thirty or seven. At eight, his secretary at the New Democrats' headquarters in Tel Aviv called to say that he was in an urgent meeting but was expected to be on his way to Acre by nine.

Issam arrived at the same time as Naftali, both of them driving up to the house on the Acre shore at half past midnight. Lilah happened to be at the kitchen window rinsing out coffee cups when the two men hauled themselves out of their respective cars.

"How about that," Lilah remarked to Michal, "they must have coordinated their late arrival."

Lilah and Michal had spent the evening waiting for their men – Issam had planned to be back from Beilinson by dinnertime – nervous and tense as they watched television coverage on the continuing fallout from Al-Bakr.

The news was not heartening. Nearly ten countries had suspended diplomatic relations with Israel as a result of the incident. The United Nations Security Council would later that day debate a resolution to "expel the terrorist-state called Israel" from the world body. The Venezuelan justice ministry was forwarding an urgent petition to the International Court of Justice concerning alleged culpability in the attack by the government in Jerusalem. Three hundred European figures had signed a petition calling for an academic and cultural boycott of Israel. Two major orchestras and a dance troupe scheduled to visit the country cancelled performances that were still months away. An international conference on osteoporosis that had been planned for nearly two years by its organizers at the Sackler Medical School at Tel Aviv University had been abruptly cancelled. Dockworkers and airport cargo handlers in Sweden and Finland said they would not off-load Israeli goods. A proposal that Israeli products be banned for sale on the continent had been fielded to the European Parliament.

In Israel, confrontations between settlers and anarchists at Bilin near Ramallah regarding the West Bank separation fence had spread and were now competing with the rioting in other Arab areas for police attention. The West Bank was afire with violent demonstrations that the Palestinian Authority forces made no effort to put down. The Hamas regime in Gaza had scheduled a martial parade, "Resolve and Honor for the Liberation of Palestine" by hundreds of lock-stepped fighters marching to "erase the Zionist entity," Israel, from the face of the earth.

All of this in just the first forty-eight hours.

The events at Al-Bakr had stirred Israel profoundly as well. At his residence, President Lustinger received a delegation of the youth movement who told him they wished to "adopt" Al-Bakr and assist its people in the reconstruction of the village. The secondary school teachers association declared that teachers in every high school in the country would devote the first day of the new school year to teaching about what had taken place at the Palestinian village and discussions of tolerance and coexistence – regardless of whether the Minister of Education approved it or not. The Israel Film Authority allocated funds for an Israeli Arab director to commence a documentary on what had occurred at Al-Bakr. It was also reported that two hundred tons of food, clothing and household goods had already been donated by the public and deposited at centers around the country.

By mid-afternoon, Lilah and Michal understood that Naftali would be delayed in coming. Newscasters reported that the Opposition leader, Knesset member Naftali Kedem, had filed an emergency no-confidence motion in the government asserting that its "failure to conclude a settlement with the Palestinians contributed to the vulnerability of places like Al-Bakr and to the growth of extremism in Israel." The Nationalists succeeded in beating back the resolution – even though six of its seventy legislators abstained from the vote. "This is a government of doom," Prof. Kedem declared after the vote to reporters. "We must bring it down before it brings down the nation," he said, the television cameras rolling.

And as he stared squarely into the camera lens, Naftali announced that a mass rally had been called for the following Saturday night in Tel Aviv's Rabin Square. He called on citizens to come to the rally to "demonstrate Israel's commitment to coexistence and justice and the people's demand for a government whose policies reflect these principles."

A shudder passed through Lilah's body as she heard one news commentator say "from Knesset Member Kedem's remarks, we can only deduce that the Opposition has decided on a strategy of direct confrontation with the Government. The question remains," the analyst added against the backdrop of a photo of Naftali, "if this man and his supporters have the power to bring the Nationalists down."

"Prof. Kedem?" Issam asked as the two men stood barely a half meter apart at the doorway of the Halaby home.

"Yes. Shalom," Naftali replied, eyeing the tall man of similar age whose drooping carriage and charcoal-colored rings around his eyes made him look as exhausted as he felt.

Lilah opened the door, admitted the two men into the foyer and introduced them. "Naftali, meet Dr. Issam Halaby, Michal's husband," she said brightly and smiled, though she stood slightly bent by the tenderness on her side.

"It is a pleasure to welcome you to our home. I have always wanted to make your acquaintance," Issam said, leading Naftali into the living room. "I have been a party member since you established the NDP – what is it – four years now?" he asked.

"Nearly four, yes," Naftali said, appreciative of the cordial reception he was being accorded. "It's good to be among like-minded people," he added.

Lilah reacquainted Naftali with Michal. Not having seen each other in nearly four decades, they searched each other's faces for memories. The memories came as they reminisced.

"Please, won't you sit?" Issam asked, offering the large recliner, "the throne," as Michal referred to the living room chair generally reserved for her husband.

"Well, thank you. It's late though," he said. "Perhaps we should get going?" he asked, glancing deferentially at Lilah. She nodded that it was alright to stay and Naftali sat down.

Conversation between the two men began slowly, but their initial reticence quickly dissipated and over several cups of strong, sweet coffee, they talked animatedly until nearly three in the morning. Their repartee ranged from the personal – a shared struggle with appetite and their expanding waistlines and a fondness for John Irving novels – to major issues of the day.

The two men had similar opinions on many matters: that there was a threat to the planet posed by environmental degradation and climate change; that the war on poverty required distributive policies as much as economic growth; that

Jews and Arabs could turn Israel into a model society if the principles of cooperation and tolerance were embraced. All this, they agreed, required a government worth its salt – the current one, they concurred, was not.

As Naftali later put it to Lilah, "We are largely of the same mind," he said of himself and Issam. "We see the world the same way," Issam would say to Michal referring to himself and Naftali. That was the evening that Naftali Kedem and Issam Halaby bonded, Lilah and Michal would later recall.

Before they parted, the two couples agreed that they would meet together and have dinner after the rally in Tel Aviv that weekend.

"How do you arrange such a thing, a mass rally?" Lilah asked Naftali as they drove toward Tel Aviv.

"How does one arrange such a thing?" Naftali began professorially. "The logistics aren't that hard to set-up, once it's been decided to proceed. Usually, though, it's organizing and mobilizing people that's the big hurdle. We have developed a good system for that. The party is built of what we call salons, modeled after the literary salons in Iraq during the 1930s and 1940s when educated people used to gather in private homes for discussions on current issues, art and literature, politics. One of the members of our executive council remembered the salons his father ran in Baghdad when he was a boy. Intellectuals, Jews, Kurds, Arabs used to meet at their homes to discuss culture and literature, new ideas. Anyway, instead of party branches like the traditional Israeli parties have with local bosses and machines, the NDP is built of salons all over Israel.

"Today," Naftali continued as he lowered the volume of the classical music station on the car radio, "with Internet communications and email, the salons are in immediate touch with one another. The party has invested a lot of money in IT, information technology, and there is a constant exchange of news and views among our members. We, at the center, are very attentive to what people in the field are thinking and need. Whoa!" Naftali exclaimed as he looked alarmingly in the rearview mirror.

"What's wrong?" Lilah asked.

Naftali slowed down the car and steered into the right lane. "This guy must be going 160 kilometers per hour," he said. "Unbelievable. They don't care," he said after he had studied the driver in the sports car that raced past him, "he can't be more than twenty years old. That's the new thing the rich are doing these days, buying their kids cars worth what it would take to feed a family of eight for a year in south Tel Aviv."

He took a deep breath and paused, trying to remember what he had been saying.

"The salons. The rally," Lilah reminded him. She was seated stiffly in the passenger seat, the dull pulsing of her bruised side sapping her. She hadn't taken anything for pain since the day before. Now she wished she had.

"Yes, well, each salon has anywhere between ten to fifty members. It's a decentralized model that encourages local autonomy. Anyway, when one member from Hadera posted on our electronic bulletin board a call for a mass protest, a demonstration like the Peace Now movement used to pull off on Saturday nights in Tel Aviv or Jerusalem, there was a groundswell of support and we realized that we had to organize such an event. Some of those demonstrations used to get tens of thousands, some even hundreds of thousands of people into the streets calling for change."

"So it's a protest rally the party is sponsoring?"

"In effect, that's what it is. We aren't directly linking the government to the recent events – there's nothing to implicate them in what happened at Al-Bakr. What we decided this evening at our meeting at NDP headquarters was to call it a rally of hope and progress. We're working on the exact formulation, negotiating the phrasing and program with our partners: the progressive religious movements, the environmental and women's organizations, other groups. But there should be no doubt. There is a lot to criticize this government for and we intend to make our positions clear. In that sense, it is a protest."

"I see," said Lilah drowsily and who, with that, fell fast asleep until they arrived at 3 HaGaon Street, just as Tel Aviv was awakening to a new day.

When Naftali opened the door and Lilah walked in, she found Ido asleep on the living room couch. He had been waiting for her, a surprise. Naftali had not mentioned that he would be there. On the coffee table in the living room stood a crystal vase with a bouquet of Birds of Paradise. Ido had bought them the evening before on his way home from maneuvers on the eastern front, the border with Syria. When his father called to tell him that he was bringing Lilah home, Ido secured permission to place his command in the hands of his lieutenant and take 24 hours of family leave.

Naftali slept at 3 HaGaon Street for several hours before returning to Jerusalem and was gone by nine. Lilah awoke late that morning and she and Ido went to have brunch at the *Namal*, the gentrified area around Tel Aviv's disused port that was now filled with cafes and restaurants, a ten-minute walk from the apartment.

They had no shortage of topics to talk about while they ate, sitting outdoors in the pleasant breeze. The breeze seemed to have disappeared when Lilah, at Ido's beckon told him about what she had experienced during the attack the week before. Ido listened as she recounted the horrors of the Coastal Road attack. He looked outwardly calm although Lilah could see in his eyes that he was seething.

Lilah then talked about her stay at Michal and Issam's home and what special people they were. She told Ido about what Issam had said around the dinner table when he returned from the long day of surgery on the Al-Bakr victims, "No people, not Jews and not Arabs – no one – is immune from this blind hatred for the other."

"Your friend Issam is right," said Ido, his eyes squinting in the strong midday sun. "There are good people and bad people in every group."

Lilah looked into her son's face. How she loved this man her boy had become. "You are so handsome," she sighed. "How do the ladies resist you?" she asked playfully.

They laughed, and Ido continued. "Issam is right about the conditions that feed the extremists. And like Dad says, 'over forty years maintaining an occupation and thirty years' worth of mostly right-wing governments run by people representing big-business, clerics and hawks, and you get a casserole that is inedible.' That's what we have now in Israel – exactly when the global economy is stalling and the planet is about to fall apart because nobody has bothered to think ahead," he said. "The situation has got to change and the New Democrats have to get ready to take the lead," he declared.

As he and Lilah walked back to the apartment, Ido responded as best he could to his mother's torrent of questions about the opinions he held. The conversation continued after they got home. Lilah found herself agreeing with much of what he said. His values were her own.

"I guess I have some reading to do," she said, "I've got a lot to learn about how we got to this situation."

Later, after Ido left to return to his unit, Lilah, though she was tired and her side was tender, went into Ido's bedroom, swallowed the remembrance that it had once been her brother's room and gazed at the books her son had collected over the years. She gathered an armful, including several books Naftali had recommended and took up a comfortable position on the couch.

And then, with a disc of soft guitar music playing quietly in the background, a small pot of herbal tea on the table in front of her and the ceiling fan turning slowly overhead, Lilah put on her reading glasses and went to work, reading as if she were cramming for a college exam. She wrote down comments and questions in a notebook that she quickly filled. She was intent on understanding how her country had gotten into this mire.

Lilah heard Naftali predict during a radio interview that "multitudes" were expected at the demonstration, which would take place under the banner "A Rally of Hope: Toward a Common Future." "It will usher in a sea of change," Naftali proclaimed.

Lilah wanted to be part of that multitude. She no longer wanted to be a visitor to her country. She wanted to be part of the landscape and among those bringing change.

Chapter Seven

Along Shlomzion Street, near Tel Aviv's old bus station, Zohar Moghrabi was well known as a man of action. Large and tough, he ran the drug trade and worked as an enforcer for the Steiner syndicate. And while years of uppers and downers and snorting cocaine had diminished Zohar's mental agility, Meir Steiner considered him a reliable protector of his interests.

Zohar's former girlfriend, a prostitute named Shira, had occasionally received johns at their apartment two stories up from where the municipal street sweepers picked up their bins early each morning in south Tel Aviv. Zohar had been decent enough to Shira. For most of their three years together, he hadn't raised his hand against her and had curtailed his cursing, which she did not care for. On occasion, he would buy her a new outfit or take her out for a nice meal. Twice he had paid for getaways to Eilat, just him and her.

Their relationship ended after two incidents involving Arab customers Shira had serviced at home. The first time, when Zohar had found her in bed with a day laborer from Jenin, he nearly killed the man and hit Shira so hard he knocked out two of her teeth. "You filthy bitch!" he screamed, "don't ever let another Arab-vermin between your legs, or you'll really get it from me." He made her douche five times over the next two days and wouldn't sleep with her for a week.

Shira had always been a *pilpelit*, of fiery temperament. She was spiteful about the beating and a few days later, she made sure that Zohar saw another Arab leaving the apartment. He then beat Shira so badly, she was hospitalized for three weeks.

Zohar Moghrabi hated Arabs very, very much.

Zohar Moghrabi was Eli Zedek's first break. The printout of data relating to the keyword "Al-Bakr" had tagged nearly thirty different documents – mostly routine lists concerning agricultural production or roadwork done on Route 443. One document, though, concerned a roster listing a platoon of Border gendarmes whose patrols included occasional visits to Al-Bakr. Eli accessed the computer files of the troops assigned to the patrol to see if any of them raised any red flags. The name of Corporal Amir Moghrabi, Zohar's younger brother did. He had twice been disciplined for using undue force against Arab detainees. One officer had noted in his file that Cpl. Moghrabi "despised Arabs to the extreme."

Eli had the younger Moghrabi questioned. The corporal claimed that he had not been to Al-Bakr over the previous three weeks as he had been temporarily assigned to a unit in the Nablus District. The alibi was checked and it held. But Eli's interrogators still harbored suspicions. The soldier was evasive in his answers and expressed no remorse, even pride, over the beatings of Arabs that had led to the disciplinary actions against him. They decided to press him further.

After a day and night of on-and-off-again interrogation, Amir let it slip that his older brother, Zohar, whom he adored, was responsible for his anti-Arab schooling.

In itself, that was hardly incriminating, but the interrogators discovered that Zohar had pressed his brother for information on "those cockroaches in Al-Bakr." Zohar Moghrabi wanted to know how to get in and out of the camp with the least chance of being seen and where things could be hidden or buried in the camp. When asked why he was so interested in Al-Bakr, Zohar told Amir that he wanted to "fuck up some Arabs, but good." Amir revealed that he had drawn a map of the camp for his brother. The map was subsequently found by Eli's men when they searched Zohar's apartment.

Eli requisitioned a telephone company truck outfitted with audio monitoring equipment and positioned it across the street from Zohar Moghrabi's apartment. The "repairmen" who worked out of the truck were members of Eli's team. Zohar was followed and conversations in his apartment were monitored around the clock. Surveillance conducted over three days and four nights revealed a great deal about Zohar's criminal activities but nothing that could be linked to the Sons of Gideon. That he cursed Arabs to the point of obsession did not constitute damning evidence of involvement in Al-Bakr.

Eli justified the expenditure of personnel and equipment involved in tracking Zohar on the basis of a single, simple fact: He had no other leads. He had to determine if the elder Moghrabi was a bona fide suspect. He hoped that the encounter with him might give him an indication.

Eli had Meir Steiner picked up on an old bench warrant and brought in for questioning to the Tel Aviv police lock-up. Eli was surprised at the crime don's appearance. In a soiled, ill-fitting suit, chalky drools of antacids trailing from his mouth and badly perspiring, it was difficult to imagine how he had managed to command the loyalty of anyone, especially the toughs in his employ.

Eli needed to be efficient and once Steiner was presented to him, he made it clear that he was being questioned concerning grave matters of national security and that Eli had wide discretionary power to deal with the individuals who might be involved. With that, Steiner became putty in Eli's hands. "I am a sick man," he appealed. "All I want to do is to get out from under my past. I want to repent. I want to spend my last years in synagogue, and in the company of my grandchildren." Steiner would cooperate. He would deliver Zohar Moghrabi.

It was agreed that Steiner would introduce Zohar to a "Mr. Haddad" – Eli– saying that Haddad was a trusted associate of his, and that he, Zohar, was to give Haddad whatever he wanted.

The meeting was quickly arranged. Steiner phoned Zohar, and told him to come right away to a south Tel Aviv *pundak* specified by Eli. Forty minutes later, the three men met. As per instructions, Steiner introduced Mr. Haddad. The thug was astonished by his boss' servility to Haddad. He had always regarded the crime boss as the all-powerful master of their world, yet now he seemed to be quivering in the stranger's presence. Steiner leaned over and whispered something in Zohar's ear. Whatever was said instantly sobered Zohar. "Got it, whatever he wants," he affirmed. Steiner then left the restaurant after assuring Mr. Haddad that all would be well.

"My friend will have your best kebab," Mr. Haddad shouted imperiously to the waiter. "How do you like your meat, Zohar, rare or well done?"

"Well-done," Zohar said.

"To drink?"

"A bottle of beer, Goldstar."

Eli ordered coffee for himself and the server withdrew. Haddad and Zohar were alone.

Zohar looked around. "Do you come here often?" he asked Mr. Haddad.

"Well, I am a part owner, but I prefer the couscous at the Cadillac when I'm in Tel Aviv," Eli replied, referring to a well-known eatery frequented by right-wing politicians and businessmen. He offered Zohar a cigarette, which he accepted.

Zohar's beer arrived. Eli eyed him, sizing him up as he poured the beer into his glass and drank in short, quick sips. Self-conscious, Zohar ventured a question. "So you are from out of town, Mr. Haddad?" he asked.

"Yes, I live in Jerusalem, although I have businesses all over the country and overseas."

"I'm an out-of-towner, too," Zohar claimed. "I mean, I live in Tel Aviv now, you know, so that I can be close to my work, but I consider Or Yehuda my home town."

"Do you?" Eli asked, feigning interest. "Well, Or Yehuda is in the Tel Aviv area, isn't it?"

"I guess so. But we have our own mayor and everything."

Eli nodded. Salads and other appetizers arrived. Zohar eyed them hungrily. "Go ahead, help yourself," Eli said graciously. Zohar ate with zest. "This is really good," he said. "My grandmother used to make an eggplant salad just like this. Boy, do I love it."

"I'm glad," Eli said, as he watched Zohar consume the salads. "Tell me Zohar, are you a family man?"

"No, not really. I have a brother, but otherwise I am free as a bird," he replied between bites. Zohar Moghrabi ate ferociously. He smiled at Mr. Haddad. A fool's smile? Eli wondered.

"Steiner tells me you've worked with him for several years now and are reliable and loyal. He likes you, you know. And he respects you," Eli said.

"Sure he likes me. His organization needs me. I look after an important chunk of his interests." Zohar then barked at the waiter for more pita bread.

"Steiner says that if he gives you a job, you do it all the way."

"If he pays, why not?"

"Then let's get to the point of our meeting together now, Zohar. I represent some people who are very interested in seeing that certain things are done, and done correctly."

"What kinds of things?"

"Let's just say things that true patriots would agree need to be done."

"Patriots?"

"Yes, you know people like ourselves who love this country like their own fathers, people who know how to deal with the enemy."

"My father died in the First Lebanon War," said Zohar. "He was captured and they tortured him before they killed him," Zohar said bitterly.

"I'm sorry," Eli sympathized. "It's a pity how many of us

have lost fathers and brothers to the Arabs."

"We have suffered a great deal. The Arabs must pay for what they have done."

"We think so, too. In fact, that's what I want to speak with you about," Haddad said, lowering his voice. He paused while the waiter served Zohar his meal, then continued when they were alone. "What did you do in the army, Zohar?" asked Haddad; Eli knew full well from Zohar's army file that he was dishonorably discharged for black marketeering during the Second Lebanon War.

"I was in a combat infantry unit. That is, until some leftist Ashkenazi officer had me driven out."

"They're always against us," Eli said with contrived empathy. He prodded Zohar to continue, wanting to know how much of a lie he was willing to tell, "What did he accuse you of doing?"

"He said I stole money and that I wasn't paying attention on guard duty."

"Too bad," Eli consoled. "No doubt you would have been proud to continue doing your duty and serving the country."

"Very much so, Mr. Haddad. I want to teach the Arabs a thing or two for all the trouble they have caused us."

"You know, a lot of big talkers say the same thing but when it comes down to it, they don't have the balls to do anything. I get the feeling, though that you are a real patriot and that you have what it takes to put the Arabs in their place."

"You bet I have what it takes," said Zohar, sitting tall in his chair. "I've already killed a few of those gnats," he claimed.

"You have?" Eli asked. He hoped that the device he wore in his ear was functioning and transmitting the conversation to his office. "You've killed Arabs?"

"Sure," Zohar bragged. "My friends and I are very good at it. Very. You've probably heard of our work."

"Really?" Eli lowered his voice to a whisper. "Say, you

weren't involved in grilling all that meat at Al-Bakr, were you?"

"Maybe we were, maybe we weren't," Zohar replied coyly. "You know, Mr. Haddad, so far you've asked all the questions and gotten all of the answers."

"You mean you'd like to know what I specifically wanted to meet you about."

Zohar nodded.

"You're entitled to know and I'll tell you. My friends and I are very concerned about the traitors who are smearing Israel's good name and protesting what happened in Al-Bakr. That kind of scum will grow like a cancer and corrupt our children, and they are interfering with Jewish settlement in Judea and Samaria. If they had it their way, we would lose the land of our forefathers."

Zohar agreed.

Eli resumed. "Now because these traitors are Jews, we are willing to give them a chance to come to their senses and help them understand why events like Al-Bakr happen. We want to warn these people against continuing their shameful protests. Do you follow me?"

"I think so," said Zohar, pushing away his plate.

"There is a big protest rally planned, you know, like those demonstrations, the peaceniks, the *Shalom Achshav* flunkies use to put on and drive the government crazy so that they couldn't take measures needed against the Arabs and traitors? You remember those big gatherings they had in Tel Aviv and Jerusalem?"

Zohar said he did.

"We don't want any more of that. The government needs order and quiet to keep up what it is doing, keeping the Land of Israel united and putting the Arabs in their place. We can't allow the enemies to interfere with what we, the people who really care about the country, know is necessary," Eli said forcefully.

Eli stared at the Arab-hater, Zohar, who boasted that he had killed Arabs. Maybe he wasn't a Gideon. Maybe he was. It was a risk. Worth taking?, Eli asked himself.

Proceed, Eli decided.

"I hear you," Zohar responded. "We need to get a message loud and clear to the traitors. They are worse than Arabs. I have always said that. The one who killed Rabin was a hero in my book. How can we finish the job so that we can finally get rid of the ragheads once and for all?"

"That's why I've asked you to see me. Maybe you have some ideas?

"First, we need to hit those Jewish wimps hard," Zohar declared.

"Well, yes. But we are hoping that they will get the hint right away, and we don't want to use more force than necessary."

"If you knock off one of the leaders, it'll probably put the fear of God into the rest of them. They'll stop soon enough."

"We don't want anyone killed," Eli firmly stated. "You have to understand that." Eli was unequivocal.

"Okay. But we can give them the feeling that there will be trouble."

"Yes, that sounds right," Eli stopped and thought: Is there enough here, sufficient suspicion to lay a trap? He believed there was. He went on.

"Alright, we see an opportunity that if handled well could get the message out to the leftists. They have announced a big rally to take place here in Tel Aviv this weekend. We think this will be a perfect opportunity to get the point across to them that we won't sit by and let them speak nonsense and confound the people of Israel with displays of weakness and doubt. We would like to encourage people faithful to the Land of Israel to speak out against the lies that come from the stage. No violence, just a lot of *balagan*, you know making enough noise so that there can be no doubt that we will not allow the nonsense they propose to pass unchallenged. We were thinking that a small, tight group of smart guys led by someone like you could create some problems, technical difficulties that everyone will know was really a display of patriotic will."

"I follow you," Zohar said eagerly.

"So do you think that you and your group could provide that kind of service?" Eli asked.

"I am sure we could," Zohar readily affirmed, then paused. "But no one lives off air."

"Of course not, and not just from patriotism either. You and your friends will be well compensated."

"How much are we talking about?"

"Several thousand."

"Dollars?"

"Fine. I could give you a portion, say a third, now as a sign of good faith, with another third just before you execute the plan and the remaining third afterward."

"It sounds acceptable to me," said Zohar, projecting the air of a businessman. "Especially if we are talking about a nice even sum like $10,000."

"Agreed," said Eli. "But I want you to understand that there is to be no violence and that I will want to be in on all the details of your plan by tomorrow night. You will tell me precisely what you and your friends plan to do, how many people will be involved and where they will be positioned? Are we agreed? Remember – no surprises."

Zohar accepted the conditions.

Zohar took up Eli on his offer of a ride and asked to be let off at the new Central Bus Station. Once there, Eli withdrew a briefcase from the trunk of his car and counted out three thousand dollars in marked bills which he gave to Zohar as a retainer. The exchange was filmed by one of Eli's agents riding in an unmarked car behind his boss.

"How can I reach you if I need to?" Eli asked Zohar before

they parted.

"You see that place, Café Mazal, over there," Zohar said, pointing. "I spend a lot of time there."

Eli looked hard at Zohar, straight in the eyes. "We have a deal, then?" he asked.

"We have a deal," said Zohar.

"And you will tell me everything about your plan tomorrow."

"Everything."

"No surprises."

"You have my word," Zohar assured Eli.

Eli proceeded to his office on Ibn Givrol Street. There, he issued instructions to double the surveillance team that was tracking Zohar Moghrabi and everyone with whom he came into contact.

ଓ ❖ ଡ଼

Sources confirmed that the security cabinet was considering banning the rally scheduled by the Progressive Bloc for Saturday night. The government would justify the action based on interests of public safety and order. The cabinet was equivocal, some ministers fearing accusations that the ban would be interpreted as a cover-up or as foot-dragging in the Sons of Gideons investigation. The decision was made to empower the cabinet secretary to negotiate an acceptable formula with the organizers.

As Eli concluded his meeting with Zohar Moghrabi that evening, Naftali Kedem was perusing a document that had been hastily drawn up by the New Democratic Party's legal department at their headquarters in Tel Aviv. A conference call was being placed to the cabinet secretary in Jerusalem. When he came on the line Naftali began speaking.

"Mr. Secretary, good evening," Naftali said in a deep baritone, his "authority voice," as Lilah called it. Ido referred to it as Naftali's "listen up, I'm damn serious" voice.

"I'm calling concerning the government's deliberations on possibly banning the Rally of Hope...Sorry?... Yes, you are correct sir. We are very opposed to such an action; that's an understatement. In that respect, I wish to inform you of a decision made a little while ago by our Central Committee...Yes, we are faxing it to you as we speak... Yes, I'll hold...," said Naftali.

Naftali sat behind his large desk, his tobacco-less pipe perched on his lower lip, fingering a fragment of an ancient mosaic that he used as a paperweight. He gazed out the window and watched the stop-and-go of vehicles on HaYarkon Street, seven stories below.

"Yes, Mr. Secretary, I am ready if you are....Fine. I'll read the resolution now," he said: "Whereas the State of Israel is a democracy with a long history in defense of civil rights and elementary freedoms, the National Democratic Party of Israel registers its deepest protest and disappointment over the prospective ban on open-air political gatherings by the government.

"The proposed ban would undermine Israeli democracy. The NDP can only interpret such an action as a blatantly political attempt to cripple the opposition forces of the country. We, therefore demand that the relevant authorities issue a permit forthwith to the Progressive Bloc to hold a protest rally at Tel Aviv's Rabin Square this Saturday evening.

"Should the government persist in imposing the ban, the National Democratic Party of Israel will instruct its members and all people of goodwill to convene as scheduled in peaceful dissent to such a decree. We appeal to the government to avoid such a confrontation and uphold the full range of civil liberties as provided under the law. End quote. End of statement."

Naftali paused before continuing. "Mr. Secretary, that is the formal statement. Now, Avigdor, what can you and I work out?"

A face-saving compromise was struck within the hour between the Progressive Bloc and the government: First, the official sponsor of the rally was to be a nonpartisan ad hoc committee and the rally would not be promoted as a demonstration in opposition to the Nationalist government. The government's second condition was that the rally be held on a weeknight rather than on Saturday evening as attendance would presumably be lower. Thirdly, a sizeable bond was to be deposited as a guarantee that public order would be maintained by the organizers and the conditions of the compromise enforced.

A meeting of the leadership of the Progressive Bloc – the two green parties, the feminist movement, the Reform and Conservative Judaism umbrella organizations, the Nature Conservancy Organization, the Union for Civil Rights, one of three Arab parties and the NDP – convened several hours later in Naftali's office. The "Committee of Hope for a Common Future," was constituted comprising the leaders of the Progressive Bloc constituents and various other public figures. A popular essayist and movie maker unaffiliated with any party was formally appointed as chairman. It was resolved that the rally would be held the following Sunday evening – one day later than originally planned – at the same location: Rabin Square. The bond was placed by a wealthy businessman, a NDP supporter who Naftali could count on for backing.

The Progressive Bloc parties immediately began posting press releases, notices and advertisements in the media while various organizational secretaries mobilized group chapters and branches in addition to the NDP salons around the country. Youth movements, labor councils and cooperatives were polled to determine how many buses should be ordered. The trade union federation contacted its workplace committees and sought commitments from members and their families to attend.

The goal was to bring 300,000 people into the streets. That would put the rally in the same league as other historical mass gatherings like the one held in the aftermath of the Sabra and Shatila massacre in Lebanon in September 1982 and the one following the assassination of Prime Minister Yitzhak Rabin in November 1995. It was, however, anyone's guess as to how many people would actually attend.

ଔ ❖ ଓ

Barely a day after his first meeting with Zohar Moghrabi, once the time and venue of the rally was confirmed, Eli Zedek headed for Café Mazal off Shlomzion Street.

The old open-air depot was bustling, a noisy bazaar where foreign workers, homeless people, artists and marginals mingled. Shops selling discs of popular oriental songs and foreign music played as tinny as the soda cans in the gutters. People lingered on the sidewalks. All of them appeared to be waiting for something – an offer of temporary work, a document – real or forged – or a social rendezvous. The air was filled with the acrid odor of rotting produce, urine, exhaust fumes and fried food.

Eli elbowed his way through the crowds. He headed for a side street where the bargain shoe stores vied for buyers. Eli found Café Mazal at the end of the street.

Zohar would return any moment said the counterman, keeping an eye on the visitor.

Eli watched as Zohar appeared on the sidewalk under the café canopy where he accepted a plastic film canister from a light-skinned youth in cutoff shorts carrying a huge backpack.

He was a mule, Eli assumed, working his way across Europe or the Middle East by ferrying drugs. Zohar stripped several large bills off a wad of cash that he pulled out of his shirt pocket and handed the bills to the courier. The transaction complete, Zohar entered the café. He was pleased to see Eli.

"Mr. Haddad. I was wondering when you would show up. Haim," he instructed the counterman. "Give Mr. Haddad a beer on my account, in a clean glass. And wipe down that tabletop. Can't you see that he is a distinguished person?" The counterman complied.

"Perhaps we ought to go for a walk," Eli suggested, his eyes shifting toward the man.

"Haim is a trusted associate," Zohar assured Eli. Eli seemed unconvinced. "Believe me, it's okay," Zohar insisted.

He and Eli walked toward a back table and took a seat. Eli got right to the point. "An official announcement has now been made about the time and place of the gathering. We wish to make use of your services."

"I am ready to provide them."

"The rally is scheduled to be held on Sunday evening at Rabin Square. We would like for you to make sure it does not happen as planned."

"It's as good as done. I've spoken to my best men. They are prepared, even eager."

"I see," Eli smiled. "How many people will you be using?"

"Five or six."

"Are they your leadership or just supporters?" Eli asked, fishing for information. He was hoping to capture the top echelon of the Sons of Gideon.

"As I said, they are my best men," Zohar answered, not having understood Eli's meaning and leaving him without a direct answer.

"Alright," Eli said, "Remember that we do not want anyone hurt. We just want you to disrupt the event. We were thinking that your forces could form into two groups, each one working its way to the speakers' platform and then storming…"

"Mr. Haddad," Zohar interjected, with feigned irritation. "We are experts with a lot of experience. Trust me, the plan we are putting together is good."

Eli had wanted to retain control by calling all the shots. He now realized that he needed to keep in Zohar's good graces. If things worked out as he hoped, he would catch the Sons of Gideon red-handed.

"Fine. Just remember that any violence will look bad and have the opposite effect than the one we want to make. No guns, knives or explosives. I want to meet your men before the rally, just to make sure we're getting our money's worth," Eli said.

They agreed that Zohar and his men would meet with Eli forty-five minutes prior to the start of the rally at a spot on the outskirts of the plaza. There, Eli's operatives could easily observe and begin tracking them in the crowd.

"Remember, Zohar, I want to meet all of your men. There may be more work for them in the future."

"I've already agreed to this," Zohar said, chafed. "Just be there alone, with the amount we agreed upon."

"I will."

"See you in a couple of days, then, Mr. Haddad," said Zohar, as he got up to leave. "You'll be very pleased."

The comment worried Eli.

The next day, the Thursday evening before the Sunday rally, Eli went to Jerusalem to brief Amos on the plan. The defense and security wing of the prime minister's bureau was abuzz, filled with nervous energy. Eli sat across from Amos and waited as he took several urgent calls from the *Kiriya*, military headquarters in Tel Aviv. Between the calls, Amos told Eli that a squad of soldiers who had been collecting field intelligence "in the eastern sector" were three hours overdue to check-in with a support unit. Urgent attempts to determine the whereabouts of the soldiers and preparations for the possible dispatch of a rescue team were underway.

While he waited, Eli looked up at the large, framed picture of the "Old Man," David Ben-Gurion that hung on the wall behind Amos' desk. Eli had always been awed by the picture, the elderly Israeli premier in suit and tie with his chin on his hands and a look of deep preoccupation on his visage. Eli imagined what it would be liked if he were still alive, what he would have thought about the latest trials of the state he had founded?

Once he was off the phone, Amos said matter-of-factly to Eli, "the foxes in Damascus seem to be cooking up something and that has to be our focus now. Until things change, your team has to hold the line against the Sons of Gideon. There's not much by way of support to you that can be spared now."

Amos listened attentively to Eli outline the plan to position Zohar Moghrabi and his group for capture. "They are a real prospect – and our only one right now," Eli explained. He described the operational plan he would implement at the rally. Amos gave him his go-ahead, a verbal consent – there would be no written authorization.

"Just remember," Amos concluded as Eli prepared to leave. "My ass and yours are on the line in this case. The whole country, the whole world, is watching."

"I know that," Eli said soberly.

"I realize you do and I know you're doing as well as anyone could do under the circumstances. You've got my confidence. But a word of advice: Moghrabi and his gang might be the Sons of Gideon, or have links to them. But nothing's been proven. Be prepared to continue if these guys don't end up being the real thing."

"We'll be prepared, either way. I'm taking nothing for granted," said Eli.

An hour and a half before the rally was scheduled to begin, Eli briefed the fifteen men under his command on the roof of Tel Aviv City Hall on the northern fringe of Rabin Square. Each agent had a single assignment: to position himself no more than two meters from each of Zohar's collaborators, to anticipate their suspect's next step and to contain him at the first sign of violence. They were to shadow their subject without arousing suspicion.

Eli completed his briefing and descended in a service elevator. As arranged, a police representative was waiting in the building's basement to supply Eli with marked bills for the second payment to Zohar. Eli was also fitted with a recording device taped beneath his shirt.

Eli left the building through the lobby and stepped out into the night into the fierce unseasonal heat, August in late November, that had crept out of Arabia and hovered over the Land of Israel like a specter. In jeans, sneakers and a loose shirt, Eli's was a feline presence as he moved along the margins of the rally, skirting the crew that placed the finishing touches on the stage and the lighting and sound system for the meeting with Zohar and his men.

Zohar saw Eli first and hurried toward him, his arms outstretched in a too familiar greeting. He wrapped his arm around Eli's shoulder. Eli instinctively tensed his back: Zohar had taken a liberty that Eli had not granted him. It was a display of bravado, an indiscretion, a bad sign, thought Eli.

"Good evening, Mr. Haddad. Meet the boys. We don't look like much, but we are dynamite," Zohar crowed.

Eli eyed Zohar's men. They were decidedly unimpressive, sitting along the curb and leaning against a pillar. Two were overweight while another two looked anorexic. One had a foreshortened arm, another had a perpetual facial tic. There was nothing to suggest that they were disciplined, intelligent and resourceful men – traits the Shin Bet profiler had associated with the Gideons. The profile had also portrayed the Gideons as calm, passionless killing machines. This crew looked feeble, dull and witless.

Did he have the wrong guys? Eli thought of his team crowded around monitors watching a video stream of these proceedings captured by the camcorder Eli had had positioned at the site earlier in the day. Eli's operatives were no doubt shaking their heads in disbelief, bewildered that these miscreants they were to shadow could have been responsible for the immaculate Al-Bakr attack.

Eli quickly retraced his reasoning for the engagement with this gang as Zohar introduced his men. Zohar was linked to Al-Bakr via Amir, his brother, the Border Policeman. Zohar claimed that he and his gang had murdered Arabs in the past. He and his crew were ready to hire themselves out to Mr. Haddad and disrupt the rally for money and a visceral attachment to extremism. By the time he shook the hand of Zohar's last man, Eli concluded that the operation was justified.

Eli turned to Zohar, "Why don't you fill me in on your plans this evening?"

"It's a surprise," Zohar interjected. "Let's just say that if it doesn't put a serious hole in these bastards' program, nothing will. People will be running in every direction."

Eli s heart fell into his gut. "I have already told you," he said angrily, "no one is to get hurt. Not from bombs and not from being trampled by a crowd in panic." Eli paused to make sure they heard his every word. "Understand that if anyone gets hurt as a result of your actions, my bodyguards will find each and every one of you by daybreak. They will not go easy on you."

Eli composed himself – he couldn't ignore the possibility that these were the Gideons and that he had a chance to apprehend them. Patience, he reminded himself, then moderated his voice and asked, "When is all of this going to happen, Zohar?"

"At 20:45, and unless someone gets really stupid, no one will get hurt. You have my word."

"Well, whatever you are going to do, you are going to do it as a single group, correct?" asked Eli, mining for information.

"No, we're going to spread out, secret agent style."

"I see," said Eli. There was nothing left for him to do or say and while he was deeply worried, he consoled himself with the observation that at least Zohar and his men did not appear to be carrying any weapons or explosives with them.

Whatever mischief Zohar had in mind, it was now up to Eli and his team to make sure that these goons injured no one.

According to the radio news broadcast half an hour before the scheduled start of the event, the police were estimating that 200,000 people were already crowded into Rabin Square. The streets of north-central Tel Aviv were virtual pedestrian malls with throngs of people pouring into the rally site. The police were keeping one route open for ambulances and emergency vehicles. Eli hoped that this route would remain unused.

The huge crowd was orderly and restrained. As they stood facing the towering stage at the front of the Square, there was a palpable eagerness and vigor among those assembled – young families and elderly couples, youth movement members and students – the faces a panoply of colors reflecting the diverse origins of the people of Israel. As Eli looked at the plaza full with people who had come from far and wide to participate in the rally, he sensed a yearning for release from the mounting grief, rage and shame unleashed by the Abed murder, the

Coastal Road attack and the Al-Bakr massacre.

Uniformed police stood along the margins of the rally site; plainclothesmen mingled with the crowd. Jeeps full of guntoting Border Police patrolmen ringed the plaza. Bomb disposal units equipped with remote-control robots were interspersed among the phalanx of police vehicles, ambulances and media vans at the ready along the edge of the plaza.

Another detachment of police guarded a nearby counter-demonstration attended by several hundred vociferous opponents of the rally. They were rambunctious and belligerent members of Rabbi Epstein's Hebrew Fighters Association and other right-wing groups.

The booming voice of one of the organizers called on the participants to isolate the counter-demonstrators in a rear corner of the plaza. From where he stood atop City Hall, Eli watched the legions of his countrymen and women move as one, repulsed by and turning their backs on the riotous groups on their fringe. They had come to demand the excision of the extremists. They wanted them expelled from their society.

Eli was fully aware that it was his task to uncover the terrorists and to extirpate them. As he stood alone and saw the masses that filled the square, he felt himself pitted against an enemy he could not yet clearly see.

Lilah, Michal and Issam walked to the rally from Lilah's apartment. They had arrived at the Square half an hour early, in time to find a spot from which they could see the stage.

As soon as the speeches began, Lilah felt an identity with the people, goals and vision of the rally. As she looked at those around her, she realized that this was her Israel: people who cared for the social "we," who identified with the Jewish collectivity, its history and future, proud Israelis who were not interested in oppressing others, people who were open-minded and progressive. She was impressed by the dignitaries sitting on the podium: a reserve general and war hero, a respected actress/poetess, an internationally renowned painter who had never before lent his name to a cause, three Knesset members, the conductor of the Israel Philharmonic, two novelists, several renowned professors, the head of the trade union federation, a soccer star and the president of the Academy of Arts and Sciences. There were six Israel Prize winners among them.

Lilah agreed with what was published the next day in *Haaretz*: "Prior to the outrage that ensued, a renewed Israel was unveiled on the stage last night, an Israel returning to its progressive roots dedicated to finding ways for the society to survive the national and global challenges of our time and blossom long into the future."

Among the speakers was a most unlikely one, a short, bowlegged man with rounded shoulders, a thin beard and *payot*, side-locks that framed his face. Shaul Ben-Yishai was introduced by the very secular-appearing master of ceremonies as the community rabbi of a small cooperative farming settlement near Nes Tziona. In the Torah world, she said, he was regarded as an *elui*, a genius and master of Talmudic law, who had been marginalized by the rabbinical establishment for his tepid opinion of West Bank settlement. His views had become increasingly condemnatory of the settlement enterprise, which he had termed it in one widely-circulated article as a "provocation" championed by "people intoxicated with power who did not know how to sift the chaff from the germ of the sacred teachings." That he also called for tolerance and rapprochement among Jews, that he backed a separation of state and religion and that he condemned the country's class of nouveau riche as "unseemly gluttons" further distanced him from the Orthodox mainstream.

The rabbi captivated everyone – not only because of what he said but because he challenged the stereotypes of the "we" and "they" that had increasingly divided Israeli Jews. Addressing the vast audience at Rabin Square where skullcaps were present but not abundant, he seemed an anomaly, an iconoclast.

In a high-pitched, guttural voice, the rabbi spoke about how he and his five brothers were sent to the Holy Land by their father. Over the course of two years, they walked from Yemen to the Land of Israel. The brothers had been separated after they arrived, and he had spent his childhood in an ultra-religious orphanage run by Yiddish-speaking Hassidim. Rabbi Ben-Yishai spoke about his brothers having very different lives from one another after having grown up separately, yet their extended family was now strong, all the stronger for their differences.

Like a biblical prophet addressing the multitudes, Rabbi Ben-Yishai bellowed, "'Justice, and only justice, you shall pursue, that you may live and possess the land.' That is what the Creator instructed us. It is incumbent on us to pursue justice among ourselves and with others as a condition of our presence on this earth." Calling what happened at Al-Bakr an "abomination of all that is sacred to us," the rabbi declared that "we are indeed our brother's keeper, including those who reside within our tents, Jews and non-Jews – and the Palestinians until they part from us and have their own state." He denounced the zealots who demanded a Greater Israel at all costs as being severely misguided and engaged in "false works."

"Disaster will befall the children of Israel if we oppress those who reside within our tents...Woe be to he who wraps himself in the prayer shawl and praises the Lord, Blessed be His Name, while standing idly by as injustice is committed against non-Jews living among us."

The rabbi spoke for a full twelve minutes. No one interrupted him. When the other speakers completed their speeches, there had been resounding applause, whistles and shouts of approval. But when the rabbi left the lectern and returned to his seat on the stage, there was silence, no one spoke. It was as if the entire assembly had been called to reckoning. Finally, someone up front began to sing a traditional hymn of peace. The singing caught on, passing in a wave until the entire Square echoed with it. Lilah felt goose bumps. Tears streamed down Michal's face. Issam was awed. "A saint," he said. "A holy man."

It was as if a hallowed spirit had descended on the rally. It remained as the next speaker was called to address the assembly.

Prof. Naftali Kedem, Member of the Knesset and Leader of the Opposition, walked to the podium in small steps, as if approaching sacred ground. The swell of pride that Lilah felt when she heard his name being called was dampened as she saw a figure, Ido, trailing his father. Their son stood discreetly behind and to the side of the speaker, intent on shielding his father should harm come his way. Ido's hands were folded at his waist. He wore a vest with a conspicuous protuberance, a sidearm Lilah realized. His feet were set a shoulder width apart and were firmly planted. It would later be explained to Lilah that Naftali had acquiesced to Ido's insistence that he accompany him to such public gatherings. The arrangement had never been formalized, but the security services did not interfere. The son as his father's protector was accepted as unwritten protocol.

Naftali seemed deeply introspective as he stood, solitary, at the speaker's podium. He removed a sheet from his shirt pocket and unfolded it. He scanned the text, cleared his throat and adjusted the height of the microphone. He closed his eyes meditatively for a moment. He then began to speak.

Lilah looked up at him, the man with whom she had been linked for most of her life but from whom she had too often been apart; how was it, she asked herself, that she had allowed that to be?

She, like many in the crowd, was perplexed by the way Naftali started his speech.

"The terrorists who destroyed the lives of dozens of people and horribly wounded many others when they attacked a passenger bus on the Coastal Road in September came from two villages near Hebron, the heartland of my people, City of the Patriarchs. As someone who seeks for the Palestinian people what I insist on for my own people – the right to control their collective destiny – the future Palestinian state will have to accommodate the Jewish communities residing in Judea and Samaria. It is their historical right to live there," Naftali declared.

Naftali's odd beginning was unexpected. His listeners couldn't fathom why the head of the Progressive Bloc started his speech in that way, from the Right.

"And we citizens of the State of Israel are duty-bound, in order to be true to ourselves, to recognize that the Land of Israel, within the State and beyond its borders, belongs to two peoples, ours and the Palestinians. Neither people can expunge the roots of the others."

The principle was well-known and broadly accepted. Where in the world is Naftali going? Lilah wondered.

The wind began to pickup.

"Both peoples must realize that their separate histories today converge in a new reality, a global one. We are not only Jews, Arabs and Druze but citizens of the world, and the future we seek for ourselves can only be guaranteed if we are part of a new consciousness, a global one, attuned to the economic and environmental dangers the world now faces."

Several gusts of wind toyed with the huge fabric posters proclaiming "A Rally of Hope: Toward a Common Future" on which the countenance of Ben-Gurion, the picture Eli had seen in Amos' office, had been pixilated. The posters were at the sides of the stage, several stories high. Both had come loose at a corner and the fabric was flapping, like some immense thunderbird waiting to take off.

Naftali paused and drank from a bottle of water and then resumed with understated power. "We must together rise to face these challenges."

"This is an age of great wealth for some but also of continuing poverty for hundreds of millions of people. This uneven wealth has bankrupted the planet. The world is today a checkerboard of the rich and poor, of privilege and injustice – which also exists in Israel, increasingly so, as well as among the Palestinians. Twenty families and a new class of affluence have dominated our lives, furthering their empires at home and abroad for their self-benefit. When petroleum resources are found off our coast, the oil barons run to persuade the people that the profits belong to them. With this government's blessing, the same appropriation is made by the real estate magnates and contractors who are granted full reign to pave over the land and construct monstrosities, the 'un-Holylands,' out of sheer greed. The same pattern is played out in the banking system and financial institutions, in the cellphone industry and the retail giants. We see it even in our supermarkets and the food industry, the manipulation of consumerism only so that the rich can get richer. These powers have no social concerns, no interest in the future.

"The day has come when a new system of sharing the planetary commonwealth – including the land and resources that both Israelis and Palestinians hold dear – is imperative. We know with increasingly clarity that our current practices are unsustainable and that the future requires us to plan together, to build cooperatively, to act responsibly and usher in a new civilization where matters of the spirit, art and culture, literature and self-enhancement replace the forces that have shaped recent history: greed, avarice, power and domination.

"Rise. We must rise," Naftali exhorted the crowd, "to

confront the challenges and realize the potentials that, we the people of Israel, possess and can share with our neighbors, the Palestinians and the other peoples of the region. We can green our common borders, cultivate our resources so that all of our people and not just the privileged among us – can rise.

"Against the backdrop of the inhuman attacks on the Coastal Road and Al-Bakr, in this age where those captaining the country steer us to waters that benefit only the oligarchic and moneyed classes, we must find a way to rise to a better future, rise so that we can bequeath to the generations that follow us the knowledge that we dared to stop the march to disaster, for our sake and theirs."

"Rise," Naftali urged. "For ourselves and the future generations, we must do so."

The entreaty, lingered over the throng of three-hundred thousand Israelis gathered in a plaza named after the assassinated peace seeker, Yitzhak Rabin. Naftali's exhortation was etched on the souls of all who heard it.

ೞ ❖ ಏ

It was 20:26, nineteen minutes before Zohar and his accomplices were scheduled to disrupt the rally.

Eli kept his disquiet in check as he stared through the binoculars. He was on the roof scanning the sea of humanity in the square below and pinpointing the location of each of his men. Eli had two of his men shadowing each of Zohar's gang, and he maintained audio contact with the two-agent teams.

Other than the ruckus caused by the right-wing counter-demonstrators and the occasional fainting of someone in the crowd below, it had been an uneventful evening. As the clock ticked down toward 20:45, Eli kept his agents focused on their targets. "Unit Dalet, you're lagging too far behind your subject.

Do you have him in view?" They did and one of the agents closed the distance between him and the suspect to a meter.

At 20:37, eight minutes before the incident was due to be initiated, Eli was satisfied that his men had Zohar's confederates surrounded and that they would take down their targets efficiently, without raising alarm among the rally participants.

The comfort of that assessment fell apart several moments later when Eli saw one of his agents clutch his chest and collapse. It would take minutes of wading through the throng for one of his backup men to replace him. Eli asked the communications specialist at the rooftop console to direct police medics toward the fallen man and ordered the downed man's partner to maintain his position next to the suspect they were tracking. "Proceed and prepare to apprehend the subject, without pause," Eli directed. The agent did as instructed.

But Eli's man was going against a stream of youth movement members that had formed in a tight knot ten people wide. The agent was effectively blocked from catching up with the suspect he had been trailing.

Eli made a quick calculation. He could not risk a loose cannon. It was two minutes until whatever Zohar had planned was due to occur. If the other teams took down their targets now, one of them could be freed to go after the uncovered subject.

"Command, command," Eli said into his transmitters, "at the count of three, execute the mission. Apprehend your targets," he shouted, and on the count, his agents overpowered their suspects in one fell swoop. All of them were contained except for one.

"Team Gimel, one of you secure your subject in a full hold. I need the other to move quickly; ten meters to the left, there is another subject moving toward the stage. Take him now."

Team Gimel placed their man face down on the ground and

in wrist constraints. One of the operatives then proceeded and in the minute and half remaining until Zohar's action was to take place, the agent reached the target, seized him and wrestled him to the ground.

Zohar and all of his men had now been arrested and were being hustled, each separately and unknown to the others, toward the point behind the office building where Eli, panting and perspiring from the tension, waited.

Eli rode the elevator to the ground floor. As he exited the building into the night, the air had grown noticeably chillier than it had been an hour earlier. He sent a text message to Amos: "Operation completed, without incident."

Zohar and his cohorts were brought one by one to the back of the building. They were placed with their backs against the wall and ankle chains were placed around their legs. Unmarked cars were waiting to take them to a Shin Bet detention center.

Zohar spotted Eli. "You?" was all he could sputter at first.

"Yes, Zohar, it's me," Eli said calmly. He intended to accompany Zohar and personally interrogate him.

"So these are the people you represent? I acted out of patriotism, you pig."

"Yes, yes. Patriotism and a nice retainer."

Zohar spat at Eli, just missing him.

Eli's agents frisked Zohar and the members of his gang. Each carried matches and small packs of fireworks. Not very high-tech. Not very sophisticated. Not very bloody – but enough to create a distraction and set off a wave of panic among those attending the rally.

Zohar's interest in Al-Bakr notwithstanding, Eli had deepening doubts that these were the Gideons.

"Drive them to the lockup," Eli ordered. "Let's see why Mr. Moghrabi here was so interested in the attack on Al-Bakr."

"I don't know anything about that," Zohar claimed.

"So why did you pump your little brother for all the detailed information he could get about the refugee camp? A man of your sentiments toward Arabs wouldn't be overly concerned about where or how they live."

"Is that what this is all about?!" Zohar practically shouted. "Steiner's heroin supplier has relatives at Al-Bakr. We were thinking of using the place to stash our supplies and wanted to make sure he could hide stuff there without anyone finding it. That's all. I swear."

Zohar's lament was interrupted by a deafening blast. The municipal building quaked and the ground shook.

Naftali had just concluded his comments and the moderator had made her final remarks. The speakers were standing together in front of the podium and as they were about to lead the crowd in *HaTikva*, the national anthem, an enormous boom reverberated off the buildings around Rabin Square.

Half or more of the people on the stage were flung off from it as it collapsed. Glass rained down from shattered windows of the adjacent buildings. People began running in all directions amid terrible screaming.

A bomb had gone off at Rabin Square.

03 ❖ 80

Issam sipped a cup of coffee as he spoke with his colleague; Lilah sat restlessly nearby on a couch in the doctors' lounge. Naftali and thirty-eight other wounded, those with lesser injuries out of a total of more than eighty, had been evacuated to Beilinson Hospital in Petach Tikva, where Issam had spent much of the past week. They had been rushed to the more distant facility after the emergency room at Ichilov Hospital within walking distance from Rabin Square had been flooded with wounded. Issam was in surgical scrubs after having assisted in several surgeries. Now, he was between operations and was consulting with a colleague about the Kedem men.

There was a gash on Ido's cheek but no other major wounds. Naftali was semi-conscious, but out of danger. He had suffered a moderate concussion and had lacerations along the left side of his body and face. The senior plastic surgeon attending to both father and son said that, in the scheme of things, their injuries could have been much worse.

Issam listened attentively, but Lilah could not.

She was focusing on the radio broadcast and trying to absorb the statement released by the Sons of Gideon:

> *At 21:00 this evening, our fighters attacked the crowd of Jewish traitors assembled at Rabin Square.*
>
> *We warn those who were there but who did not directly suffer our wrath that if you persist in such traitorous activities, you will be similarly punished. Give us a free hand to take care of the Arabs. Give us our liberty....*

Lilah struggled to contain her fury. She was enraged, not only by what had happened to Ido and Naftali, not only by the dead and wounded, but also by the fact that these madmen were so inaccessible, so beyond reach. Who could they be? she wondered. Who are these monsters?

She listened as Ambassador Ephrati pleaded yet again for the public's help in identifying and apprehending the Sons of Gideon.

It was then, listening to his appeal, that Lilah decided how she would contribute to ending this plague. She would capture the Sons of Gideon – capture them on film.

CHAPTER EIGHT

In the cab from Beilinson Hospital to Tel Aviv, Lilah left the window half open. The air, drier and cooler than it had been since her return, lightly lashed her cheeks and forehead. It was refreshing, cleansing, though dry. The land of Israel was still thirsting for the start of the winter rains.

Lilah did not see the urban landscape sweeping past her on the highway. Instead, her mind's eye was focused on a kaleidoscope of seared images, a photo album – "The Crucible" she would have titled it – of the four months since she had been back: Fatima Abed in her long dress with three black holes on her chest and fish strewn about her where the assassin had felled her; the little girl clutching both her doll and her dead mother as a smoky haze hovered shroud-like over them as she squatted on the Coastal Road; the old man behind the child, hollow-eyed with metal nails embedded in his neck and cheeks; the photographs of Al-Bakr laying in ruins as though some maniacal legion had sacked it of all but its misery. And the fresh images: the crowds fleeing Rabin Square after the bomb blast at the Rally of Hope, Knesset member Naftali Kedem on a stretcher being rushed to an ambulance and his son – his own face bloodied – one of its bearers.

At dawn, Lilah was still awake. She sat at the kitchen table, her laptop open. Michal and Issam had come back with her to 3 HaGaon Street and were asleep in her bedroom. Ido was in his room, the Percocet for the pain where his face had been stitched having plunged him into deep slumber.

Lilah, in contrast, had not felt so awake in a long time.

"Blood-anger, disappointment, rage, a desire to protect and console, to strike out is what I felt," Lilah wrote to Lucian. "I am calm as I write to you now, my dear friend, but in me there is lava boiling and a loud voice screaming: Who has done this to my country?"

She wrote on, the words could not be constrained:

What can I do? I wondered as I watched the rescue teams untangle the dead and wounded that these beasts had left behind. I could no longer cry. I have my power – my eye and my camera – and with it, I will dig and dig and dig until I find something that identifies them.

I will flush them out into the light of day.

Lilah sent the email off to Lucian. She showered and left a note on the kitchen table for Michal and Issam to make themselves at home. The photographer-hunter selected several cameras, packed her bag and then made her way to Rabin Square.

Traffic was just now being allowed on the streets surrounding the plaza. The square reeked with an industrial odor, the smell of spent explosives. Lilah positioned herself at the northwest corner near the steps up to city hall and scanned the concrete vista. She then began shooting at a furious clip, collecting a mosaic of images around the square and the buildings that surrounded it.

Lilah was determined to find the wretched souls who were behind this one.

Lilah wasn't the only one to come back to Rabin Square that morning. Eli had also returned, sobered by the realization that his gambit had failed. The wager he had made by betting on the only card he had in hand, Zohar Moghrabi and his gang, had been exploded by the Gideons' bomb. He kept his self-recrimination in check and acted on the one emotion that could be channeled productively: a raging desire to find the terrorists. He and Lilah passed each other that morning, impervious to the other. They were seekers in pirouette, hunters in tandem, pursuing a common quarry.

Within hours, the preliminary findings showed that the bombs were made of a sophisticated explosive used in mining operations. Parts of several detonators were recovered, and the specialists were able to deduce that the bombs had been buried in concrete. Given that a permit to hold the rally had only been issued three days previously, the window of opportunity when the explosives could have been placed at the site was between Wednesday evening and Sunday morning.

Eli sent for the municipal employee in charge of physical grounds and infrastructure in the area of Rabin Square. It was ascertained that a private contractor with a work order issued on the letterhead of the Israel Landmarks Authority had presented himself on Friday and claimed that he had been commissioned to install new planters alongside where the stage was being erected. Fragments of the planters were discovered beneath the collapsed platform. They had been assembled elsewhere, thereby enabling the perpetrator to spend as little time as possible at the Square. It was soon determined that the Israel Landmarks Authority had not ordered any work done at Rabin Square that week.

At the time, the municipal inspector had asked the contractor to register. The name he had scrawled on the log was either Ya'akov Shimshoni or Shimshon Ya'akov. Eli had checks run for data on Shimshoni or Ya'akov on the computer servers of the Interior Ministry, the National Insurance Institute and several licensing boards. There were twenty-three men with those or similar names in the central region alone. The names were immediately checked against police, prison service, court and probation office records. Military records were also cross-referenced.

An IDF data bank entry provided an exquisitely relevant lead: An "S. Ya'akovi" had registered at the office of the Coordinator of Government Activities in the Territories at Beit El a week before the Al-Bakr massacre. He had produced a requisition order from the unit's headquarters to install cement bases for streetlights in the Al-Bakr refugee camp. According to a notation made by the duty officer in the relevant log, Ya'akovi was a civilian contractor.

Eli sent for the officer who had been on duty at the Coordinator's office the day "S. Ya'akovi" had presented the requisition order. By 11:00 a.m., the lieutenant was sitting with a police artist to create a composite likeness of the man who had identified himself as S. Ya'akovi at Beit El. The duty officer and the Rabin Square grounds supervisor agreed that the man was large, muscular and powerfully built and in his mid-to-late forties. The inspector claimed that he was clean-shaven and bareheaded with blond hair. The man the IDF officer remembered was described as having a red beard and sideburns and wore a beret and sunglasses. By noon, both images were released to the press as being those of individuals wanted for questioning with respect to the attacks on Fatima Abed and at Al-Bakr and Rabin Square.

Concurrently, Eli initiated the most extensive manhunt in the history of the State of Israel.

The search focused on those suspects began at around noon on Monday, fifteen hours after the bombing at Rabin Square. A nationwide review of files, ledgers, databanks and registries was set into motion. The media, anxious for a role other than merely reporting another attack or a lack of progress in the investigation, complied with the government's request that descriptions of the masonry contractor suspected in the attacks be broadcast continuously and be featured on the front pages of the dailies. The public was highly responsive; tips were pouring in on the police lines. The Nationalists and the religious establishment, frightened by the deteriorating situation, could not ignore the public's outrage. They denounced the Gideons and their actions as "contrary to State interests" and "opposed to the principles of Judaism."

Eli and his investigators sifted through all the information that was flowing in from multiple sources; initially, none was very compelling. But late that afternoon, something promising caught Eli's eye: a landlord in Jerusalem's Romema neighborhood had contacted the police. He had rented an apartment some months earlier to a person that fit one of the descriptions in the media and the signature on the lease was Ya'akov Ben-David Shimshoni's.

Eli's men were either at Rabin Square or at his office; it would take them nearly an hour to get to Romema. Eli contacted the Shin Bet and asked for a squad of investigators to descend on the Jerusalem apartment with instructions to eviscerate it and search for evidence. Eli left Tel Aviv immediately for the capital. By the time he arrived, the Shin Bet contingent had gone through the apartment with a fine-toothed comb and had begun to interview the neighbors.

The picture that emerged of Ya'akov Ben-David Shimshoni was consistent with the description of the contractor who had installed the planters at Rabin Square. Significantly, neighbors also reported having seen someone resembling the description of the contractor who had worked in Al-Bakr, although none had had more than transient conversations with him. Shimshoni was described as exceedingly reserved. He was obsessed with fulfilling the daily religious rites and commandments and passionate about the practice of religious law.

Once the neighbors learned who Shimshoni was suspected of being, they were keen to talk to the security men. Eli saw the fear in their faces, a fear he had increasingly encountered among ordinary Israelis wherever he went as the violence mounted. They were terrified by the Sons of Gideon, distressed by the fury the group had vented in so short a time. Like a bucket brigade hoping to douse a wildfire, they poured out anything they could remember about the stranger who dwelled among them.

According to the neighbors, Shimshoni's Hebrew was good but odd and inflected; he was clearly not a sabra but an immigrant, perhaps from an English-speaking country. No one had any real idea of his background.

The landlord reported that he had rented out the apartment six months earlier in response to a flyer he had placed on a community bulletin board in the Jewish Quarter of the Old City. Shimshoni had paid the landlord a year's rent in advance – in U.S. dollars. He had mentioned that he had come to Israel to study under a well-known rabbi – the right-wing zealot, Yehezkel Epstein. He was not employed, but money did not seem to be a problem for him.

In the living room of the apartment, the security men discovered reams of anti-Arab propaganda printed by Epstein and other extremists. A closet in one of the bedrooms was stocked with timers, batteries, spools of wire and electronic gadgetry including switches for remote detonation. Shimshoni had set up a workbench in the bedroom complete with tools and other paraphernalia useful to a bomb maker. Folded neatly on one shelf were work clothes, construction boots and heavy gloves.

There was also a selection of Israeli military uniforms: army, navy and various units of the police and Border Police, as well as an air force jumpsuit and infantry battle gear. Shimshoni had two sets of the flak aprons, body armor and helmets worn by police sappers.

Shimshoni had not been seen by his neighbors for approximately four weeks. An elderly man who lived in the building did report having seen someone fitting the description of the man suspected in the Al-Bakr attack on several occasions, coming and going at odd times of the day and night and carrying construction equipment. Both men had been observed separately using the same van.

The suspect wanted in connection with the Al-Bakr attack had been seen much more recently than Shimshoni, in the days leading up to the Al-Bakr massacre, and then on two occasions in the last week. He had been covered in dust and grime when he entered the apartment. The man appeared physically tired, but energized – "like a watch spring," recalled the elderly neighbor.

In a single hour, more had been learned about the Sons of Gideon than in the nearly four months since Fatima Abed's murder.

Word of the discovery of the Gideons' hideaway had gotten out, and the area around the apartment building was soon thronged with the media, curiosity seekers, people from the neighborhood and outraged citizens from elsewhere in the capital who had arrived in droves. Both major television news networks as well as foreign television crews had edged their vehicles as close to the site as the police would let them. All other traffic around Romema was redirected.

On the margins of the site, in sharp relief from the plump, wigged Hassidic women with children and baby carriages in tow, appeared an attractive middle-aged woman in jeans clutching an Olympia camera and with a gear bag on her shoulder. Careful to intrude neither upon the security forces nor the neighborhood residents, Lilah took close-ups and long shots of the vicinity.

In the area around the old *Jerusalem Post* building, there had gathered a quorum of the Hebrew Fighters and Keepers of the Faith. Still humbled by the trouncing their compatriots in Tel Aviv had suffered at Rabin Square the previous night, they were uncharacteristically restrained – as if whatever little sense they had told them that some kind of presence, even more noxious than theirs, had infiltrated and assumed their guise.

Lilah observed it all. She took many pictures.

Chapter Nine

The late November winds carried no rain and the leaf-shorn branches on the tall trees seemed to scratch impatiently against the panes of the hospital room windows.

"We are all the same in our johnnies and when we return to our Creator, Blessed be He," Naftali said as the Arab physician, Issam, adjusted the drip rate of the IV in the rabbi's arm.

Michal, wiping the rabbi's face with a washcloth, looked warily at Lilah. Coming from the head of the secular opposition, such allusions to divinity seemed odd.

"The key," Rabbi Ben-Yishai added, "is for human beings to recognize that we are all equals even when we are not in johnnies or in our graves."

"Quite right," Naftali agreed

"Yes, of course," Issam acceded.

Thirty-eight hours after the Rabin Square attack, the five of them – Michal, Issam, Lilah, Naftali and Rabbi Ben-Yishai – had congealed into a community. In that time, both the rabbi and Naftali had been operated on – the rabbi to repair a shattered arm and Naftali to remove his spleen, which one of his broken ribs had pierced. The two men had been in nether worlds of pre-op fasting, anesthetics and painkillers. Both were now out of danger and stabilized. "Blessed be the Name," they both said on their common good fortune, their having been delivered from even worse fates as a result of the blast.

During their bantering about the inedible hospital food, the constant interruptions of their sleep, the interminable needle pokes they had suffered and the vile medicines that had been forced on them, the rabbi and the Knesset member found themselves talking about matters of consequence. They had begun with gentle probes of each other's views but quickly found that there was much they concurred on. They agreed that things had evolved badly and that the society had been poorly captained. It was woefully clear to them both that government policies had sapped education and culture of their humanistic elements and that they had been subverted to the service of technocracy. They had reached the common conclusion that religion had been hijacked by right-wing clerics who had forgotten its true meaning and proselytized a dangerous romanticism. They were of one mind regarding the Occupation: It was unjust to both Israelis and Palestinians and its dismantlement was long overdue. They both felt that society had been lulled into believing that the interests of the business tycoons would guarantee the future of the state. They were both aggrieved by the Nationalist policies that had so alienated the rest of the world from Israel. They reached the common conclusion that the road the State had been set upon would lead only to disaster.

"Israel is in trouble," Michal said as she adjusted the rabbi's pillows.

"Yes, it is," the rabbi said regretfully. His wispy beard was unkempt and his thin arms stuck out of the yellow hospital garment like sticks. His black skullcap hung topsy-turvy atop his crown. His deep-brown skin looked blanched and his eyes were weary and downcast. "The danger Israel faces is that we have become beguiled by a world of appearances and fakery. The people have been led to believe that material things are all that matter, that life should be lived quickly and that the more we possess, the greater is our salvation," he said, shaking his head, a prophet's lament.

A roar from the television suddenly interrupted their conversation, and an image of a race car came across the screen. It was a commercial for a cell phone provider urging shoppers to upgrade to its latest model, "Get with it! Join the crowd and race to a better life!" the announcer shouted.

"Too much diversion, too much rushing, too many things," the rabbi decried.

"It has become a material world, not only here but all over the world," Michal commented. "Some places have too much and other places too little."

"And few have enough of the things that are really important," Issam said as he sat down in the drab-green recliner by the rabbi's bed, the IV flowing evenly now. "Not enough caring about each other. Not enough respect for life."

"And not enough caring for the planet," the rabbi added, grimacing as he changed position in his bed. "The earth is in real trouble and we, human beings, are responsible. The bounty conferred on us by the Creator, Blessed be His Name, has been squandered and degraded. We have taken his great gifts and squandered them."

"Don't tell me you're an environmentalist?" Naftali asked approvingly.

"If that means protecting what the Creator has given to us to sustain our lives and enjoy its wonders, then yes, I am an environmentalist. What is destroying the air and water and earth is also destroying us. Greed and power and disrespect are destroying everything."

"Disrespect for life," Issam was quick to agree.

"Right, like the Sons of Gideon. They don't seem to place much value on life at all," said Michal. "They seem to prefer a world without people who are different than them. I wonder what they plan for the rest of us after they are finished with the Arabs. Of course, since I am married to a son of Ishmael I guess they won't keep me around. Not Jewish enough for them, but more than enough for Hitler," she said bitterly.

Her tone took Lilah back to when they were in middle school. She remembered sitting in Michal's room and listening to her downstairs, pleading with her father not to move out of their home after he and her mother had decided to divorce. "He says that he loves me and that I didn't do anything wrong but he can't take me with him. I guess that I'm just not good enough, so he's leaving me behind," she had said, heartbroken to Lilah.

"Michal, if the Gideons and their ilk ever get to power – which won't happen," Naftali declared, "because we won't let them – but if it does come down to that kind of repression, you won't be alone in that line of prisoners. I'll be several places ahead of you. And there will be plenty of good people to keep us company in any prison of their making, and we will fight and take back the night from them."

"Why wait for that before we organize ourselves?" the rabbi asked. "I believe the will of the people is against the extremists. I believe that Israelis, both Jews and Arabs, have had enough of the fanatics. I think the majority would like to cast them out," he added.

"The New Democratic Party is attracting members, right?" Issam asked. "We haven't been waiting patiently on the sidelines."

"Yes, but we are a political party that is slowly building on the ruins left from the collapse of the Labor movement," answered Naftali. "We operate in the context of a system of government run by coalitions based on power politics, not popular representation. We have years of work ahead of us before we change the political system," he said pensively, then urged: "Don't wait for us. The way to bring about change now is to stop the advance of this wave of hatred through a grassroots movement. Change the society from within the society – don't rely on the politicians on Mount Olympus," he counseled.

He paused, and then offered, "I will you help you," he said, his eyes turning from the rabbi, then to Issam, to Michal, finally stopping on Lilah. "The people must take matters in their own hands. The country's leadership has been taken over by corrupt men, small-minded and interested only in wealth and power. They dismiss the importance of an enlightened, progressive state, democratic and sustainable with equal rights for all; it's simply not in their frame of reference. They think that our security and future can be maintained by armed might alone and that justice is a weakness in the face of the enemy. It might be that Jews have always been among the most enlightened people in the world, but right now it's the most unenlightened forces that dominate our own country. It's time for us to drive away the darkness before it consumes us. It's up to us, the people to do so," he insisted.

Naftali asked Lilah for a drink of water. She lifted a glass to his lips and he drank from it gratefully and though he looked exhausted, he remained impassioned. "The buffoons must be shaken from power," he said with more fervor than one could expect from a man in his condition. "Go build a movement," he said, his voice low but clear and commanding. "Get the people to rise up and throw off this gang of reactionaries and Neanderthals. They endanger us as much as any external enemy could."

From Naftali Kedem's injunction made in the hospital room where he and Rabbi Shaul Ben-Yishai were convalescing, the Movement, an energy, a spirit that would reform and renew Israel was born. Its name came from Naftali's speech at the Rally of Hope replayed on the television news that evening.

"Rise. We must rise to confront the challenges and realize the potential that we, the people of Israel, possess," Naftali had exhorted the masses of citizens at Rabin Square.

Na'aleh, Rise, became both the name and the credo of the movement that, like the winter rains, was much awaited by the people of Israel. It had been born in the hospital room where Naftali Kedem and Shaul Ben-Yishai had been brought to heal.

☙ ❖ ❧

The first ad appeared on the third day after the Rally of Hope. Under a picture of Prof. Naftali Kedem delivering his remarks at Rabin Square the text read:

THE TIME HAS COME TO RISE
HELP BUILD ISRAEL ANEW
NA'ALEH, RISE

People throughout Israel heeded the call and in the ensuing groundswell Lilah found herself in the role of "movement spokesperson" without having time to get her bearings. She realized this after an Army Radio producer dialed her phone and button-holed her into giving an interview on the ten o'clock magazine program.

After hanging up the phone and finding that she had agreed, Lilah wanted to kick herself – she was petrified – but she quickly recovered. She was determined to make this work. She brought a spare phone into the room and plugged it into an outlet. Michal would listen in and bail her out if need be.

"You say that your agenda has nothing to do with politics. If you are not political, what are you after?" asked the sharp-tongued soldier-journalist.

Lilah paused before answering. Michal sat next to her, clipboard and pencil in hand. In large letters she scrawled "the *real* Israel, prophets, justice, equality, tolerance." Lilah, surprising herself, fluently wove an appropriate reply: "We're searching for the *real* Israel. The Israel of the Prophets and of Jewish ethics. We want this to be a country of justice, equality and tolerance," she replied.

"Isn't that more than a little naïve? A sentimental notion, given what the country has experienced recently? How can you be apolitical? Are you on one side of the fence or the other?"

"We represent those who will not resign themselves to blind hatred and bigotry. Politicians use the instruments of power.

Ours is a people-to-people approach," Lilah answered, prompted by keywords Michal scrawled on a notepad.

"Who are you and the other founders of this so-called movement?"

"We come from diverse backgrounds. My parents were members of the founding generation of Israel. They came here from Europe and Turkey. I am a secular Jew and was born and raised in Tel Aviv. I am a photojournalist who lived abroad for many years. Rabbi Ben-Yishai came here from Yemen. He is the spiritual leader of a small, rural, devoutly observant community; he is a *Talmid Chacham* and heads a yeshiva. Michal and Dr. Issam Halaby are the other founders. Michal has a very similar background to mine. She is an artist and actress who lived for many years in Paris where she met her husband, a distinguished cardiovascular surgeon, who was raised in an Arab village in the Galilee. They returned to Israel from France: two Israelis, one Arab and the other Jewish.

"As you can see, we are all very different. But we all, directly or indirectly, experienced some aspect of the recent attacks. For example, I photographed Fatima Abed shortly before she was murdered by the Sons of Gideon. I then was personally a victim of the Coastal Road terrorist bombings. Dr. Halaby has been performing emergency surgery on the wounded of Al-Bakr. Rabbi Ben-Yishai is still hospitalized after being injured at the Rabin Square bombing," Lilah paused for a moment and thought. She decided not to mention her connection to Naftali and Ido though she wasn't sure why. "All of us have had enough. We want the violence to stop," she continued.

"I see," said the broadcaster. "What kind of people do you hope to attract to your campaign?"

"Ordinary Israelis. People like us: Jews, Arabs, Druze, Ashkenazim, Ethiopians, Sephardim, Russians. Men, women, workers, farmers, managers, shopkeepers, veterans, new immigrants, Orthodox, secular. The whole rainbow of Israel."

"To what end?"

Lilah thought. "Our program is dynamic, a work in progress. We know that we want to build ties of mutual respect and equality among all the groups that make up Israel. We seek a society where the various sectors coexist. We oppose those who seek a segmented, divided, closed society. We believe that a majority of Israel's citizens want a society where a person is not just typecast as a member of one group or another but is viewed as an individual. Of course, an immediate aim is to isolate the extremists, both Jews and Arabs, who have caused so much bloodshed recently."

"Do you really think that a small band of do-gooders can accomplish what the security services have not been able to do?" asked the interviewer.

Lilah looked at Michal but did not betray a word – that she was pursuing the Gideons. That was a private concern, a pact she had made only with herself. She would not involve anyone else in her hunt.

"We have no intention of interfering with the security people," she said resolutely. "Perhaps we can help them by having those who identify with us deny extremists of all groups the cover they have operated under."

The interview came to an end. "This has been a production of "People and Places" on Army Radio. We've been speaking with Lilah Kedem, a founder and spokeswoman of Na'aleh."

Lilah and Michal didn't even have time to consider her performance on the interview. The phone began ringing immediately with people wanting to help out in some way; they found themselves deluged by support. Among those who had phoned were acquaintances of Lilah's and Michal from the distant past, school friends and people from the youth movement, people who had grown up with the two of them and Yonatan. They invited several of them to the steering committee meeting in her home that evening. Na'aleh needed the input of as many like-minded people as could be found. To Lilah's surprise, the cavalry promised to come.

And come they did – including many who were complete strangers. Among those who arrived at 3 HaGaon Street that evening, were an architect, a jazz musician, a prominent poet, the dean of an Arab teachers' college, a psychology professor, a chemist, the owner of an electrical appliance factory, a banker, a housewife, a taxi driver, and a farmer who grew roses. The tasks the organization would undertake were divided among them. A social worker agreed to organize the volunteers. A retired magazine editor and radio journalist agreed to coordinate Na'aleh's media contacts. Programming, outreach, logistics and liaison committees were created. And all the while, the phone kept ringing with more offers of help.

Something magical was happening here thought Lilah as she watched the determined faces of the people gathered in her living room. It seemed as though people long in search of kindred spirits had finally found each other. Lilah thought of her parents and how fitting it was that this meeting was taking place in their home. She felt a tremendous connection with them, a passing of the torch.

When the discussion turned to what the organization would actually *do*, a call was placed to Rabbi Ben-Yishai and Naftali, who were waiting in their hospital room like satellites orbiting the meeting. It was the rabbi who came up with the idea for the "Drown out the Darkness" campaign. The lighting of candles as a symbol of hope and affirmation was deeply rooted in Jewish life and would be used to express the Movement's spirit. Each evening, Na'aleh supporters would place a candle on a windowsill or outside their homes to identify with the campaign against intolerance and violence.

It was decided that Na'aleh would proclaim "Democracy and Unity Day" – teach-ins at universities, secondary schools and workplaces. That night, the steering committee conceived the "Know Your Neighbor" project that would foster salon meetings where Arabs and Jews would meet in homes and try to reverse years of estrangement. A "Voice of the Victims" campaign was adopted entailing newspaper advertisements, wall posters, and art and photography exhibitions that would document, through texts and visuals, the human cost of extremist acts. Finally, a 'Lobby of Israel United' would be created to work for parliamentary and government action against violence and bigotry.

It was all so ambitious, terribly ambitious. There was change in the air, in her, too, Lilah thought as she watched the Movement come alive like a beating heart in her living room. She felt enveloped by a huge and humbling emotion: was it really possible to chase the evil winds from the land?

After the meeting, Michal went to bed in Ido's room. In her room, Lilah sat on the cushioned bench by the window just as she had as a young girl. She gazed out at the sky, clear as crystal, a multitude of stars overhead. But instead of the unadulterated wonder she had felt back then, another set of feelings, something gnarled and bitter invaded her consciousness,

In her mind's eye, there arose the memory of blood spurting from Ido's cheek as he struggled with the other bearers of the stretcher on which an ashen Naftali was carried from the collapsed stage at the Rally of Hope. She thought again of Fatima Abed laying shot on the ground, of the child on the Coastal Road next to her lifeless mother, of the photographs of Al-Bakr.

Lilah felt a surging determination to apprehend them, the demons responsible for the entire cycle of bloodletting.

She thought of a statue she had once seen, of Diana, the Roman goddess of the hunt. That this spirit might now inhabit her heart made Lilah shudder.

She wondered, had she let herself feel these same emotions then, after Yonatan had been wrenched from her, would she have stayed in exile those thirty odd years.

CHAPTER TEN

It was six weeks after the Rabin Square bombing and the new calendar year was about to begin. A television documentary on the events of 9/11, now more than a decade past, left its impress on Eli Zedek's mood. When would the Gideons next pounce? The question had plagued Eli since the Rally of Hope.

It was quiet in the late night, the traffic sparse in the streets below. Eli ate a few forkfuls of the couscous and *kubeh* he had brought back to his office hours earlier. He had returned after retrieving the Shin Bet report he had asked for, the one on Na'aleh, that group that seemed to be everywhere now: candles on windowsills, posters, newspaper ads, gatherings of Jews and Arabs. The reading was absorbing and as Eli concentrated, the couscous spilled off his fork and flecked the hair on his strong arms and hands, specks of yellow against fields of deep brown.

"The General Security Services' domestic organizations division is monitoring Na'aleh on an ongoing basis. The following is a summary report, current as of December 20th of this year.

"HISTORY: Established in the immediate aftermath of the Rabin Square bombing on November 2nd, Na'aleh is believed to comprise individuals adhering to loosely-defined humanitarian principles rather than a specific political ideology; clearly, however, the group is of a liberal-left orientation.

"GOALS: Its goals as described in the attached brochure are: promotion of mutual understanding and respect between the majority and minority sectors of the society; safeguarding the democratic foundations of the State of Israel; promoting the civil liberties of all citizens; urging tolerance among different ethnic, religious and ideological camps of the society; and revitalizing and expanding the dialogue between Israel and its Arab neighbors to advance coexistence and cooperation.

"The Na'aleh Movement has acquired growing visibility in

the public eye. Its recognition is due in part to the Sons of Gideon and Coastal Road attacks last summer and throughout the fall in response to which the organization first arose. It uses large newspaper advertisements extensively to photographically describe the murder of Fatima Abed, the Al-Bakr attack, the incident at Rabin Square and numerous threats received by progressives and their groups – all of which are sent in the name of the Sons of Gideon. The organization, it must be noted, presents a balanced picture and also strongly condemns Arab terrorist attacks against Jews such as the Coastal Road bus bombing last summer. It has also issued a strong statement critical of the Palestinian Authority's lack of recognition of the right of Jewish self-determination in parallel to the rights it claims for the Palestinian people. Na'aleh recognizes this right for the Palestinians, including statehood.

"Significantly, many of the founders of Na'aleh witnessed and/or were injured in these attacks. One of the founders of the group who is also its spokeswoman, Lilah Kedem, was wounded as a result of the second bomb that exploded in the Coastal Road attack. Her husband, Member of Knesset Naftali Kedem (from whom she had been separated) and their son, Lt. Col. Ido Kedem, were injured in the course of the Rabin Square blast. Another founder of the Movement, Rabbi Shaul Ben-Yishai was also badly injured at the Rally of Hope bombing.

"AFFILIATIONS: Na'aleh professes independence from formal political programs and established parties. Nevertheless, informal ties with the New Democratic Party are assumed, given the latter's endorsement of the Movement and the fact that Lilah Kedem and the New Democrats' party chairman, Professor Naftali Kedem appear to have reestablished their relationship.

"Na'aleh includes among its constituents Israeli Jews, Arabs and Druze. It is largely secular, although Rabbi Ben-Yishai, the head of the Ein Baruch Yeshiva, is a founder and leader of the organization. He has brought a growing number of religious figures and groups close to the movement."

"FINANCES: As far as can be discerned, the group is financed by contributions, the majority of which are believed to be relatively small sums. Given the group's estimated expenditures in newspaper ads and printed matter alone, this means that it has a comparatively large number of contributors.

"Na'aleh is not a membership movement and in the words of one leader, it conducts a 'collective, decentralized dialogue among its supporters.' It is guided by an informal national secretariat; the individuals serving on this body include prominent cultural, academic and public figures (Appendix B). The Movement uses Lilah Kedem's apartment at 3 HaGaon Street in Tel Aviv as its headquarters and has branches in Acre, Haifa, Nazareth, Jerusalem, Beersheva, Dimona and Eilat (Appendix C).

"Na'aleh has adopted a number of high-profile activities intended, in its words, 'to sensitize and educate the Israeli public to the cycle of bloodshed threatening to engulf our country.' Among these activities: evening prayer vigils outside the Prime Minister's Office organized by Rabbi Ben-Yishai and led by distinguished rabbis. During these gatherings, dozens and sometimes hundreds of yeshiva students pray for peace and for the speedy arrest of the Gideons by the government and for the healing of the society. The police have had to physically separate the vigil from a much smaller but vociferous demonstration organized by the Nationalist Youth Movement, Keepers of the Truth and Rabbi Epstein's Hebrew Fighters Association. The latter often employs violence to disrupt the Na'aleh vigils.

"A second project launched is the 'Drown out the Darkness' campaign, which aims to heighten awareness of the organization's existence, promote solidarity among Jews and Arabs and 'affirm our resolve to keep both Jewish and Arab extremists from usurping our society.' Intelligence indicates that the 'Drown out the Darkness' campaign has become popular in many areas, particularly in middle-class neighborhoods. The Movement claims that between 20,000 and 30,000 households across the country regularly burn the bright blue candle on a windowsill each evening. While we can neither confirm nor deny the Movement's estimates, it is clear that the endeavor has become increasingly popular despite instances of threats and neighborhood ostracism of those who display the candle.

"A third area of activity sponsored by Na'aleh is a series of gatherings in Jewish and Arab households throughout the country. The 'Our Neighbors, Our Selves' effort brings together Arab and Jewish Israelis to acquaint each group with the values, lifestyle and home atmosphere of the various sectors. Several of these gatherings were filmed and featured on the Friday evening television news magazine on December 3. Although the activity is said to have directly involved a few dozen families, it has resulted in enhanced relations between the two sectors. At least two incidents have been reported (in Tiberias and Beersheva) of extremist youth breaking into homes where the gatherings were taking place and disrupting them. In both cases, several hosts and guests were beaten before police could restore order and carry out arrests.

"IMPACT: The Movement is coordinating an intensive lobbying effort among Members of the Knesset. The reception accorded the group by elected representatives is closely related to the Right-Left divide, although Na'aleh's popularity has also gained some interest among moderate nationalists. Local government officials have tended to respond along political lines to the group although, again, some nationalist-affiliated heads of local councils have embraced the movement in view of its rising profile. Many local officials have expressed special interest in the group's planned 'Democracy and Unity Day' on January 15, which will be marked by numerous activities and rallies at the municipal level.

"In the brief period since its formal founding, Na'aleh has unquestionably made its mark on the country. One seasoned observer writing in *Ma'ariv* commented that the group 'has already matched or exceeded the impact of the older protest movements of both the Right and the Left in the pursuit of its aims. If this should continue, Na'aleh could play a catalytic role in altering current national trends.'

"Participants in cabinet meetings report that on several occasions, the organization has been the subject of discussion. It is said that the Prime Minister and his close advisors are concerned that the organization's success could affect government policy and create a situation in which the Movement's concerns are placed on the national agenda.

"Extremist right-wing elements have attempted to neutralize the Movement's effectiveness by coordinating hostile challenges to their programs. One far-right Nationalist Knesset member has denounced the group as 'traitorous revolutionaries strongly influenced by the Communists' (there is no evidence supporting this claim), while Rabbi Epstein's Hebrew Fighters Association has declared the Movement 'Public Enemy Number One.' Several groups have filed suit against the State for failing to declare Na'aleh an illegal organization on the basis of existing laws outlawing organizations hostile to the State. We do not believe these efforts will succeed in the courts unless new supporting evidence is presented.

"SUMMARY: Despite continuous probing, we have no reason to label Na'aleh a subversive organization or one whose goals are injurious to State interests. The use of traditional Jewish symbols and concepts, the movement's independence and the group's nonviolent tactics all serve to refute the claim that Na'aleh is in any way a dangerous group."

Impressive, Eli thought as he slid off the remains of his

dinner and washed the plate at the kitchenette's sink. Na'aleh had had a stellar rise. Nothing like it had stirred the country since the heyday of the Peace Now movement and that of its nemesis, Gush Emunim, the religious-nationalistic settler's movement that began in the 1970s.

It wasn't surprising, thought Eli. The government served only the agenda of the privileged classes and their alliance with the clericalists and right-wingers. The situation was deteriorating without peace and always the rumblings of war in the background. We have turned our back on the world even as the threat on the Eastern Front, Syria, Hezbollah, Hamas and Iran mounts. People out of work, disaffection. Of course the movement would grow.

As he coursed through the streets of the capital and other cities as part of the investigation into the Gideons, Eli was struck by the sight of home after home displaying the Movement's candle, its 'Drown out the Darkness' campaign. On several occasions after meetings with Amos in Jerusalem, he had seen hundreds of people attend the group's prayer vigils throughout the city. He was intrigued by the intimate pictures the group had somehow obtained of the attacks against Fatima Abed and in the aftermath of the Rally of Hope. Eli even had an analyst probe the photographs for clues into the attacks. This is a sophisticated group of people, Eli thought. They warrant respect.

And, it occurred to him, the ire of those who oppose them.

What would the Gideons make of Na'aleh? Eli wondered. The zealots must be enraged by the success of the group that was conceived to defeat them. The Gideons might be glad for the convenience Na'aleh afforded them, bringing together in one group the traitorous "bleeding hearts" that so poisoned the country's spirit with their message of goodwill and fraternity between Jews and Arabs. The filth was easier to attack that way, assembled together, the Gideons might reason.

Opposites attract and Eli thought it plausible that the assailants would want to strike at Na'aleh – just as they had at the Rally of Hope. They probably would be present at the Movement's events, looking for vulnerabilities that could be attacked to weaken and possibly destroy it. The Gideons had proven proficient at concealing themselves, but now they were without doubt homing in on Na'aleh, like a predator zeroing in on its prey. If the Sons of Gideon would not show their hand directly to Eli, perhaps the best way to snare them was by way of their disdain for the do-gooders.

Eli thought it prudent to take greater notice of Na'aleh. Perhaps he would start observing its activities. Perhaps there was a trail to the Sons of Gideons from there.

ೞ ❖ ಒ

His cousin's wedding was the first time Eli had seen his family in weeks.

"Lior, give your uncle a kiss!" Eli's sister prodded her son. "Quit being so stubborn. It hasn't been that long!" The six-year-old had refused to open his bedroom door. "He's angry that you haven't been over to see him lately. He cried all during his birthday party after we told him you couldn't come."

"Lior, it's Eli. Please come out. I've brought you a present and you don't want it to drive away, do you, Lior?" Eli called out softly, "I'm sorry I couldn't come to your party. I tried to call but you wouldn't come to the phone. I promise to make it up to you. I'll tell you what. Remember the water park you liked so much at the kibbutz? On Saturday, I'll take you. Just you and me. Then we'll have pizza for lunch. How about it? Do we have a deal?"

"That place with the long slide?" Lior asked from behind the door.

"Yes. And we can go for a ride in one of those little pedal boats in the lake."

"You promise? And pizza too, just you and me?"

Eli looked at his sister. She nodded affirmatively.

"I promise. Now open the door so I can give you your birthday present," Eli said.

The little boy opened his door a crack, glanced at his uncle and brought his hand to his mouth, trying to hide the smile that broke across his face. Eli held out the gift-wrapped present and the door opened a bit wider. Finally, Lior threw open the door and leapt into his uncle's arms.

Eli and Lior were playing on the living room floor with the fire truck when the boy's father opened the apartment door. Leaning on his arm was Simon, Eli's father and Lior's grandfather who was walking slowly, tentatively. He had lost his sight and was frail. The old man's feet shuffled in his frayed, open-heeled shoes. Eli watched the shrunken and feeble figure of his father. He was a shadow of what he had once been. In Libya, within the Jewish community, Simon Zedek had stood tall and proud, a much-respected dentist who often appeared fit in well-tailored suits. Look at what they've done to him, this place. Look at what they have made of him. He no longer carried an air of distinction about him. His dignity had been taken long ago.

"Father, it is so good to see you," Eli said. He buried his sadness as he bent over the old man and kissed him on each cheek.

"How are you?" the father said to his son as he groped for Eli's arm, and finding it, grasped it hard.

"Good, very good."

"Your sister says that you are working hard. Too hard."

"Just the usual," said Eli.

"Grandpa," Lior said as he tugged the old man's sleeve. "Look at what Eli brought me," he said lifting the fire truck up to his sightless eyes.

"I am sure it's very nice," the grandfather said. He sat quietly for a minute, running his fingers through the boy's hair. He began to cry.

"But father," said Yair, Eli's brother-in-law, "it's a happy day. We have a wedding to go to." He held the old man by the shoulder. They were used to tears whenever they were all together. "I am so sorry that Deborah is not here. How she would have liked to be at this wedding," Simon lamented. Eli's father especially missed his murdered wife at such times. And whenever her name came up, so did Eli.

Lior sat in the backseat of the car between his grandfather and uncle, his parents in front. As they drove out of Jerusalem, Eli felt himself beginning to relax for the first time since the events at Rabin Square. He settled back in his seat as they headed for Ramla. He peered out the window like a little boy, watching the city blocks give way to the broad vistas of open space.

They arrived in Ramla and found the neighborhood where the bride's family lived and the wedding was being held. Eli's cousin was marrying into a traditional Yemenite family and all the splendor of that community's wedding rites were enacted. An entire street had been barricaded off for the ceremony and celebration.

At dusk, the guests were summoned to gather near the bridal platform. The wedding contract had been signed and witnessed. The black-garbed rabbi piously officiated over the marriage ceremony beneath the bridal canopy. He intoned the ancient blessings, somberly presided over the exchange of rings, the drinking from the wine goblet, and the seven ritual encirclements of the groom by the bride. Finally, he instructed the young man to crush the glass with his foot, symbolizing both the destruction of the ancient Temple and the couple's fusion as husband and wife. The groom made the blessing and stomped on the glass wrapped in foil. The crowd enthused.

Eli loosened up, reassured that he had not lost his ability to enjoy a good party. He made sure to make the obligatory rounds, greeting family and making small talk with relatives he saw only at such occasions. He was accorded respect by anyone who knew who he was. After all, he was a member of the family who had made good – in the military, at university, in the security services. His advice was much sought after. One uncle asked him to talk a cousin out of incipient delinquency. A cousin ten years Eli's junior requested a few minutes so that he could spill out his guts about a love affair gone awry.

Eli ate well. He laughed at jokes, sang along with others, and danced with the ladies. He spent quite a bit of time with a particularly attractive second cousin once removed with whom he strolled to a nearby park and spent an hour talking.

It was well after midnight when one of his cousins gave Eli a lift to his apartment, a pleasant end to a night he had enjoyed. Eli was a little tipsy and fully exhausted. He walked straight into his bedroom and fell asleep on the bed, fully clothed.

The incessant ringing of the phone at five in the morning drove Eli out of deep sleep. Amos was on the line, his voice tense. As Eli gathered his wits, Amos gave him a bare sketch of what appeared to be the latest strike by the Sons of Gideon. Within minutes, Eli was in his car headed for the Tel Aviv-Jerusalem highway.

Eli arrived at the Messubim intersection just as the rescue workers were starting to put the nine corpses in body bags. A dozen ambulances, their emergency lights piercing the end-of-night darkness, were lined up along the shoulder of the road where paramedics were attending the wounded. Police were directing a trickle of traffic around the carnage while crime-lab technicians began collecting evidence.

Eli walked behind the cordon where some of the

eyewitnesses, mainly workers from the Territories, stood and gazed at the scene. He was briefed by the first police officer to reach the scene, a few short moments after the assailant had torn off into the night on a speeding motorcycle. There wasn't much the officer could offer by way of information. He had arrived after the attacker had already sprayed the crowd with machine-gun fire and taken off. Eli would get a more complete picture from a labor contractor who was assembling a crew of workers from among the victims when the attacker struck.

"All I can say is I've never seen anything like it in my life," said the contractor, his voice raspy and choked. "I was in Lebanon three times and I never saw anything like it. He just began shooting, cool and calm, into the crowd. He gave no warning. It was a massacre."

"You saw him firing?"

"Yes. I could have been killed myself. He was as close to me as I am to you right now." The witness took a long drink from a bottle of water that an officer offered him. Then he resumed. "I was standing over there, where that first ambulance is," he said, weakly, lifting his timorous hand and pointing. "I had parked my van – that's it over there, the green one – and walked over to a worker I've used before on a couple of jobs. He spoke some Hebrew, so I started to negotiate wages with him for a group of them. I chose the men I wanted and was heading back to the van with them when this guy on a motorcycle slows down and pulls over to the side of the road. I didn't think anything of it; all sorts of people are out here in the early morning. Anyway, the guy jumps off the motorcycle and takes off his gloves. Despite the heat, he's wearing a knee-length coat, black, like the Haredim wear, and I remember thinking that was pretty strange. The next thing he does is slowly unbutton the coat and then, bam, he does it."

"He did what? What exactly did he do? Hey, buddy," Eli touched the man's forearm. "It's very important that you tell me everything you saw."

"He shot them. Took out an Uzi and just let the bullets fly. Haven't you heard?" he asked Eli incredulously. "Nine people were just killed out here!" the man shouted.

"Easy, easy," Eli said softly, attempting to calm the witness, "help us catch the guy. Tell us all you can remember."

"It happened very quickly. The shooter came over to me. He was a huge man – no youngster but damn, he was strong. I mean huge – and with the back of his arm, he shoves me out of his way. I flew, really flew and he yells, 'Be careful, brother Jew' or something odd like that. I'm on the ground and the guy is as cold as ice. He holds the Uzi at hip level and lets loose a volley. Damn, it was loud. He wasted the workers; they fell to the ground like sacks of potatoes. All of the blood and the screaming. It was horrible. I couldn't believe what was happening."

"Did he say anything else?" probed Eli.

"Yes. After the shooting, he tucks the gun under his coat and lets out a howl like a dog and then does this crazy dance, stomping his feet and reaching to the sky. He had madness in him, I swear. I couldn't believe it. And he kept shouting in English, something like 'Scorched earth, Scorched earth,' with this look of joy on his face."

And then?"

"All of a sudden he stops. He becomes very quiet, almost sad. He walks back to his motorcycle, starts it up and speeds off. One of the other contractors carries a gun, and he started shooting at the guy, but the guy was too fast."

"Did you get a good look at him?"

"The murderer? Oh yes. I'll never forget what he looked like as long as I live. He seemed crazy."

"Can you tell me some more details about him? You said he was big. How big?"

"Very tall and very heavy. A mountain of a man."

"What color hair?"

"He had his helmet on but took it off for a minute to wipe his forehead. He was light-haired, with light skin."

"So he wasn't Middle Eastern-looking?"

"No, he looked European or American."

"Hebrew?"

"He didn't say much, but what he said to me was in Hebrew. With an accent – English or American."

"How was he dressed?"

"That's another thing. He was dressed like a Haredi, black slacks and white shirt with fringes hanging from his waist."

"Beard or mustache?"

"A thin beard."

"Did he limp or anything? Any scars or anything noteworthy?"

"Not that I saw."

"You say he wasn't young, about how old."

"You know, it's funny, He looked in his late forties or early fifties, but he had this baby face about him."

"You're sure he was using an Uzi?"

"Yes, I'm sure."

"What about his bike?"

"It was a big BMW."

Eli reached into his wallet and took out the composite sketches the police artist had put together after Rabin Square. "Did he look anything like one of these men?" Eli asked. A television crew had arrived and begun to film the scene.

The man looked at the two sketches and said nothing.

"Mister?"

"That's him," the contractor said, pointing to the picture of the man who had installed the cement bases for the streetlights at Al-Bakr.

Thirty minutes passed before Eli saw Carmi's hulking figure walking toward him. Carmi's face was red with fury. Eli was supervising the crime-scene technicians at the site of the shooting attack.

Eli confronted Carmi, "Motti, no one ordered roadblocks. We have an excellent description of the assailant that an eyewitness gave us. There's a good chance that we could have picked him up not far away."

"Listen, Zedek," Carmi shouted heatedly. "You don't give orders or instructions to my men, understand? After Rabin Square, you are nothing. My men don't answer to you. So get into your car and drive away. We'll take it from here."

"I'm sorry, Carmi," Eli said sarcastically. "I keep forgetting just how fragile your ego is. Even so, you ought to remember that I don't take orders from you either," Eli replied furiously, his body taut with contempt and anger. He paused, controlled himself and continued. "Amos told me to get down here and assume control, and my authority exceeds anyone's on the scene, including yours. If you don't order roadblocks to be set up this minute, you are going to have hell to pay."

Carmi refused to call for the roadblocks. Eli then phoned Amos' office, had him contact the internal security minister, who in turn contacted the police commissioner and ordered Carmi to put up the roadblocks. Forty minutes later – nearly an hour and a half after the motorcyclist had left the scene – the checkpoints were finally erected, far too late to be effective.

As Eli returned to his office following the attack at the Messubim interchange, he had a thought that staggered him. He had been thinking about there having been too many glitches and too much incompetence surrounding the Sons of Gideon case, too many missed opportunities to apprehend them. Gradually Eli thought of a possibility he had considered inconceivable, what was for him an unthinkable thought: maybe it wasn't just "glitches or incompetence" and maybe Carmi wasn't as inept and negligent as he appeared. Perhaps the oversights and lapses were intentional.

The notion revolted Eli, it made his mind swim. But under the circumstances he had to consider anything. And "anything" now included the possibility of a conspiracy, maybe involving big players in the government or the security establishment. The possibility sickened him. But he could not dismiss it.

☙ ❖ ❧

It was still early on a quiet, hot Thursday morning before the day's activities got off to a start. Michal had spent yet another night sleeping in Ido's room, the cultural committee meeting having concluded too late for her to drive all the way back to Acre. She had gotten up early and had just returned from a walk along the shore. She had heard about the incident off the radio in the kiosk where she had stopped to buy the newspaper.

Lilah was finishing getting dressed when Michal walked into her bedroom.

"Bad news," said Michal, handing Lilah a cup of coffee.

"What could have happened in four hours? I heard the 3:00 a.m. news before I went to bed and there was nothing special going on," said Lilah, gratefully accepting the mug.

"Three workers from the West Bank were killed, and another five wounded, at around 4:30. Someone on a motorcycle drove up to a spot where day laborers wait to get picked up for work, and shot them. He had a submachine gun, and indiscriminately fired at the men."

Lilah's face froze.

"Yes, and you can figure out who was behind it. The Sons of Gideon telephoned a statement to Israel Radio at a quarter to five, taking full responsibility. As usual, they promised more of the same," Michal reported. "We had better prepare a response," she lamented. "We are going to have to do something visible, demonstrative, not just another statement."

Lilah was no longer listening. Her thoughts were fixated on where she would go and how she might snare the Sons of Gideon on film.

Chapter Eleven

The wind blew blisteringly hot through the car as Issam drove across the Galilee from Acre to Tulazine. A mid-December day, such weather was unheard of; it should be chilly and wet. As he looked out on the fields devoid of green, Issam's heart ached. Whoever doubted climate change has his head buried in the sand, thought the physician as he drove.

In the early morning light, the terrain was already awash in blazing white sunshine. The *sharav* deadened the normally busy road, now forlorn and empty except for an occasional police car or lumbering truck. As a headache worked its way upward from the nape of his neck, Issam wondered if perhaps he should have stayed home.

The fields that lined the approach to Tulazine were empty. The olive trees appeared even more twisted and gnarled than usual. Cars littered the village's single, paved road as though they had been abandoned by drivers fleeing a tidal wave of heat.

As he stepped out of the car at the clinic, Issam felt like he'd walked into an oven. Even the leather handles of his medical bag seemed to sweat. The dry dust invaded every pore and crevice of his sandaled feet.

The clinic door was wide open. Inside, the benches were filled with weary, troubled, poor people whose listlessness was a metaphor of their lives. One child was coughing relentlessly and her skin was flecked with scaly red patches. Other children too sick to play or to get into mischief rested their heads on the laps of women in long black dresses. Grizzled old men with stubbly, hard-beaten faces silently fingered their worry beads. A wilted receptionist sat behind the counter, looking decidedly uncomfortable. A small ineffective fan was mounted on the wall.

"Good morning, Sali," Issam said in Arabic to the

receptionist as he eyed the patients in the waiting room.

"Good morning, Doctor Issam."

"Any emergencies?" he asked the rail-thin young woman. He leaned down and inspected the little girl with the skin condition.

"Nothing too urgent, I'd say."

"Has Dr. HaCohen come in yet?" he asked referring to the retired physician, a member of a nearby kibbutz who volunteered at the clinic three mornings a week. Issam unbuttoned the little girl's blouse and checked her torso for patches.

"His wife phoned a little while ago. She said a man his age shouldn't be volunteering as many hours as he does and that she wasn't about to let him come here in this heat."

"Yes, well, he really shouldn't be outdoors on a day like this," Issam said, studying a large red patch on the girl's chest. "I'll see this patient first," he said to the receptionist. "Send her to examination room 1," he continued. It was as if the girl's mother, a Bedouin from one of the unofficial settlements on the hill overlooking the village, wasn't even there. That was the aristocrat in Issam, an educated son of the affluent Galilean elite, a surgeon who had been a Parisian and beneficiary of its noblesse for many years. A Bedouin woman was well beneath him, an *enfant*. The child, though, required his immediate attention.

Issam went to the examining room and scrubbed his hands with soap and water. He unlocked the supply cabinet and removed the medicines he knew he would need: antibiotics for infections, serums for intestinal worms and parasites, antiseptics, painkillers and analgesics. He removed needles and tweezers and checked the supply of bandages. The essentials were there, though the inventory of syringes and vials had dwindled – budget cuts by the Ministry of Health had taken their toll. The government was committed to de-socializing medical services in favor of privatized health care. Its policies were being felt.

The mother gently carried her daughter into the room and gingerly placed the little girl on the exam table.

"Doctor, she burns up at night and cries constantly from the pain and itching," said the Bedouin woman. Her eyes averted his as his did hers, and Issam began examining the little girl under a magnifying lamp.

"What has her temperature been like?" Issam asked, as he placed a thermometer into the girl's mouth.

"She cries all night long," the woman repeated. Issam knew she hadn't understood the question and almost certainly hadn't taken her child's temperature.

"It's a fungal infection," Issam pronounced. "Where does she sleep at night?" he asked the mother.

"In this heat, I keep her next to me near the water tank in the chicken run, where it is cooler.

"You mustn't do that," Issam directed. "The combination of the dampness and the chicken feces is probably spreading the infection. Keep her skin dry, don't let her pick at the scabs, and make sure she drinks a lot of clean water, not from stagnant pools. I will give you a slip for a prescription. I want you to put the cream on her skin when she goes to sleep at night and in the morning," Issam instructed. He removed the thermometer and read it. "She has no fever now. If you take good care of her and do what I said, she'll be fine in a few days." He signed the prescription, gave it to the mother and dismissed her with a nod.

The next patient was a young woman dressed in jeans and a fashionable blouse; her hair was covered. She walked uncomfortably, her face flushed, though not with fever. She came in with a young man who had a beard and was dressed in blue work clothes. Presumably, he was her husband, or maybe a brother.

"Hello, I'm Dr. Halaby," Issam said pleasantly.

"I know who you are," the man said. His face was hard, angular, his chin jutting out and his eyes suspicious.

Issam asked the woman to sit down on the examination table and describe what was ailing her. The woman looked deferentially at her escort.

"She has pain," he said roughly.

"Pain where?" asked Issam, though from the man's tone he had a pretty good idea of where in the body the woman might be feeling discomfort.

"Down there, in her womanhood," the man answered.

"What sort of pain?" Issam asked the woman. "Does it come and go? Is it constant?"

"Constant pain. It aches all the time," said the woman. She answered the rest of the doctor's questions the way she began, gazing at the man who accompanied her.

"I'm going to have to examine her," Issam said. "Please remove your slacks," he said to her, while looking at the man. The escort said nothing and made no move toward the door; he stood like granite where he was. Issam knew it would be fruitless to ask him to leave.

"You must allow me to examine you, please. It is necessary," Issam said. The woman unbelted and lowered her trousers and underpants and removed her sandals. She placed her feet in the examination table stirrups.

As he pulled on surgical gloves and squeezed lubricant on his index finger, Issam felt as if the man's eyes were searing holes into the back of his head. Seated on a revolving stool, Issam turned around for a moment and looked at the man. Fires of hatred burned in the dark brown pools of his eyes. Why was he so full of enmity for me? Issam wondered.

As Issam eased his finger into her, the woman let out a sharp, piercing cry. Issam knew that the pain must be considerable; he felt a mass in her uterus the size of an orange.

He quickly ended the examination.

"I want you to see a specialist as soon as possible." Issam scribbled a note to the office assistant. "Give this to Sali. She'll see to it that you get an appointment with Dr. Lapid."

The woman, hurriedly dressed, nodded to Issam and left the room with the note. But the man stood by the open door. "I don't need another Jew or a man married to one enjoying my wife's private parts," he said scornfully. "I will take her to a doctor who is a real Arab, in Nazareth or al-Quds," he declared, slamming the door behind him.

Issam's initial impulse was to run after the man and knock the bigotry out of him. The insult was personal; it was known that Dr. Halaby was married to a Jewish woman and half of the Galilee hated him for it.

But Issam took a deep breath and calmed himself. There were other patients in the waiting room and he was the only doctor on duty today. More than that, the enormity of the prejudice defied any prescription he could give.

A ragtag group passed under Issam's care that morning. Most were poor residents of Tulazine and the surrounding hamlets. Some were chronically ill and had been coming regularly for years to be treated by a native son – albeit an errant one, someone fallen as he had married out of the faith. Issam had been volunteering here for years. It was his mother's family village and some of the patients, especially the older ones, trusted only him to handle their allergy or flu injections, remove sutures and casts, and calm frayed nerves.

Issam had seen what he thought was his last patient before going to a second village where he volunteered in the afternoon. The waiting room was empty and Sali had just about completed the paperwork when a late-model Mercedes Benz arrived outside the clinic. The driver parked on the sidewalk so that his passenger would be only a step or two from the building.

Out stepped an expensively dressed, middle-aged man, one

of the Arab Galilee's wealthiest businessmen. He entered the building, his neck bedecked with gold chains, and several large gold rings on his fingers. On one wrist, he wore a heavy bracelet, on the other, a Cartier watch.

"Hajji Miari!" Issam greeted the man, a cousin of his who he disliked and distrusted and who he took pains to avoid. "What a nice surprise. I hope you are not ailing," Issam said falsely.

"No, thank Allah, I am well," the man said as he half-leaned, half-seated on the examining table. Issam's intuition was to distrust the man's smile. When Ibrahim Miari asked him how he was, there was something about the question that made Issam uneasy.

The silence during which Miari stood gazing at him, seemed to Issam to drag on forever. Miari just stood there, his tailored European attire not quite concealing his obesity. He wore a *keffiyeh* that framed his eagle nose, jowls and carefully groomed goatee. He was unruffled by the long pause, and seemed satisfied to stare faintly but malignly at Issam with an inscrutable smile on his heavy, pursed lips.

Finally, Issam's patience expired.

"Hajji, to what do I owe the pleasure of your visit?"

"Is it forbidden for one cousin to pay a visit to another?" Miari replied coyly.

"No, of course not. You are most welcome at any time. But why not come to my home in Acre? Why inconvenience yourself by coming to this clinic? I cannot host you here with the hospitality I would like."

Miari said nothing. He turned away from Issam and looked out the window, fingering his worry beads and infuriating Issam by lighting a cigarette, despite the no-smoking signs throughout the clinic. Finally, he spoke again. "Cousin, you are sorely missed in your village."

"How is that?" asked Issam, trying to keep his calm. "After all, I visit the clinic here at least once a week, not to mention family visits."

"Yes, well, you know you can be here without truly being present," Miari said enigmatically.

"What do you mean?" Issam asked firmly, his patience tried by Miari's Levantine circumlocution.

"Some people are afraid that you are forgetting us, that you are so busy with extraneous matters that you are neglecting the affairs of your people."

"Forgetting what, exactly?" Issam asked, trying to mask his mounting anger.

"Your community," Miari said matter-of-factly, his eyebrows raised in a strange gesture, as if he were seeking assurance that those who accused Issam of such wrongdoing were mistaken.

"Oh, I see," Issam said, now with his anger bared. "You mean I am not fulfilling my obligations to the Arab community, to the Arab nation."

Miari puffed his cigarette wordlessly.

"Be assured that I am a proud Arab and that I will help my people all my days. But let there also be no mistake that I am an Israeli."

"Yes, by circumstances forced on us, you are an Israeli."

"I voluntarily returned here from France," Issam quickly added, but to bolster what point, he did not know. By saying so, he had walked into the trap.

"Yes, well there are a number of interpretations one might ascribe to that," Miari said dryly.

"What precisely is it that you want?" Issam asked, dropping all pretense of cordiality.

"I'll tell you, Issam," Miari began, launching into what sounded like a prepared speech. "In the past year, you have lost some friends here. People in the village feel you have forsaken them. Your name appears alongside those of known Zionists in newspaper advertisements, for example. I have been asked to tell you that we view your behavior as aberrant."

"Why? Because I am part of a movement of Jews and Arabs who want to live together peacefully?"

"They are Zionists. Some wonder if you are not one, too."

"I told you – I am a proud Arab Israeli. Before anything else, I am a human being who believes in progress."

"That's a nice slogan, but what kind of progress are you for? For whom do you want progress? We are the ones who lag behind the Jews," Miari piously placed his hands together.

"What kind of progress?" Issam asked rhetorically. "This kind of progress: this clinic, for instance, schools in the villages, electricity, water, roads, money. We vote. We are more or less free citizens in this country. I think there has been a great deal of progress since the region stopped being ruled by certain fat cat landowners who did not care about anything but lining their own pockets."

"I see," said Miari. He put out his cigarette in a metal instrument tray, having clearly grasped Issam's insinuation. "There are those in the family who cautioned me against coming to see you and reasoning with you. They warned me that it was futile to ask you to come back to us, to embrace your village and your people. I wanted to try. Perhaps they were right. Sadly, I am afraid I won't be able to influence those who are now asking that you no longer serve in this clinic. You are no longer a son of Tulazine, in their eyes. You are not welcome here."

"What?" Issam asked threateningly as he moved toward Miari; it took everything he had to restrain himself. Miari began to back out of the room as Issam thundered: "Do you and your cronies think you are my masters? The masters of this village? The masters of the Israeli Arab community? You and your chums do not control anyone, least of all me. I will continue to serve my people in my profession wherever and whenever I can. There are those here who need my services and I will not deny them. Do you understand?" Issam shouted.

Miari fairly waddled down the corridor, turning around apprehensively to see if Issam was coming after him. He hurried out of the building, got into the car, and ordered his driver to speed off.

Issam was livid. Face to face with Miari he saw the past struggling against the present. Issam thought for a moment. He picked up the telephone and dialed a friend of his, a good man who was the director of the youth center in the village. Issam asked if he could pay him a brief visit. The friend said he was at the football pitch and that yes, Issam was invited to come at any time.

Issam left the clinic and walked swiftly to the center where he found his friend.

Issam put a proposal to him: Na'aleh would be interested in sponsoring a soccer match between the Tulazine team and the leading team of the regional kibbutz youth league. But the rosters of the two teams would be mixed, with Arab youth playing with the kibbutz team and Jewish youth on the Tulazine team. The director of the Tulazine youth center enthusiastically endorsed the idea, and was certain the kibbutz league would back the proposal, too. He volunteered to set up the match.

That pleased Issam. It would help drown out the darkness that had long ago descended. No less on Arabs than on Jews.

Chapter Twelve

Lilah felt silly about her reticence. After all, she and Michal had shared so much those past few months, their renaissance as Michal called it.

Michal had been devoting herself night and day to the Movement, functioning as de facto office manager and committees coordinator. The Movement was entrenched at 3 HaGaon Street. Rather than undertake the long commute to Acre each day, Michal established herself in the extra bedroom and went home on the weekends. Issam tried to be understanding and joined her at Lilah's whenever he could: Michal was away, after all, for the "cause."

"What is so important that you can't make the program committee meeting tonight?" Michal challenged.

"I just feel I need a break. I miss my camera. The soccer game will be a good opportunity for me to get some fresh air and shoot some film."

"But we're supposed to be finalizing plans for Artists' Night. You're the one who's been pushing it."

"You're in charge of the program committee, not me," Lilah countered. She wasn't keen on the charade, didn't like perpetrating the subterfuge and sought a change of subject. "Here, let me beat the eggs. The whites have to be stiffer," she said, and took the bowl and whisk out of Michal's hands.

"I am perfectly capable of baking a cake by myself," Michal bristled.

"I know you are. You can also run a meeting without my being present. I think I am entitled to a night to myself," said Lilah.

"You are entitled to a lot more than that," Michal relented. She lay her hand gently on Lilah's shoulder. "It's just that things go so much better when you are around."

"I don't know why you are laying the guilt on me," Lilah

said, aiming to anchor her ruse. She was frightened enough about the hunt and dearly wanted to share her intentions – to capture the Sons of Gideon on film – but she didn't dare – for Michal's sake. It was enough that she was willing to endanger herself looking for the demons.

"Why would you accuse me of trying to make you feel guilty? Damn it, what's with you lately?" Michal asked.

"Ask yourself the same question. Then you'll have the right to ask me." Lilah turned her face away. She hated being deceptive.

"What are you saying? I've been by your side, virtually night and day, for more than a month. I've been more devoted to you and Na'aleh than to my husband, even after you started acting as if you've been entrusted with some big state secret. Then you turn things around and accuse me of... Oh, just forget the damn cake," Michal broke off in tearful exasperation, dashing out of the kitchen and heading for the guest bedroom. In the whirlwind of recent Na'aleh activities, she, like Lilah, could barely tell where the Movement ended and she began.

Lilah wanted to sink into the ground. A quarter of an hour passed as she thought through her plans again. Was it really so necessary for her to be so secretive? Was the role she had chosen for herself of apprehending the Sons of Gideon on film so important that she had the right to hurt others – Michal of all people? She couldn't bear to hear Michal crying. Lilah went to her room.

"I'm so sorry," she said, as she hugged Michal. "I was totally out of line."

"After everything you've been through, you are definitely entitled to an evening to yourself," Michal said.

"I didn't mean what I said. It was horrible of me."

"Oh, come on." Now it was Michal's turn to be consoling. "You were upset."

"Yes, but you are the last person in the world I should

mouth off to. I don't know how I would have gotten through all this without you. I've found a long-lost sister. More than that – it almost feels like I've fallen in love."

"Oh, stop it," Michal blushed. She embraced Lilah.

"No, I mean it. I love you dearly," Lilah declared.

"It's a good thing no one is here to overhear all this. All Na'aleh needs is rumors that its spokeswoman and one of its main activists are having some kind of lesbian love affair."

"That's nonsense. Nobody would say something like that."

"Is that so? Lilah, you really don't realize that you are playing in the big leagues now, do you? Whether you like it or not, you are the face of the Movement. You are what the public sees. And in politics, anything goes in neutralizing the competition. You've got to face up to the fact that you speak for a national movement that is beginning to carry weight in this country. Things are being said and written about us. We've got a lot of supporters, but there're also a lot of people out there who would love to dig up some dirt on us – or make some up, since there isn't any."

"Stop talking that way," said Lilah. "You're frightening me."

"That's the way it is, my dear. But I'm sure you can handle this, and you will. You've just got to face reality... Anyway, I'm sorry for my part in the argument."

"I'm sorry, too," said Lilah.

"And I think it's a great idea, you going to the soccer game. It's good for the common people to be able to rub elbows with their leader."

"Michal!"

"And it's good for the leader to be shoulder to shoulder with the masses. Come on, we've got a cake to bake before you leave."

The quarrel was resolved. The levity and warmth between them restored.

Just as she was preparing to leave the house, Lilah received yet another "black call," an anonymous threat, another "we're-going-to-get-you" message. She had become accustomed to them, though she was far from immune from their effects. It wasn't that she had become inured to such depravity, she had not, and she felt the tension of the threats in her body and soul constantly. She hung up on the caller in the middle of his rant. Determined not to succumb to her fears, Lilah collected her equipment bag, said goodbye to Michal and left the apartment before the program committee members began arriving.

Established in 1930 by socialist Zionist intellectuals from Poland, Kibbutz Ramat Zion had been ideologically fortified by successive waves of left-wing immigrants – a group of Holocaust survivors who had fought alongside Communist partisans in Italy, South African radicals opposed to apartheid, even former aides to Salvador Allende, the assassinated Marxist president of Chile –ensuring that Kibbutz Ramat Zion remained faithful to its founding leftist ideology. Over the decades, it had given many of its sons to the defense forces' most elite units and as a result, had suffered its share of bereaved families whose sons had fallen in action. With many distinguished officers among its sons, the kibbutz was renowned for its contribution to national defense.

That served the Ramat Zion well in spearheading the kibbutz movement's resistance to the Government's "land reform" program, which entailed the privatization of public and collectively-held lands. The policy was aimed at denationalizing state lands and weakening the communal settlements to extinction, a longstanding aspiration of the nationalist movement ever since Menachem Begin was elected premier in

1977. Privatizing land also served to keep the contractors, important contributors to the Nationalist Party's coffers, content and generous. Now, the kibbutz movement with Ramat Zion at its lead was defying the trend and was actually growing in its number of members. It was attracting people who wanted a less stressful life and who were attracted to the greening that had taken place on the settlement. Also, Ramat Zion's wind turbine and drip irrigation industries had brought the members a comfortable economic base.

As a result of its standing, kibbutz members unabashedly pursued their progressive programs – including the tradition of furthering Jewish-Arab coexistence in the western Galilee. Well-known for the friendly ties its members had cultivated with neighboring Arab villages, Ramat Zion's willingness to host the sponsored soccer game was surprising to no one.

Kibbutz members had worked for the better part of three days to extend the bleachers and install lighting fixtures along the soccer field. Signs of welcome in Hebrew, Arabic and English had been placed throughout the public areas, and a generous spread of fruits and pastries had been prepared on tables near the bleachers. Kibbutz vehicles shuttled spectators and players from the neighboring Arab villages to the collective settlement.

The game had been scheduled for early evening. By the time Lilah arrived – early enough she thought to discreetly position herself – the access road to the kibbutz was already filled with vehicles and pedestrians. In the waning light, traffic marshals directed cars and buses toward makeshift parking lots that in another season served as cotton fields.

Lilah parked along the road and walked nearly half a kilometer to the main gate. All the while, her eyes were busy, scrutinizing anyone and anything that could be considered "suspect." Initially, as she approached the main gate of the kibbutz, Lilah did not notice the milling crowd that had gathered. But as the din grew louder and angrier, she stumbled her way up a nearby slope and watched a confrontation unfolding.

The crowd had surrounded a small bus filled with brown-shirted members of Rabbi Epstein's Hebrew Fighters Association. The rabbi himself was there. Handsome and deceptively genteel, he was standing next to the vehicle.

"Epstein, I am ordering you and your followers off the premises," commanded the kibbutz secretary, a robust Holocaust survivor who had spent time in Generalissimo Franco's security prisons after the War and who did not cower in the face of adversary. "You are not welcome here," he asserted.

"But the supporters of terrorism are?" asked the rabbi, smiling in disregard of the jeers erupting from the crowd that dwarfed his own group in number. "According to the newspapers, this disgrace is open to the public. We want to make a proud Jewish presence felt," he said cockily.

"The only supporter of terrorism here is you. We can't guarantee your welfare here, and your presence constitutes a danger to public safety. You can either leave of your own free will or we will force you off our land," said the kibbutz secretary.

The crowd surrounding the bus swelled and grew livid. Just as it appeared they would pounce on Epstein and his supporters, one of the settlement's farm combines arrived at the site. The driver positioned the vehicle in front of the bus, jumped out and secured it with heavy chains to the harvester.

"Traitors! We will crush you yet," Epstein cried timorously as he was placed in the vehicle now being towed away by the combine. Epstein began to lead his followers in chants against "Jewish traitors and Arab dogs." At that, someone in the tense crowd began a cheer in Hebrew: "Fascists here will never pass/Out of this Land we will chase them/Jews and Arabs stand united." The chant immediately caught on as the minibus was pulled out of sight.

Throughout the row, Lilah furiously gunned her camera. And all the while, Eli Zedek was standing only a few meters from her. Outwardly, he seemed no different than the other spectators. He tried to look as inconspicuous as possible, though his eyes never stopped scanning every person that passed under his gaze, every large object and vehicle he saw, and the windows and roof and doorway of every building he had passed on the grounds of the kibbutz as he made his way to the soccer field.

Lilah's eyes were also scanning, though she was frustrated by the realization that she did not know what exactly she was looking for. How do you capture a specter? She decided on coverage, getting as much on film as she could: the spectators, the nearby buildings and any place where an assassin might lurk.

Once the burgeoning crowd – an estimated three thousand people had come to Ramat Zion – had found seats on the bleachers or along the pitch, the teams were chosen. Each player drew lots; chance rather than ethnicity, would compose the teams, the organizers had decided. Then, the kibbutz secretary, calm now that Epstein and his hooligans had been ejected, welcomed the guests, first in Hebrew and then in the fluent Arabic he had painstakingly studied ever since he had arrived in this land. He spoke about the importance of such encounters, how the kibbutz was honored to host the match and how imperative such events were to advancing Arab-Jewish understanding. His words were plain, earnest. He then introduced Dr. Issam Halaby, who welcomed the attendees on behalf of the Na'aleh Movement. It was Issam, after all, who had initiated the event. Accordingly, the Board reasoned that he was the most fitting to represent the Movement that evening.

Issam addressed the crowd, first in Arabic and then in

Hebrew. How distinguished he looked, thought Lilah as she stooped down and trained her lens on him. Issam saw her and grinned from ear to ear – he'd had no idea that she would be there but was thrilled that she was. He then composed himself, collected his thoughts and continued speaking. His voice was strong, confident, commanding.

"Friends, on behalf of Na'aleh, I welcome each and every one of you to the Friendship Match of Arab and Jewish Unity," he said, his voice rising with enthusiasm. A cheer went up among the spectators.

"The purpose of this evening is to strengthen ties between Arab and Jewish Israelis. Through events such as this, we intend to prove to those who oppose fellowship between our two peoples that we will not capitulate to their message of hatred. They will not succeed in sowing the seeds of discord, because justice and democracy are infinitely stronger than hatred and bigotry," he said.

"The Na'aleh movement belongs to all the people of Israel: Jews, Arabs, Druze, every citizen. We are a movement of equals who are committed to rescuing this country from the hands of bigots and reactionaries," he said.

"Speaking as an Arab Israeli, the past few years have been difficult ones for me personally," he said. "I returned from living abroad and have chosen to remain in Israel not because I am a Zionist, but because I want to live on the land of my parents and their parents before them. This soil and the sky above it reaches deep into my heart. It may have been easier to live elsewhere, but elsewhere is not my home."

"Frankly," Issam continued, "for a time in my youth, I wished there weren't any Jews in this land. I once thought that this was an Arab land, Palestine, but the truth is that it is Zion as well. It is revered by both Jews and Arabs, and nothing that either community does will alter that fact. It is an irreversible condition of our lives."

The crowd was silent. Issam was laying out a painful truth, and it denied both absolute absolution and vindication to Arabs and Jews alike; the truth was that there was no black and no white in the conflict, only shades of gray.

"It is the fate of Arabs and Jews to live together, but the relations between us can take several forms. We can ignore each other, interacting only when necessary. We can hate each other and continue to generate rivers of blood. Or, as I hope, we can embrace each other, not by neglecting our differences but by transcending them. Open your hearts and minds. Pass on this message to others. Convince those who have resigned themselves to the violence and hatred that they must defy it. We must struggle together – or this land that we love in common will know only misery.

"And now dear friends, let's enjoy the game. We have named one team Shalom; the other is called Salaam. There are Jewish and Arab athletes on both teams. Let us cheer on both groups, so that we can all be winners!"

And with the roared approval of the crowd, the players ran onto the field.

Throughout the game, Eli and Lilah moved in a kind of blind tango, unaware of their common search. Eli was placid but alert as he scanned the faces of the spectators, searching for bulges around people's waists or ankles. Lilah was less at ease. Her stomach was tense with the worry that she wouldn't know a Gideon if one fell on her. Still, she kept shooting, shifting from one angle to another around the playing field, moving from telephoto to wide-angle lenses as she covered the perimeter over and over again.

During the game, a mass of clouds began drifting overhead from the south and east. The temperature was rising and a dry, grainy wind began to blow. It was the start of another winter *sharav*, a phenomenon observed only over the last few years, a sign of the change in climate. It was as if the sky was pregnant but could not release its bounty, inhibited by the conditions of these times.

Suddenly, just after halftime, a kibbutz marshal raced to the sidelines, almost as if part of the unsettled weather. He spoke with alarm to the kibbutz secretary. The older man took the announcer's microphone off the table and spoke urgently.

"Ladies and gentlemen," said the secretary, "kindly rise, and calmly – again, calmly – leave your seats immediately and walk away from the area. Move to the fields on the far side of the buildings behind me. Proceed quickly. An abandoned package has been found that has aroused suspicion."

The crowd rose, gathered their belongings, took their children in hand and hurried off the bleachers. The marshals directed them to a cotton field several hundred meters away.

Eli had identified himself to the head marshal when he arrived at the kibbutz. He had thought it prudent to do so, not quite a premonition that things would develop here but just in case. After the abandoned bag was found beneath a bleacher pylon, he was summoned. By the time Lilah intuited what was going on, Eli was on his knees and hunched over the parcel. He gazed into the large green fabric sack. He was focused on the contents, a coil poking out of its side. Lilah moved past the marshals and stood nearby in the crypt-like silence that had gathered. She began taking pictures.

Focused on the bag, Eli had not looked up at the person with a camera who stood nearby and was clicking away, having evaded the marshals occupied with shepherding the crowds. Eli found it distracting and barely glancing her way ordered the photographer away. Lilah yielded, satisfied to take the next series of photos from further back. She had no desire to betray her purpose or to interfere. She had no idea who the man was probing the sack that quite possibly held a bomb. But in trying to disarm the device, he had placed himself in harm's way and there was heroism in that, Lilah thought. With his noble, broad, intelligent face, the man looked remotely familiar to her, and while he seemed experienced and in control, Lilah was worried for him.

Eli's shirt was damp with sweat from the heat of the *sharav* and the tension. "Several things have to be done immediately," he said to the head marshal. "Have your people keep the spectators on the field where they are now standing. Do not let anyone approach the bleachers. Also, I need more light. Please have someone set up halogen lamps or spotlights." Eli looked around at the buildings and sheds that separated the bleachers from the cotton field. "What's in there?" he asked, pointing at a large structure near where they were standing.

"That's a factory. Volatile materials are stored in there," said the head marshal, anticipating Eli's next question and his own concerns.

"How far is the kibbutz from Tiberias?"

"Half an hour."

"And from Safed?"

"About the same."

"We can't get a bomb disposal team here quickly enough." Eli paused for a moment. He removed his wristwatch and placed it out on a flat stone.

Eli caught sight of Lilah, who had threaded her way back to where he stood. "Lady," he called out to her, an anxious tremor in his voice, "for your own good, get the hell out of here."

Lilah had moved onto the field when an announcement was made over the public-address system, asking the owner of the cloth green shopping bag to identify him or herself. No one claimed the bag, but several people reported seeing someone with it. Lilah overheard the description offered by one witness of the person seen with the bag. The bearer was a woman between the ages of 40-50, large-boned and husky, with light-colored skin. She had stood out, since in spite of the heat, she wore a long-sleeve white blouse, a dark, heavy, checkered skirt, stockings and heavy shoes. A kerchief also covered her head. Her modest dress suggested that she was haredi, devoutly observant.

Lilah remained at Ramat Zion long enough to hear that the bomb had been dismantled and that had it exploded, given where it lay, it would have caused the deaths of a great many people. Early the next morning after little sleep, Lilah pored over the contact sheets with a magnifying glass. She had at least three photos of the woman with a green, cloth shopping bag partially concealed in two prints, but plainly visible in the third. She enlarged the photo to 400 percent, large enough to show the features of three-quarters of the woman's face and revealing a long-sleeve blouse, a dark plaid skirt and a head covering that matched the description given by the witness to the kibbutz marshal.

Lilah stared at the picture for a long time, awed by the prospect that she may have captured one of the Sons of Gideon on film – the first time anyone had succeeded in doing so.

She phoned Naftali in Jerusalem.

"I think I have a picture of one of the Sons of Gideon," she said.

"Is that a fact?" Naftali asked skeptically. "What did they do, send you a snapshot?" Issam had told him that he had seen Lilah at the kibbutz but could not find her after the area around the bomb was evacuated. Naftali had been worried and irritated that Lilah hadn't called him to tell her she had been there and that she had returned safely.

Lilah told him she had been at Ramat Zion and that she had taken many photographs including several of the woman suspected of bringing the bomb to the kibbutz. She asked him for advice: Who should she show them to? Naftali assured her that he would find out who the chief investigator was and that he would try to arrange for her to meet him.

By 9:00, Lilah was on her way to the headquarters of the Central Investigations Unit for a meeting with Commander Mordechai Carmi, the man officially in charge of the Sons of Gideon case.

Chapter Thirteen

Eli's brother-in-law was awakened by the sound of someone fumbling with keys outside the front door. He looked at the clock on the nightstand. It was barely three in the morning. Whoever it was – and Yair had a good idea who it might be – was having a very hard time getting in. But Eli had let himself into the apartment countless times with his own key. Why was he having such a difficult time now?

Yair opened the door. Eli was slumped against the doorframe, in a state of disarray, his hands and clothes soiled, his hair wild. "Lord," said Yair as he half-dragged Eli into the apartment. "What have they done to you now?"

"Was Lior terribly disappointed about me not coming for him on Saturday?"

"He'll survive. Look at you, though. We were right to be worried."

"I'm okay," said Eli, as he collapsed onto the couch. He was pale, his shirt was soaked with sweat, and his eyes were bloodshot. "I'm sorry I woke you."

"It's alright. It doesn't happen every day. What can I get you to drink?"

"Coffee would be good. And a glass of water."

Yair returned from the kitchen and Eli gulped the water thirstily in one long swig. Yair got him another glassful. He returned to find his brother-in-law lying on the couch limp as a sheet and looking ever so troubled.

"You know what happened to me tonight?" Eli began. "I came a hair's breadth away from meeting my maker."

Yair settled into a chair. He said nothing.

"I am working on a very important case – you've probably already figured out which one. There was a bomb, and it was up to me to defuse it. I have never had to dismantle a live bomb."

Yair's face hardened with worry. He and Dinah had discussed that whatever it was that her brother was up to those past few months, it was taking too heavy a toll on him.

"A lot of people, me included, came within a minute or two of getting blown up," Eli continued. "One wrong move and enough explosives would have gone off to throw a loaded dump truck into the air. Only by the grace of God did I get through this," Eli confessed.

There was pained quiet, a pause filled by Eli's heavy breathing and Yair's gathering will. The worry was affecting him and his wife too. He finally broke his silence.

"I hate seeing you like this," said Yair. "How much longer can you walk around with the weight of the entire country on your shoulders? There's only so much one man can take," he said, exasperated, now fully awake.

"You don't know the half of it..." Eli said. And he began to talk, baring his soul – and details of his professional life – as he had never done before. His long practiced circumspection, his near refusal to reveal anything about his work had been broken by the incident at Ramat Zion. He felt that he had to speak to someone and Yair was the only one he could ever conceive of confessing his burdens to. Eli spoke of his frustrations over the lack of leads to the Sons of Gideon, about their audacity and how little he had to work with. He spoke about how the Syrian threat had orphaned him from Amos and the security establishment. He talked about Carmi and confided his suspicion that there might be a conspiracy or a cover-up in high places, protecting the Gideons.

Once he voiced that, Eli grew both sadder and less laden but no less intense. In the late night quiet, Yair could see the fires of passion stoking deep within Eli. "I'm going to see this through. These madmen have got to be stopped," the investigator pronounced. "They are committing crimes against innocent people and against the State, out of hatred and contempt. I won't stand for it." He took a couple of sips of coffee, thought hard, and then continued, "It's as if they are a bunch of ghosts," he said of the Sons of Gideon. "It's as if I am tracking a group of phantoms. They have got to show their faces sometime, stand still long enough to be photographed."

"I want to thank you for seeing me on such short notice," Lilah said, shaking the hand that Carmi feebly offered.

"Yes, well, your husband or lover or whoever he is to you has a lot of influence in certain circles and I was told to see you. Not that I have the time." Carmi said coolly as he fished about his desk for something that he then proceeded to read without as much as looking in Lilah's direction.

Lilah had already summed up this crass man, Carmi. She would not bother to clarify her relationship with Naftali to him. Not only wouldn't the police inspector be able to comprehend it, it wasn't relevant.

"I understand that you are heading the Sons of Gideon investigation," she said.

"That's right," he said self-importantly, continuing his reading.

"Perhaps you have heard of the organization I am active with, Na'aleh?"

"Yes," Carmi said, with obvious disdain.

"We sponsored an event last night at Kibbutz Ramat Zion and as you have probably heard, there was a bomb."

"I know that, too," he snapped as an anorexic secretary knocked on the door and entered the office. She placed a cup of coffee on the officer's desk. He took a sip from the cup, without offering his visitor the same. The secretary asked Lilah what she would like to drink.

"Nothing, thank you," Lilah answered. A cup of coffee might lengthen the time she would have to be in the man's presence, a prospect she found loathsome. "Getting back to why I am here, I was at the kibbutz last night. I am a photographer by profession, and I shot a great many pictures prior to the discovery of the bomb," she said, as she pulled the proofs and prints out of a manila envelope.

Carmi nodded as he continued his reading.

"I happened to be within earshot when some spectators came forward and described the woman who was seen carrying the bag in which the bomb was later found," Lilah said, raising her voice to draw Carmi's attention. "I spent much of the night developing the film to see if I had any photos of anyone matching the description of the woman with the bag. Then I came across this one," she said, picking up one of the prints. "It's a little blurry because it's been enlarged, but you can definitely make out the woman's profile."

Carmi took the photo roughly, unconcerned that his fingers were smudging the gloss. He glanced at the shot and peered at Lilah over the rim of his glasses. "All I see is a poor-quality photograph of a woman in a crowd of people," he patronized.

Lilah took a breath and explained, "What's important is that the subject matches the description provided by the witnesses of the woman who carried the bag containing the bomb. Additionally, given the way she is dressed, she is probably religiously observant. A sporting event geared to enhance Arab-Jewish solidarity taking place on a secular kibbutz up north is not the sort of venue one usually associates with haredi spectators. She doesn't look at all like the others who were there, and more closely resembles someone who might have sympathies for or be active with the Sons of Gideon."

"And what would you have me do with the photo?" asked Carmi.

"I would think that your investigators would want to find this woman and have a talk with her. There is more than a passing chance that she's involved. I would think that you and your men would want to check any possible lead, given the fact that there have been so few."

"Look here," said Carmi, leaning forward aggressively in his thickly cushioned chair. "I know what you leftists are about, and I don't mind telling you that I don't like it. I think you are irresponsible, and more than a little weak in the patriotism department. All your group does is criticize."

"Excuse me, Inspector Carmi, but I am not interested in your opinion of my organization."

"All you have been doing is criticizing the security services even though we are doing all we can to resolve this case. You bend over backwards for the Arabs, and I don't see any of them giving a ..."

Lilah interrupted Carmi's lecture. "Now you listen to me," she said angrily, "you are an officer of the State and I am a citizen. My stand on public affairs is my business, not yours," she said, surprised by her assertiveness. "Let's set the record straight: First, Na'aleh does a lot more than criticize the authorities. We are engaged in constructive activities aimed at bringing citizens together, not spreading discord. Second, in view of the sorry state of the investigation and my reception here today, I would say that we may have been a little bit too trusting of the people in charge. The government claims it has not unearthed any evidence that would help identify the attackers. I'm trying to give you what might be an important piece of evidence, possibly a photograph of a would-be terrorist. And you don't appear to be the least bit interested. I don't understand."

"We have a number of leads that are being vigorously pursued," Carmi said as if reading from a press release. "Besides, this is not our only case. But there is something I don't understand. You people make a big deal over the rights of Arabs, but you don't seem to care that your picture implicates someone who may be entirely innocent, her only crime being that she resembles a description provided by someone who no doubt was anxious and panicked. The woman in the picture aroused your attention because she may be haredi. As far as I know, that's still not a crime in this country."

"I'm not telling you to put her in shackles and torture her. But there is very good reason to think that she is involved. Look, you're obviously not willing to listen to me, and I see that I don't have much of a chance of changing your mind. Just know that the people in my movement are too committed to what we are fighting for to let people like you stop us. And we will continue to try helping anyone interested in stopping the Sons of Gideon. You may think you don't need the public's help – despite what the government says. But if you don't take steps to act on these kinds of leads, we'll take the initiative. Then you'll have to explain your failure to act. I assure you, the information – in this case, the photo – is going to find its way to the public."

"Fine. Suit yourselves. That's your right. Go ahead and act irresponsibly on evidence that we professionals would be extremely wary about accepting at face value. Know this: I'm going to be watching you people. One transgression of the law, the slightest interference with the official handling of this or any other case, and I'll come down so hard on you, you..."

"Traitors?" Lilah suggested.

"Your word, not mine."

Lilah rose, "Thank you for your time. I'm sorry if I interrupted your work," Lilah said sarcastically as she left the room.

Carmi went back to what he had been doing before Lilah's arrival: reviewing summonses issued to diplomatic vehicles parking in tow-away zones.

‍ ଓ ❖ ଔ

"It's all too fishy. Something is definitely wrong," said Ido, munching on the sandwich his mother had made for him. He was in uniform, on a break from briefings across town at the Defense Ministry compound. "I think any responsible official would agree that the photograph is an important piece of evidence that should be pursued."

"What do you think is really going on?" asked Michal. She was seated across the table from Ido in Lilah's kitchen.

"I don't know. All I can say is that some of my friends are wondering how interested the security community and the government are in solving this case. There should be more progress than there has been, and a government cover-up isn't so far-fetched."

"One idiot, even a high-ranking one in the police, doesn't make for a conspiracy," Lilah said, as she sat down.

"That's right," added Michal, "and whoever the Sons of Gideon are, they are not your run-of-the-mill criminals. They're sly, elusive and sophisticated."

"Granted, but with this much effort going into breaking this case, there should be more to show for it."

"Carmi claimed they were working on some leads," said Lilah, trying hard to balance Ido's skepticism, though she had plenty of doubts of her own.

"They haven't made any arrests, as far as I know. These guys don't seem too worried about being found out."

"The security services have been interrogating settlers. Some of the more extreme right-wingers have been repeatedly questioned and detained. It's not as if the government has been entirely passive."

"Good," said Ido, who had finished his sandwich and potato salad and was rummaging through the refrigerator. "Maybe once we treat the Jewish extremists the same way we treat Arab security suspects, we'll begin to get some answers." He cut himself a hefty slice of cake, returned to the table and consumed it with vigor.

The phone rang and Lilah picked up. It would be a long call, and Lilah went into her room to take it. Michal and Ido were alone. After a few minutes, it was Ido who changed the subject.

"I'm really proud of Mom," he said.

"So am I. For someone who only a couple of months ago didn't know who the cabinet ministers were, she's become a remarkable leader."

"She doesn't want to admit it. It frightens her," Ido said, stretching himself, long and muscular, across two chairs.

"She'll get over it soon. There's no choice," Michal said confidently. "Once you've appeared on all the talk shows that she's been interviewed on and your name is printed in the papers as often as hers has been, things become different. The public persona starts to assume real proportions. Being a leader suits her, don't you think?" Michal asked.

"Yes, I think so, too," said Ido, swirling an ice cube in his empty glass. "I've always thought she was a born leader."

"She's been there before, you know," Michal continued. "Back when she was the head of the youth movement, nothing went on in this country without Lilah having something to say about it. People were predicting a Knesset career for her. Nothing was beyond her grasp."

"So what happened?" asked Ido.

"I imagine that her choice of profession had something to do with it. You can't go running around the world shooting photographs *and* have a political career back home. But there's more to it than that."

"Like what?" Ido asked.

"I am sure the two of you have talked about it."

"No, we haven't. Dad has always been the political one. There's enough in him for us all. My mother just didn't seem to be the type."

"No, there's more, a lot more. Certainly you know about

your uncle?

"Of course. I feel like I've known him my whole life. Sometimes I feel like he and I are the same person. Army, politics. I supposedly even look a lot like him."

"Yes, you do. Both of you are the type of man that women take notice of. I don't know you that well yet, but I did know him. I knew him very, very well. As you know, your mother and I were very close back then and I practically lived here. Yonatan was as close to being a brother as I ever had. But he belonged to Lilah. That's something she never allowed me to forget. Though they could fight like cats and dogs, she adored him."

"So what does my uncle have to do with my mother rejecting politics all these years?"

"I think it played the biggest part in her choice to give up politics. You know how your uncle died, don't you?"

"Of course. Aside from all the newspaper clippings and articles, we also studied what happened the night he died in officers' school. It was a brilliantly executed counterinsurgency attack, though my uncle was either crazy or unbelievably courageous to go out and infiltrate behind enemy lines all by himself."

"He was a very brave man. And he went into that abandoned village alone to eliminate the terrorists' scouts because he didn't want to unnecessarily endanger his men."

"He achieved his objective. His deputy followed his instructions exactly and caught the attacking raiders off-guard. No other Israelis were killed. The planned attack never materialized. It was neutralized," said Ido, sounding very much the military professional.

"Yes, all went well except for what happened to your uncle."

"I know."

"Do you know what happened, how he was caught and

despite being tortured, did not reveal what he knew about a certain operation?"

"That's the official story."

"The official story is wrong," said Michal. "That information had been de-classified a few days earlier. Yoni died protecting so-called secrets that his commanders, I mean the ones at the very top, neglected to let filter down. The information had already been cleared for publication. There was a breakdown in the chain of command, and your uncle died withholding information that he could have traded for his life."

There was a sharp silence in the room. Ido was shocked. The "chain of command" – in his family and in the army – had never told him what had really happened. It was Michal who revealed it to him, now.

"Are you saying that the government knowingly sacrificed my uncle?"

"Your grandfather, of blessed memory, checked that possibility thoroughly. No, it was just plain negligence. And it was enough to make Lilah associate politics with the totally unnecessary death of her brother," Michal lamented. "It was hard for me to get over it. Imagine what it was like for her."

"Alright," Ido began, "I understand. But people get over things, especially when they are married to someone as involved as Dad."

"Not always," Michal corrected. "Sometimes when something withers, it just withers, and not all the care in the world is going to revive it. When her brother died, something in Lilah died, too. A deep channel of grief has been running through her ever since."

"Alright," Ido said somberly. "You react the way you react. But why did it cause the breakup of their marriage? What did Dad have to do with Yonatan's death? I've always heard they were the closest of friends."

"Your mother just couldn't cope with what happened and because your dad and Yonatan were so close, your mother just associated the tragedy with your father as if he was in some way responsible. It's that simple."

"What a shame. You know, they still seem to love each other, even after all these years."

Michal nodded in agreement. "I think they are deeply in love. Anyway, in terms of public life and political change, Lilah is making up for lost time now, whether she wants to or not."

"I'll say. She's much more involved these days than I am."

"Yes, but she's not a lieutenant colonel in the Israel Defense Forces." Michal paused for a moment, and then asked, "How do you reconcile the two – your military career and your politics? On the one hand, you serve and protect the State as directed by the government; in fact, you've pledged your life to it. But then there's your politics, so to the Left. I don't see how they mesh."

"There's no contradiction, as far as I am concerned. I have no quarrel with the State. I am quite a Zionist, you know."

"But the positions you take are so at odds with the policies of this government."

"They most certainly are. I could probably count on the fingers of one hand the issues on which I agree with this government. That's why I am so politically active."

"You've been involved in politics for years."

"I was aware and made my commitments when I was still quite young. My parents raised me on the values of social justice, and our elected governments have become increasingly unjust, so I have strong disagreements with them."

"But you execute their commands on the battlefield?"

"Not theirs, my commanders. On the battlefield, in defense of my people. An army relies on officers issuing orders and soldiers executing them. But the government hasn't earned my obedience in civilian life."

"And if you disagree with orders?"

"I've never hesitated to express my disagreement to my commanders. The Israeli army is different than most, in that you can question orders, though not in the middle of battle."

"Alright, I accept your position. They're sound and principled. You know, when I was your age, even younger, I was intolerant of Israel. I was radical to a fault, out of a romantic notion, a belief in being holy rather than human when it came to judging my people and my country. I saw everything in black and white. I moved to France, which I believed was freer, more progressive and just than my own country. And then I saw the anti-Semitism of the French Left, and began to realize that things weren't as perfect there as I had believed. I learned that life consists mainly of grays. It took some time, but I sobered up. I agree with you. Israel isn't the monster it has been made out to be. In fact, Israel's right to exist and be defended is far greater than many other states – including almost all of the regimes governing our neighbors," Michal concluded.

"That's right. But there's the other side of the coin, too," sighed Ido. "We are facing a major struggle. We are battling for the soul of our country. I believe with every fiber of my being in the justice of the creation and survival of the State of Israel. At the same time, I believe, that this government, so right-wing and closed in its policy, acts unjustly toward the people of Israel and in its dealings with the Palestinians. And they keep getting elected. The electoral machine works to their favor since every tiny interest group can buy into their coalition as long as they give voice to their mantra: fatalism and insularity. 'They're-all-against us' and 'Wealth is redemption.' We are somnolent, as Rabbi Ben-Yishai says. And with people like Mordechai Carmi in charge of law and order, my disgust just gets deeper."

"I couldn't agree with you more," Michal said. "We've got to keep struggling for what we believe in. We've got to make things better."

Lilah came back into the kitchen. Her face was red with anger.

"Come on, Mom. Put this Carmi thing to rest. Let it go," said Ido. Then, from the look on her face, he understood that something else had come up.

"There's been a terrorist attack in Jerusalem, apparently perpetrated by Palestinians. An entire wing of the Malha Mall has collapsed and it sounds as if there are a lot of people trapped in the debris. There are no casualty figures yet, but it doesn't look good," Lilah reported, sliding onto a chair as if her legs had been cut down from under her.

The attack on the Malha Mall was the bloodiest attack Jerusalem had known in years. A Hamas splinter group had already phoned the Agence France-Presse and taken credit. The emergency rooms of the capital's Hadassah Medical Center and Sha'are Zedek Hospital were overflowing with wounded. As reports came across his radio on the savagery, Eli considered – briefly – whether the hunt for the Sons of Gideon was justified: maybe their approach was right, an eye for an eye. Then he heard that Rabbi Epstein had already arrived at Malha, and the Border Police were having a hard time controlling the angry crowd he was inciting there and at the hospitals. Eli concluded that his contribution to containing the madness was to reset his sights on the menace he was already stalking, the Gideons, ensconced somewhere deep underground.

Eli's investigators had come up with an ID of the owner of the motorcycle used in the Messubim Juncture attack; a traffic surveillance camera along the highway had captured its tag number. It had been found at Beit Jala, outside of Jerusalem in the West Bank and had been reported stolen six months earlier. Apparently due to a clerical oversight, a license had recently been issued for the motorcycle, despite it being listed as stolen. The new owner of record was a woman, Shoshana Ya'akov and the application form carried the signature "S. Ya'akov," – the same name used by the contractor at Rabin Square.

Eli had the motor vehicle bureau run a computer check and found that a motorcycle permit had been issued at its Holon facility to S. Ya'akov early the previous February. The address listed on the license application was an absorption center for religious new immigrants in Jerusalem's Bayit Vegan neighborhood. The height and weight listed on the application indicated a tall and heavy 43-year-old female with auburn hair. The photograph that accompanied the application was inexplicably missing.

The manager of the motor vehicle bureau, apologizing profusely over the phone, could not account for the missing photograph. Eli told him to go through his files again. For his part, Eli would pay a surprise visit to the immigrant absorption center that was Shoshana Ya'akov's last address of record.

The small, dignified building tucked behind the trees on a quiet street of Bayit Vegan was nearly empty. "The economic crisis is discouraging immigration right now, and most of the Orthodox newcomers are going straight to West Bank settlements," said the director of the immigrant absorption center, an owlish, fragile-looking man in a suit and tie as he led Eli into his office. A certificate of rabbinical ordination and diplomas from British universities, including a master's of social work from Leeds were prominently displayed on the office wall. The dark wood shelves were lined with works of Judaica, sociology, psychology and other books of scholarship.

"Officer, how can I help you?" the center's director asked Eli solicitously as they sat down.

"I'm with the office of the Prime Minister's security advisor," Eli told the man. "We're interested in a woman who we believe was living here – maybe still is."

"What is her name?" asked the director.

"Shoshana Ya'akov, or a version of that. She gave this center as her home address when applying for a driver's license last February."

"Last February," the man thought out loud, "I was abroad for most of that month. But the name does ring a bell. Let me check the files."

The director went into an adjoining room and returned with a folder. "Her family name is Ya'akov?" he asked as he scanned the contents. "Yes, of course – I knew the name sounded familiar. You must be speaking of Sandra Jacoby. She began calling herself Shoshana Ya'akov. I should have known."

"And she resided here last February?"

"Yes, she came in the fall and stayed through winter, if I remember correctly."

"She is tall, heavily built?" Eli ventured.

"Yes, that's Sandra. Poor woman, she really wants a family but with her, let's say bulky appearance and her introverted nature, she'll likely have a difficult time of it – not to mention her age, of course."

"I thought she was married," Eli said.

"Married? Sandra, no, not that I know of. Why would you think that?"

"She was wearing a head covering," Eli answered.

"Oh, that. Well, she was always trying to be as observant and modest as she could be, more than required. During our interview she told me that she was dedicated to making up for all her years of transgression. As for being married, given her age, she was petrified that she would never find a spouse."

"Her age?" asked Eli.

"Around forty-five, I would imagine. Maybe older."

"What else can you tell me about her?"

"Well, where do I begin? I know, let me get her file. That will jog my memory and enable me to be a bit more precise." He returned to the adjoining room where he opened and shut the drawers searching for the file. After several minutes, he called in the secretary to help him. They checked exhaustively but the center's director returned empty-handed to his desk, looking quite discomfited.

"This is highly peculiar. We keep very careful records of the people passing through here, but we don't seem to have Sandra's, eh, Shoshana's file."

"Nothing at all?" Eli pressed. He was disappointed – and increasingly suspicious. "Maybe on a computer back-up or something else?"

"I'm afraid not. We only began keeping computer records this summer," the director said apologetically. "I am a bit of a technophobe," he admitted. "It's odd, though. I don't recall a file ever being displaced or lost. Fortunately, however, all of our files are copied and stored at the Ministry of Immigrant Absorption."

"That's good. As it happens, they are already photocopying some documents related to Ms. Ya'akov. Perhaps they can collect all the material and put it aside for me. Do you mind if I phone them from your office?"

"Not at all," said the director, as he dialed a number and passed the phone to Eli.

Eli spoke directly to the director-general. She promised a prompt check and within five minutes had called back quite ruffled: The file on Sandra Jacoby, aka Shoshana Ya'akov, was missing there, too. Eli's face grew stormy as his mind filled with thoughts of conspiracy and obstruction.

"She's in trouble, isn't she?" said the director of the absorption center. Eli nodded. "I don't know what happened to her or what she's done, but I would like to help," he told Eli in a tone that left no doubt of his sincerity.

"Thanks. Let's start by going back a few steps. Tell me everything you remember about her."

The man thought quietly, then said, "It was hard to get to know her. She was very shy and quite the loner. She is a troubled soul, some kind of personality disorder – though that's my personal impression, not a clinical determination."

Eli was growing impatient. He wanted facts, not impressions.

"She's very sensitive. One incident that comes to mind was how terribly distraught she became when she found a dead sparrow in front of the building. The bird must have flown into a wall or something and broken its neck. You know, things like that happen from time to time. You would have thought she was a child the way Sandra – Shoshana – carried on. She wept and wept and cuddled the bird in her hands, rocking back and forth. She couldn't stop sobbing. I couldn't console her. She's so gentle, she wouldn't hurt a fly."

Eli didn't say a word. "How about her friends? Did she have a roommate?"

"We don't have roommates unless two residents make a request. With so many empty rooms, we find that people are grateful for a little privacy. As for friends, I don't know of any. She spent virtually all her time alone. My wife and I had her over for Shabbat lunch once. Our children were away and our other guests couldn't make it at the last minute, so she had our full attention. But she said barely a word, though she's exceedingly polite. The house mother here commented several times on her solitary ways. It was as if she didn't want to be close to people."

"Did she tell you anything about her background?"

"Little. From our conversations with her, we learned that she became religious on her own. It wasn't how she was raised; apparently she had lived among non-Jews most of her life.

When we made the blessings on Shabbat, she hardly seemed to know them, much less the traditional songs or customs. It was as if she went through the motions of Orthodoxy by rote. She seemed detached, like an automaton without knowledge or feeling. As for her family, she didn't mention them. I didn't know she had a brother here in Israel until he came to the absorption center shortly after she left."

Eli had been taking down every word, noting "brother" in large letters.

"What were the circumstances of her leaving?" Eli asked.

"She went away one weekend, and simply did not come back. Her brother came a few days later saying she had decided to move to one of the West Bank settlements. He, the brother, retrieved her belongings and said she was in bed with the flu and that she couldn't come herself. He came with a note from her instructing me to let him have all her possessions, so I complied." He started up from his chair as if to retrieve something but then sat down again. "I'm sorry, but I am sure we left the note in her missing file."

"What can you tell me about her brother? Start with his name please," Eli said. He was taking notes assiduously, absorbing every word like a sponge.

"I don't remember his name. He didn't appear to be religiously observant. In fact, I found him to be a rather disagreeable sort, particularly in his appearance, his demeanor and his manner of speaking. He rode a motorcycle and was unshaven. He seemed uneducated and rather crude. Quite different from Shoshana."

"He didn't tell you where she was?"

"No. I asked him where I could forward her mail, but he avoided answering."

"Has she received any mail?" asked Eli.

"Off hand, I don't know," the director answered. "I could check if you like."

"Please."

As the director left the office, Eli considered the emerging facts. It was a family affair, evidently. Sandra Jacoby – also known as Shoshana Ya'akov – and her brother, using the identity of Shimshon Ya'akov also known as Ya'akov Shimshoni, were implicated. Finally, Eli had names of people who either were Gideons or close to them.

The director walked back into his office. "No, there was no mail. But something was left behind when the brother took Sandra's belongings. I have it here if it's of any interest to you," he said and handed Eli a magazine enclosed in a postal wrapper.

Eli unceremoniously ripped off the wrapper. The invasion of his client's privacy seemed to disturb the director. "I have an open warrant in this case," Eli informed him. Eli stared at the cover of the magazine and began leafing through it.

"Is it in any way illuminating?" the director asked.

"I think so," said Eli, as he placed the issue of *Gunfire! Holy Writ for Today's Man of War* in his briefcase. "Tell me, did Shoshana Ya'akov ever express her politics?"

"Not to my recollection."

"Did she identify with any movements, say, the religious youth movements, or express support or admiration for any particular political party or political figure?"

"No," said the director. "I don't think that would fit her personality. Oh, wait. When I first interviewed her in this office," he said slowly, "we were talking about the challenges faced by new immigrants in Israel and about the need to contribute to the betterment of society. Suddenly she said – it shocked me at the time although I subsequently put it out of my mind – she stated quite resolutely that Rabbi Epstein, you know, of the so-called Hebrew Fighters Association," he pronounced the words acidly, "she said that Rabbi Epstein wasn't 'strong enough' and that 'much more has to be done to get rid of the Amalekites, the Arabs.' I believe those are the words she used."

Eli took a moment to commit what was said to paper. "Anything else?" he asked.

"I don't thing she said anything else. Maybe she concluded that I didn't share her thinking. She's in serious trouble, isn't she?"

Eli nodded as he rose to leave.

"It's hard to think of her in that way. I don't know what this is all about but it would seem to have something to do with the extremists. For my part, I find them utterly repulsive, a blot on the Jewish soul."

Eli nodded and handed the man his card. "It would be helpful if you could call me at this number if either Shoshana or her brother comes here, or if you hear anything about their whereabouts. I know it's unlikely, but just in case, or if you think of anything else. Also," Eli continued as an afterthought, "if you suspect that someone has been going through your files without authorization or if more records seem to be missing, please let me know."

"I most assuredly will."

Eli walked out of the immigrant residence into the unseasonably hot, dry air of the evening. The bizarre weather seemed a metaphor for these people, the Gideons. If only it would finally rain, thought Eli, perhaps it would wash the evil away.

Eli proceeded to the Ministry of Immigrant Absorption. That evening, he had its offices torn apart in a search for Shoshana Ya'akov's photo.

The new information about Shoshana Ya'akov and her brother added greater depth to the Gideons' profile. Among them were religious zealots and social marginals prone to violence; they canonized hatred for Arabs; they, at least some of them, were based in Jerusalem's religious neighborhoods; there were both men and women in their ranks; they were resourceful and had access to funding; they had recruited new immigrants; they possessed diverse skills from masonry to electronics – in addition to expertise in weapons and explosives. They seemed not to fear capture.

It wasn't much, but it was something. Enough to power Eli further through the sea of reeds and into the marsh.

og ❖ ৪০

Issam was in Tulazine attending a town council session. He had requested to address the scheduled meeting. He was determined to have the council condemn the bombing at Malha.

The reception bestowed him was hardly welcoming.

"But they have denounced every incident of Jewish terrorism that has taken place against us," Issam appealed, his Arabic sounding especially guttural as if he was trying to swallow the resistance he was encountering. "Groups like Na'aleh have defended our rights and now we aren't willing to reciprocate? Not to condemn the shopping-mall bombing is to slap our Jewish friends in the face, especially since it was perpetrated with the help of Arab citizens of Israel."

"The Jews have slapped us in the face all these years. When an individual Israeli Arab commits a crime, we all get blamed. Enough. I am not in favor of humiliating ourselves. That's what they want, to keep us down."

"Why are you making it so complicated? It is a simple issue of humanity," Issam countered. "Innocent people were killed by terrorists," he said, the sweat dripping off his brow and cheeks from the stifling heat in the cramped room. "There is a growing movement among the Jews – I don't see any of you running to be part of it – that is reaching out to us. And we won't reach back? I don't understand."

"It is we who don't understand you," said an irate university student with an angry, taut face. He was a first-term councilor, and much taken with himself. He sounded as if he were campaigning. "You speak Arabic, you come from an Arab family, but the interests you care about are Jewish ones." There was a subtle but discernible wave of agreement among many of those in attendance. Issam was shocked.

"I don't have to take such abuse from a green sapling like you," Issam spewed. "You play exactly the same game as the Jewish extremists, viewing the problems in terms of "us versus them," Arabs against Jews and vice versa. The problem is not ethnicity, but simply a question of good and evil."

"Yes, you are right. Good and evil. The Arabs are good, the Jews evil," said a wealthy businessmen who, like Miari, nominally lived in the village, but who spent the bulk of his time abroad.

"You say that even knowing full well that Tulazine's record in producing extremists is well above the average for the Arab Israeli sector. There are sons of this village with blood on their hands, and you say we are all good and the Jews all evil?"

"We have been provoked," declared a councilor whom Issam had counted on as a moderate. There was fear in the man's voice.

"Provoked to kill innocent, unarmed and unsuspecting people?"

"Terrorism is not the way to meet our goals. Dr. Halaby is right about that," said another member of the council. "But they feed it. Look at us here. We are meeting in a schoolhouse because there is no funding for a municipality building. The children have to sit in this oven all day looking out through cracked window panes. There isn't a proper playground in the entire town, never mind a youth center or a place where the old folks can spend their last years in pleasant surroundings. Our people have to walk a kilometer-and-a-half to catch the nearest bus. And when we do get on the bus, the Jews stare at us, certain that we are going to plant a bomb or that we're infected, or criminals."

"Do you blame them for being suspicious? In the past months, there have been two major incidents of Arab terrorism. And it's not going to stop until good people on both sides speak out. That is why I want us to issue a condemnation."

The debate continued. The pragmatists and moderates nearly prevailed, but in the end the councilors were hopelessly deadlocked. At length, a short, bland statement was issued regretting the loss of innocent life. "But let no one think that we do this wholeheartedly," said one councilor, bitterly.

Wicked winds blow over this land now, Issam thought to himself as he left Tulazine. The drought seems to have stricken both the land and the people. There is so little meeting ground, little upon which to cultivate peace. It is hard to know how to change things, make them better. Let it rain, Allah, please bring the rains.

At an emergency meeting taking place in Tel Aviv at the same time as the councilors convened in Tulazine, Na'aleh forcefully denounced the Malha Mall bombing and called on the Palestinians to do so as well. In a resolution distributed to the press, the Movement declared that "whether committed by Jews or Arabs, terrorism condemns both Israelis and Palestinians to perpetual bloodshed."

Also during the meeting, the Na'aleh board decided to publicize the photos of the Sons of Gideon that Lilah had taken at the Ramat Zion soccer game despite the likely rebuke it would bring from the government. "With full cognizance of the authorities' objection to our doing so, we believe these photos must be released to the public at once," the Movement declared in announcing that it would hold a press conference to release the pictures.

Ironically, Eli would finally get his photos of a Gideon – from the pages of the next day's newspapers where Lilah's pictures of the would-be bomber would appear next to a photo of Malha Mall, an entire section of which lay in ruins.

CHAPTER FOURTEEN

It was a cold night, the weather finally resembling something more seasonal than the long, hard heat that had scoffed at winter's arrival.

Lilah felt emboldened as she sat at her kitchen table and wrote to Lucian on her laptop:

> *So much has happened…I hardly know where to begin. My life has become so different from what it was in Cambridge, yet nothing could seem more right than what I am doing now…being part of the struggle for the soul of my people.*
>
> *We may have Sons of Gideon among us, the Rabbi Epsteins and their fighters and other sowers of hate, but there are many people in this society who believe in the vision of the prophets. We are alive, Lucian, alive, determined to fight the hatemongers and build a society fitting of our true heritage. I have rediscovered my people – in Michal and Issam, Rabbi Ben-Yishai, my son and his father, the many others who surround me in Na'aleh. We live, Lucian. We will win this struggle.*

In the night cold and its silence, Lilah felt a warmth welling in her, a creative impulse. She imagined images she had taken over the last months, photos she had taken that could constitute a new collection, *Arise Zion* she might call it, documenting the emergence of Na'aleh and, she was certain, its eventual victory. Such a project appealed to her and she would give it due consideration – once the Gideons had been put down.

ଓ ❖ ଚ

The archives of the Ministry of Immigrant Absorption had been scoured from top to bottom, but produced no file on either Shoshana Ya'akov or Sandra Jacoby. Other than one citation stating that a file had been opened in her name and that she was living at the Bayit Vagan absorption center, nothing was found. The search for her brother also led nowhere.

Eli went mining for more information. Through Amos' office, he convened an urgent meeting of security directors of relevant government ministries. While the precise reason for the meeting was not announced in advance, the reference to a "national security crisis" brought the officials running. At nine that evening, the conference room at the Prime Minister's Bureau was full.

"Some of you know me," Eli began modestly, nodding to those, not a few, veterans of the security community whose paths had crossed his in the past. "For those who do not, my name is Eli Zedek. I work with the Prime Minister's Office of Security Affairs. I apologize for requesting your attendance at this meeting on such short notice but I assure you that in light of the domestic security crisis, this meeting is absolutely necessary. We have very little time." A wave of lightheadedness, the consequence of a lack of sleep and stress, caused Eli to pause, take a sip of water and collect himself before continuing.

"I assume you have already guessed what security crisis I am referring to. I cannot share any details of the Sons of Gideon investigation with you other than to say that despite vigorous efforts to solve the case, progress has been slow. There has been a development that may help us apprehend some of the principals –assuming we can get more information than we now have in hand. This is where you come in.

"We are hoping to learn more about two individuals, a brother and sister with the last name of Jacoby, Ya'akov or some variation of that. The woman goes by the first name of

Sandra or Shoshana. The brother has given Shimshon as his first name. We believe that the sister arrived as an immigrant in Israel late last fall from an English-speaking country, most probably the United States or Canada. The brother has been here at least as long as the sister. Both speak some Hebrew. She is religious, tall, husky and is not, shall we say, a beauty queen. She is in her mid-forties to early fifties.

"The brother is about the same age. He rides a motorcycle and is apparently not religiously observant. He has a thorough knowledge of explosives and electronics. Both brother and sister are fair-haired and light-skinned. It is believed that both individuals have been involved in acts of extreme violence," emphasized Eli.

He paused, giving his listeners time to complete their notes.

"That's all you can tell us about them?" someone from the audience asked.

"That's all we know," Eli confirmed.

"How about photographs?"

"If only we had one," Eli lamented. "The nearest thing we have to a picture is composite portraits of the brother drawn by a police artist. You've seen the drawing on television and in the newspapers. Eyewitnesses have told us they are not especially accurate."

There were other questions, though Eli had answers for few of them.

"I wish I could tell you more about these people, but that's exactly the problem with the Sons of Gideon: They cover their tracks like spirits in the night. I ask you," Eli continued with controlled but certain gravity, "to help us find these people. Any information we can gather about them or anyone associated with them, no matter how unimportant it may seem, will help us make progress. We ask that you have your agencies and ministries search carefully for any and all data on these two names: Please use whatever resources you have at your disposal. People's lives are, as we have already seen, at stake."

Eli had inspired the audience. They rose as one and joined the pursuit for the terrorists.

A first call the next morning came from the Ministry of Housing. The director of its Rental Housing Division was on the line.

"Our records indicate that a Shoshana Ya'akov rented an apartment in Ma'ale Adumim for someone named Moshe Ben-Avraham. We have the address of the apartment."

"What information do you have on Shoshana Ya'akov? A checking account, identity card number, anything."

"She paid for Ben-Avraham's apartment a year in advance in cash. We don't have anything else."

"And what have you got on Ben-Avraham?" Eli asked, as he opened a new computer file in his name.

"Only his signature on a standard lease. Would you like me to fax you a copy?"

"Would you please?" said Eli, and gave his fax number.

Within minutes of hanging up, Eli had a small team on its way to Ma'ale Adumim. The massive dragnets he had previously set up around the Romema apartment as part of the manhunt for Shimshon Ya'akov, and the search in the Jerusalem hills for the motorcyclist after the massacre at Messubim interchange had failed to achieve results; only the motorcycle, not its operator, had been found. But Eli was more hopeful now. A track was being uncovered.

Barely half an hour after receiving the call from the Housing Ministry, Eli was on the road to Ma'ale Adumim, which, at 35,000 residents, was Israel's largest settlement in the occupied territories. As he drove, Eli was deep in thought, contemplating what he might find there. He was coming out of a sharp curve as he passed near Al-Issawiya, one of the villages near Ma'ale Adumim when he was startled by a loud crack, the sound of something striking his car.

His first thought was that it was a gunshot. He brought the car to a hard stop, jumped out, pulled his pistol from the holster at his ankle, crouched behind the open door and aimed at the first sign of movement. His lungs were pumping hard when he realized that he had taken aim at a group of Arab children, the source of the projectile. They had been throwing stones at passing cars with Israeli plates. Eli had aimed his gun at the children but had refrained from pulling the trigger. The children darted up the hill, screaming with fear and running as swiftly as their feet could carry them.

Eli was horrified; he had been moments away from firing. He slowly re-holstered the gun; it was suddenly abhorrent to him, what he might have done with it. Israelis had died after being struck or distracted by rocks thrown at them in the West Bank. He, like other targets, could have gotten out of the car and started firing, claiming self-defense.

It took Eli several minutes to catch his breath and steady his legs. He sat in the car and waited until the cold sweat stopped streaming down his face. The children had disappeared, scattered, frightened out of their wits. They may have had it coming, but he would forever regret that. Besides, he was after other prey now, one who threatened them all.

He composed himself and continued driving to Ma'ale Adumim.

The GPS directed him to a street along the southeastern edge of the town in an area of new construction. Eli parked at the foot of the hill where the paved street ended and a new neighborhood was being built. Eli entered the building where the apartment leased to Ben-Avraham was located.

"Eli?" someone whispered from the dark hallway, not far from where he was standing.

"Who's that?" Eli called out mutely. A figure in jeans and sneakers stepped out of the shadows clutching a pistol. Eli recognized one of his agents. Eli stared at the gun. "Sorry," apologized the agent, "but I realized I didn't know a thing about Ben-Avraham and that I had no idea what he looks like or who to look for. It's dark in here."

"I understand," said Eli. "Is the rest of the building empty?" he asked.

"I think so. All the front doors are open except for Apartment 2, the Ben-Avraham apartment. That door is shut and locked."

"Okay. You and I are going in. Is your partner with you?"

"Yes."

Eli whispered, "Have him go around to the back of the building. Tell him to be prepared for anything coming out of apartment 2," Eli directed. The agent nodded and whispered instructions to his partner into his cell phone.

"We'll knock," Eli instructed. "If the door opens, watch out for a gun or knife and grab who ever opens it. In the meantime, I'll sweep the rooms. If no one answers, I'll pick the lock and go in first, you cover as I sweep." The agent nodded.

"Take a good look at the door frame; it might be booby-trapped. The only thing we know for sure about this guy is that he's close enough to the Gideons to have one of them sign a lease for him. Be careful. Be very careful. Let's go."

They rounded the corner and approached the door of Apartment 2. Both men drew their pistols. Eli knocked on the door, then pounded. He paused, then ran his fingers around the doorframe, feeling for a booby trap. He then took out a locksmith's pick he carried in his wallet and inserted it into the lock; it gave way. Eli kicked the door wide open.

Eli and the agent moved through each of the rooms, pistols held full-handed and ready to fire. No one was in the flat. They admitted the man who was covering the back door. The three began to search the apartment.

There was no electricity; the building was not yet connected to the grid. A kerosene lamp was on the living room floor. Next to it was a sleeping bag, neatly laid open. An empty upside-down five-liter can served as a makeshift nightstand: stacked on it were an English-language Bible, a can opener, a rabbit's foot and a notebook.

It wasn't the English that made the contents of the notebook incomprehensible to Eli. Rather, the characters formed a string of symbols and phrases, some kind of code. The third entry, for example, read: "Sheepshead melt k2!!fgy; ;== cute mousey in a heap." The ninth entry was: "*Lo9**54 is over, round mountain, northstar, xxx8!!! Doused:hooray gook!" The other 53 entries were similarly unintelligible, written in a code that demanded a cryptologist's focused attentions.

They found nothing else of interest in the apartment. It had the same sterile order to it as the Romema apartment, but far fewer furnishings and possessions. There was little they could find to dust for fingerprints.

"I'd like you guys to continue staking out the apartment," Eli said. "I'll see to it that you are relieved by late afternoon. You have communications gear that can tie into the security network, right?"

They did.

"Water?" he asked. They did.

"Stay put, then. If anyone shows up, sit tight and call me. Don't move in unless he tries to leave. If he does, take him. Have your dispatcher forward regular updates to me every quarter of an hour. You know how important and difficult this case is. So handle things right, all the way around."

Eli took the notebook, left the building and walked hurriedly to his car. He placed the binder on the seat next to him. It was prime evidence, possibly full of fingerprints and other identifying information. Eli considered going to Amos' office but decided that it would be more efficient to take the notebook to National Police Headquarters in East Jerusalem. There were cryptologists there.

It took Eli seven minutes flat to make the trip.

If he could have heaved himself upward through the elevator shaft to the top floor of the building he would have done so. He half-burst into the quiet, darkened lab where the cryptologists worked. Eli sought out the chief. He found him and within half an hour of its discovery, the Ma'ale Adumim codebook was being scanned into one of the country's most advanced computers. Within the hour, some of the best minds in the country would assault it with full fury.

ය ❖ ෩

Lilah felt uneasy even before the press conference began. Firstly, the briefing at Beit Sokolov, the journalist association's center on Kaplan Street in Tel Aviv had to be moved into the main auditorium instead of the briefing room where such events were usually held; the press, domestic and foreign, had come en masse.

That delayed the start of the briefing by half an hour. The number of foreign journalists was much larger than expected and the supply of press kits was quickly exhausted. The photocopier was arthritic, and it was nearly an hour after it was called that the conference began.

Tension was already high when, shortly after the opening statements pandemonium erupted.

"Are you or are you not alleging Government complicity, direct or indirect, in the spate of terrorist attacks against Arabs?" asked the correspondent of a left-wing British newsweekly considered hostile to Israel. As he was staring at Naftali, the New Democratic chair felt he had no choice but to reply.

"We are not a commission of inquiry, nor do we profess to have all the facts," he declared from the podium where Lilah and Issam, representing the Na'aleh board, and Naftali and various other New Democratic leaders were sitting. Television cameras and sound booms hovered over the table, which had been draped in bunting and bore a placard with the logos of the party and the Movement.

"The Government contends that it has been making every effort to track down the Sons of Gideon. We take those assurances at face value but also call the public's attention to the fact that Chief Inspector Mordechai Carmi, who is purportedly directing the police investigation, refused to accept or release to the public the photograph you are holding in your hands. At a time when the investigation is going nowhere and there is supposedly little evidence with which to identify the terrorists, we find it puzzling that Chief Inspector Carmi would not welcome what could be a crucial piece of the puzzle."

"How certain are you that this photograph is what it purports to be? Couldn't you be mistaken? The police surely receive numerous tips and leads from the public that are not what the sender thinks they are," said a reporter for a an Israeli news service.

"I believe that question would best be answered by Lilah Kedem," said the New Democrat's spokeswoman, who was serving as moderator.

"We are not certain of anything," said Lilah. "We cannot say with complete confidence that the woman in the photo is a Gideon or one of their confederates. However, I can say that after reviewing the exhaustive set of photos of those who attended the event at Ramat Zion, there is no one who more closely resembles the eyewitness description of the woman carrying the shopping bag that had the bomb inside it."

"So your conclusion is reached on the basis of an association of a woman with an ordinary bag. How seriously do you expect the police to take your assertion that this individual is affiliated with the Gideons? Isn't that somewhat of a leap?" asked a red-faced reporter for *The Nationalist,* the governing party's newspaper, as he disdainfully waved the photo as though it were pornography.

Lilah was losing her patience. "There is simply no one else who matches the description of the person who was seen with a bag that was the same type that contained the bomb. How many people bring shopping bags to such events? What are the chances that there was more than one similarly dressed and presumably Haredi woman carrying such a bag at Ramat Zion? I think that common sense more than validates the assumption that this woman is the carrier of the bomb that night."

"I'd like to comment on all this, if I may," Issam said calmly but firmly. "I think the entire point is being missed. The facts are simple and easily understood.

"One of our leaders, who happens to be a professional photographer, found a photograph among the pictures she took of the crowd. The subject of the photograph closely resembled the description given of the person who was seen carrying the bomb. A meeting was then arranged with the senior police officer in charge of the investigation. He was offered the photograph, but elected to turn it down. We want to know why. Given the lack of progress in solving the case and the government's stated desire to enlist the public's assistance in identifying these criminals, why was this potentially key piece of evidence so brusquely and illogically refused by Chief Inspector Carmi? His response was so contrary to the government's call for assistance and that creates all sorts of suspicions.

"We seek an answer to the question: Why has no discernible progress been made in this investigation? We appeal to the government: Help us dispel the suspicions that you are behind these attacks or are concealing information about the parties responsible. With the whole world watching, we ask you to ease the concerns that we Israelis have developed about official motives and policies."

"Issam Halaby," said an Israeli reporter well-known for his ultra-nationalistic stance as he made his way to the front of the auditorium. Shaking with anger, he shouted, "Your only qualification for speaking on such matters comes from the fact that your home village is a hotbed of real terrorism, Arab terrorism. That's the main issue that should be addressed here, not the misguided actions of a group of Jewish patriots seeking to protect the State. How dare you impugn this Government's intentions? You do not deserve the right of citizenship as you surreptitiously serve interests that are antagonistic to the State of Israel."

The journalist's remarks elicited counter-accusations and catcalls from the audience. The uproar had just begun to die down when Rabbi Epstein and his brown-shirted followers jauntily entered the hall, shouting their own accusations. "Supporters of terrorism!" "Self-hating Israelis!" they cried at those sitting on the dais, chanting as they made their way toward the front of the auditorium. With the television cameras rolling, the rabbi was in his element, lapping up the publicity while posturing humility and righteousness.

From among Epstein's followers, a diminutive woman with a bad limp appeared clad in an oversized Hebrew Fighters Association T-shirt. She suddenly pulled two plastic bags of red paint out from underneath it and heaved them at the Na'aleh and New Democratic Party members on the podium. A burst of blood-red paint hit Naftali in the chest.

"This," began the rabbi, speaking in a carefully modulated, sanctimonious tone, while pointing to the splashed paint, "symbolizes the blood of Israel that self-hating Jews and traitors have helped to spill throughout history. The people sitting here, reciting fabrications and telling lies, are the self-haters and traitors of today," he said.

The audience had had enough. A burly reporter for the

kibbutz federation's website rose out of his seat and shoved two Hebrew Fighters members out of his way as he headed for Rabbi Epstein. "This seems to be the only way to deal with fascists like you," he said as he grabbed Epstein – who, judging by his mocking smile, seemed to delight in the spectacle – and propelled him down the main aisle. Epstein had been thrown halfway to the rear exit when five Hebrew Fighters members overpowered the kibbutznik. Others came to the latter's aid, at which point a general free-for-all broke out. It was ten minutes before police arrived in sufficient numbers to clear the room.

All the while, Naftali, Issam and Lilah maintained their composure. As they waited for the briefing to resume, the journalists gathered around them and sought their reactions to the incident.

"I don't think any further comment is necessary. By their actions here today, Rabbi Epstein and his thugs have demonstrated the danger we Israelis face in these times of great upheaval," Naftali stated as he, Lilah and the moderator wiped away the red paint on his shirt and face as best they could.

"Our struggle will continue unabated," Issam said, facing the cameras. "As the brave people who struggled for civil rights for all in the United States promised, 'We shall overcome.'"

"I'd like to say something," said Lilah having retaken her seat and speaking into a table microphone, steady as the Rock of Gibraltar. "I turn to the people of Israel who I am sure will be shocked when they see on the television news what happened here, and I appeal to Jews and Arabs alike to put an end to this madness, to the terror and violence. Let us stand together and stop the extremists before they destroy us all."

The press conference ended shortly afterwards. No one could predict when the outrages would stop.

ೞ ❖ ೂ

Eli's men and Shin Bet agents continued the stakeout of the Ma'ale Adumim apartment into the night and the following day. With the search for the Ya'akovs/Jacobys at a dead-end, finding Ben-Avraham took on increased priority.

A deluge of information on Moshe Ben-Avraham began to arrive by email and fax. The National Insurance Institute had records on five individuals by that name: two were elderly, a third resided abroad, while a fourth Moshe Ben-Avraham resided in an Ministry of Defense nursing-care facility for the war-wounded.

The fifth Ben-Avraham was of relevance: like Ya'akov/Jacoby, he was a new immigrant. The Ministry of Immigrant Absorption reported opening a file for a 35-year-old British immigrant who had arrived in the country the previous December via the port of Eilat. The Interior Ministry reported that the outpost settlement that Ben-Avraham listed as his address had been disbanded well before his arrival in the country. He, too, it seemed, was prone to giving false addresses.

The passport control office informed Eli that Ben-Avraham had departed the country in April on an El Al flight to New York. There was no record of his return to Israel, yet the Transport Ministry reported that a license to operate a tractor-trailer was applied for and granted to Ben-Avraham in June. The Jerusalem address that Ben-Avraham gave as his place of residence on the Transport Ministry application was the same as the work address he listed on income tax forms. The police officer that Eli dispatched to check on the address found that it was a small paper factory that had closed years earlier.

For all the new data that came in on Ben-Avraham, no agency was able to comply with Eli's request for a photograph; all of the photos needed for the various applications and forms had inexplicably been removed from their records.

By mid-morning on the second day of surveillance, the

morning after the Na'aleh press conference, Eli was sure that the Ya'akov/Jacoby brother and sister and Ben-Avraham were key activists in the Sons of Gideon. Eli had never pursued people who remained elusive for so long; no one had ever remained so obscure. The lack of a visual record was crippling. If only he had a photograph, even if only of one of them....

And so, when his secretary entered his office, dropped a copy of the morning newspaper on his desk, and pointed to the outsized photograph on page one, Eli was thunderstruck. The caption of the photo read: "Why did the authorities ignore this photo of a potential Gideon?" Eli grabbed the newspaper and gazed at the grainy image of a modestly-dressed woman carrying a bag like the one containing the bomb he had defused. "What is this?" Eli asked in astonishment. The woman in the photo bore close resemblance to the description of the person seen carrying the bag, as provided by eyewitnesses at the scene. Eli hurriedly searched the newspaper for the full story behind the picture:

At a press conference at Journalists' House last night, leaders of the Na'aleh Movement and the New Democratic Party released a photograph they claim is of the woman who carried a bomb onto the grounds of Kibbutz Ramat Zion on Wednesday. The bombing attack took place during a soccer game dedicated to Jewish-Arab coexistence.

Professional photographer and Na'aleh leader Lilah Kedem disclosed that she had found the picture among numerous photos she had taken during the soccer game, which was organized by her organization. After hearing witnesses give the authorities a description of the woman carrying the bag where the bomb was found, Kedem reviewed her off-prints to determine whether any of her random shots of the crowd had captured an image of the alleged assailant. The picture here (right)...

Eli's memory carried him back to the woman with the camera at the kibbutz, the one he kept ordering away from the package. "Get me a phone number and address for this Lilah Kedem," he directed his secretary. He continued reading the story in the paper:

> ...*Prof. Naftali Kedem, the New Democratic Party chairman, told a large crowd of reporters and correspondents that Chief Inspector Mordechai Carmi, chief of the National Police Investigations Unit and the officer in charge of the police search for the Sons of Gideon refused to accept the photograph that was offered by Lilah Kedem during a meeting initiated by Ms. Kedem earlier this week.*
>
> *Although Carmi acknowledged that the authorities had failed to obtain even a single photograph of a Gideon, the chief inspector purportedly dismissed Lilah Kedem's offers of cooperation and reportedly made disparaging comments about Na'aleh and about Ms. Kedem personally.*
>
> *Declining to characterize Carmi's rebuff as implicating the government or police as being behind or covering up for the Gideons, Opposition leader Naftali Kedem did say that such behavior does not cohere with the government's claim that it is doing all it can to apprehend the Gideons and put a stop to their activities... .*

Eli stared at the photo on the front page. He then consulted his notes and personally telephoned several of the eyewitnesses who had seen the woman carrying the shopping bag with the bomb in it at the kibbutz. He asked them to get a hold of the newspaper and look at the photo. Three of them confirmed that the photograph was that of the woman carrying the bag at Ramat Zion.

Fuming, Eli then phoned Carmi's office. Kept on hold for the better part of ten minutes, he cut promptly to the chase, once Carmi came on the line.

"Is it true that you were presented with the picture last Monday?" he asked Carmi when he came on line, dispensing with the formalities.

"What picture is that?"

"Just answer the question," Eli said harshly.

"I don't have to report to you or anyone else," Carmi barked.

"So you did see it and you didn't have the sense to get it to the media, or at least show it to me?"

"I don't conduct my professional affairs irresponsibly. I don't humor every crackpot who comes my way."

"You know what, Carmi? I hope the leftists nail you. I look forward to the day when the Israel Police finally gets rid of one of the biggest jerks that ever wore its uniform," Eli yelled into the receiver before sending it crashing onto the cradle.

Half an hour later, Eli was at Lilah's door.

"Lilah Kedem?" Eli asked.

"She isn't in now," Michal replied.

"Do you know when she'll be back?" Eli asked, as he inserted himself into the apartment through the half-open door.

"She won't be back until late this evening. Who are you?" Michal asked.

"I'm with the security services," Eli answered. "Where can I find her?"

"She's speaking at a meeting in Rishon LeTzion."

"Do you have her cell phone number?" Eli asked as he eyed the surroundings.

"She didn't take her cell phone. She seldom does. Is something wrong? Has someone been hurt?" Michal asked apprehensively.

"No."

"Then maybe I can help you. Has it to do with the Hebrew Fighters Association incident last night?"

"No."

Michal tried a different tack. "I suppose you people weren't terribly pleased with the bad press you got at last night's press conference. You know, Lilah really wanted to give the photo to the right people. If your superior Carmi had acted on it in the first place, we would not have gone public with it ourselves."

"Carmi isn't my superior. Besides, that's history now," Eli said dismissively. He asked for something to drink and while Michal went to the kitchen, he picked up a copy of the pamphlet that accompanied the "Drown out the Darkness" campaign. "May I take one?" he asked one of the volunteers. She said he could, and gathered some other Na'aleh literature for him.

"Here you are," said Michal, handing Eli a glass of juice. He drank it thirstily. There was something about this place, something subdued. It quieted his angst.

"I'd like to see Lilah Kedem right away," his voice sounding gentler. "Do you know where she is exactly?"

"In Rishon LeTzion, at the Labor Council hall there..." Michal said, then regretted telling him that; she had no proof that he was who he said he was. "It's an important meeting for us, so if you could wait." she tried.

"It is urgent that I speak with her immediately. Thank you for the information, the juice and the background literature," he said, moving toward the door and departed. The man was driven and determined, thought Michal. She worried about Lilah being the subject of his pursuit.

Eli drove straight to Rishon LeTzion.

There was not a single parking space to be found within proximity of the Labor Council building. Anxious to speak with the woman who had taken the Gideon's picture, Eli parked his car on the sidewalk in front of the small hall and placed his blue roof light conspicuously atop the dashboard near the steering wheel. In the early evening darkness, Eli approached the building with respect: Simon, his father, had served several terms on the Labor Council in southern Jerusalem and had been active in the workers committee at Hadassah Hospital. Eli had not inherited the fire of Simon's labor spirit, but he surely respected it.

Police were milling around outside the building. A white bomb-disposal van was positioned on the sidewalk nearby, and a jeep filled with Border Policemen was double-parked on the street. Eli entered the building.

The large, drab hall was packed to the rafters. Every seat was taken and people were standing in the sloping aisles or leaning against the walls. Eli eyed the speakers sitting on the stage of the auditorium. He recognized one of them as the woman with the camera at the kibbutz last week. But as he thought back, he realized that he had seen her not only at Ramat Zion but before then. He flashbacked to Jaffa the past summer, the murder of the old Arab woman, Fatima Abed. Eli kept gazing at the woman with the elegant oval face framed by a handsome mane of dark curls. Yes, she was the same woman he had encountered at Ramat Zion. She had been an annoyance then as he sweated elbow deep into the cloth sack while trying to neutralize the bomb. As Eli observed her now though, a mood surfaced, tenderness, the feeling he had looking into his mother's eyes. This woman, Lilah, evoked that in him.

The Na'aleh meeting was about to conclude. The moderator thanked the speaker, Lilah Kedem, for her remarks and the ensuing applause was intense; people rose to their feet. Lilah was besieged by well-wishers as she walked down the central aisle toward the back of the auditorium.

"Excuse me," Eli said, as he firmly took Lilah's elbow and extracted her from the crowd.

"Don't I know you?" Lilah asked, disoriented by seeing Eli

in this context. "Yes, I remember, it was at the kibbutz last week. You dismantled the bomb."

"I need to speak with you alone," Eli whispered. "Please excuse us," he said to those who were waiting to speak with Lilah. He shepherded her out of the auditorium toward a secluded corner of the building.

People continued to trail behind them, intent on sharing a few words with the leader of Na'aleh. But Eli persisted: "I absolutely have to speak with you now. It's a matter of national security. Please come with me," he said, leading her intently through the lobby toward the front doors of the building and then outside.

"Lilah, what about the salon meeting?" one of the organizers called from the doorway.

"I'll be right back," she called out, then turned angrily to Eli. "I'm not accustomed to people grabbing me like that. Who are you, anyway?"

"My name is Eli. I am with the security services and that's all you need to know. You have acted irresponsibly," he said, but then when he saw his mother's eyes again in Lilah's, the recollection of her, Deborah, mellowed him. "Come," he said, "let's sit in my car, where I can get in a few sentences," he said, opening the door to the passenger seat of his car.

"If you think I am going anywhere with you, think again.

"Don't worry. I am not taking you anywhere," he said. He relented, persuaded that she would not enter the vehicle. They stood next to his car.

"What is it that you want from me? I am irresponsible? Why? For doing what you people should have done?"

"Security matters are very delicate. Investigations can take a very long time and inexperienced people with good intentions can cause a great deal of harm. Such things are best left to the professionals," Eli explained, regretting his gruff manner at the start of the encounter. Her eyes spoke to him; they were disarming.

"And when the professionals aren't being professional? Worse, when they seem to be in collusion with the criminals, what is a concerned citizen to do?" Lilah strained.

"Do you have anything solid to back up such a serious accusation?"

"I don't have proof. Not yet. I am hoping there isn't any cover-up or conspiracy to prove. But from the way you're supposed professionals have handled this, there aren't too many other conclusions that can be rationally drawn. And if you think you can intimidate me from speaking out, don't waste your breath."

"I have no intention of convincing you of anything or preventing your activities, not at all. I just want information. Did you really meet with Carmi and offer him a copy of the photograph?"

"I'm not a liar, Eli."

"And he refused to take it?"

"Yes, he refused."

"Did he say why?"

"Nothing that made sense. Mainly, he just insulted me."

"I have seen you before, before Ramat Zion, even," said Eli. His tone had become far gentler.

"I've been warned about people like you following me."

"No, I wasn't following you. I've been too busy trying to catch the Gideons – regardless of whatever prejudices you have about the security services." He paused, then changed the subject. "I saw you at the beginning of all this mess, outside the home of that murdered old woman in Jaffa."

"You did? I don't remember you," Lilah said, a touch of fright in her voice.

"I was watching from my car. Why did you even try? Did you really expect that old Arab to accept your goodwill? You're lucky he didn't send his grandson to strangle you."

"Oh, yes. The Arabs are like that, you know," Lilah said facetiously.

"Why were you taking pictures at the kibbutz?"

"Why? I wasn't aware it was a legal transgression. Why do you wear tight-fitting shirts?"

Eli sighed wearily. "Did you have any reason to believe you'd be able to photograph one of the Sons of Gideon?"

Lilah hesitated. She decided not to reveal her hunt. "I am a professional photographer. I think Na'aleh should have a visual record of its work."

"That's it? No warnings, no tip-offs?"

"Look, I get about ten death threats a day. One fellow calls each day at midnight to tell me how he is going to kill me the next chance he gets. Other than my regular fear of Gideons lurking in every shadow, I had no special reason to think they would be at the event that evening – although they would certainly prefer that such events not happen and are apparently prepared to take steps to ensure that they don't."

"Do you have any other pictures that would be of interest to us?"

"I don't know. Let me think about it."

"Please. I can use anything you have. Look, this is how you can reach me," Eli gave her his card. "From now on, if there's anything you think will advance the investigation please contact me directly, immediately. You don't have to go through Carmi any more. I am in charge of the investigation and I am very interested."

Lilah became curious about Eli. Something about him seemed frank, decent. Her pose slackened and she grew less defensive. "How do I know I can trust you? You haven't even told me your full name."

"Zedek, Eli Zedek. And we can't afford not to trust each other."

CHAPTER FIFTEEN

"I've got to get away. We have to get away," Lilah declared as she sat on the rim of the tub in the her bathroom and watched Naftali gingerly towel himself dry. He had gotten off most of the red paint from the attack by the pathetic zealot at the press conference.

Six weeks had passed since the Rabin Square bombing and Lilah looked dejectedly at the large, sickly-yellow remains of the bruise on Naftali's torso. X-rays had shown that his ribs had healed beneath the pink scar where the surgeons had removed his punctured spleen. There would always be, Lilah knew, remains of the Gideon's attack on Naftali's body and soul. Then, too, the entire society had been badly bruised by the Gideon's mayhem.

Lilah watched Naftali slip into briefs and an undershirt. He winced as he raised his arms and reached into sleeves of the shirt. "You've certainly paid the price of your convictions," she said sadly.

"Yes, well..." Naftali answered dismissively as they moved out of the bathroom and into the bedroom. "It's Thursday night; the weekend is here. If you are still serious about wanting to get away, I can try to get us a room somewhere."

"I think we've earned a day or two away together. I think we need it," Lilah said firmly.

"How far away do you feel like going?" Naftali asked as he passed a brush through his hair, as thick as it had been when he was young though now charcoal gray. Despite his middle-age paunch, as she watched him dress, Lilah realized that she was still attracted to him, even after so many years. And for a moment she pondered: After all they had gone through alone and apart, can we really make things work, live the rest of our lives together? "How far do I feel like going?" Lilah asked after Naftali repeated his question. "With you, to the ends of the earth."

He made a call. A friend arranged a room for them in a boutique hotel at Mitzpeh Ramon. The settlement was perched on the edge of Ramon Canyon, which had once been a seabed and was now the largest erosive gulch in the world. A geologist's wonderland and a nature-lover's dream deep in the Negev desert, Mitzpeh Ramon is also one of the most isolated places in the country.

It would be midnight before they arrived there. They drove south from Tel Aviv on Route Six and then turned southeast onto Route 40 just before Beersheva. There, as they left behind the city lights, the wilderness arose. In its nocturnal outline, the landscape was spare and disinviting.

In their vehicle, the handsome couple rode in solitude. They spoke little as they drove, content to let the soft instrumentals of classical guitar, melodious and cadent, playing off the car stereo, fill their space. In the glances they exchanged, in the small gestures they shared, a growing intimacy was developing.

As they drove, Lilah thought of a painting that she loved, Monet's *Morning on the Seine, near Giverny*. It was displayed at the Museum of Fine Arts in Boston, near Camera Distincta House on Huntington Avenue. She would return to see it time and again. She loved its verdant greens, the lilac and blue hues along the river-melded-sky, an organic picture of a whole, pieces in harmony. After each visit, Lilah would take the image away in her heart where it would reside and make her serene for days at a time. As unsullied as the nature in the painting, she wished people would be that way, too; that was the message she found in the picture.

"I love you," Lilah said, spontaneously as they traveled along a long stretch of road devoid of all life but the two of them.

"I love you, too," Naftali responded.

A moment passed, then Lilah asked, "What's going to be?"

she inquired.

"With us?" Naftali asked, surprised. "What will be with us is what we are making of it. I think we're alright, getting better. Don't you?"

"I meant what is going to be with the country, with Israel," Lilah clarified.

"Oh, that," said Naftali, his voice dipping.

They passed a sign; they were drawing near Midreshet Sde Boker, the campus David Ben-Gurion had established for the study of the Negev and to further the greening of the desert. Adjacent to the campus was Kibbutz Sde Boker and, beyond that, the Wilderness of Zin.

"The Old Man is buried there. He and Paula," Naftali commented, referring to Ben-Gurion and his wife.

"I suppose he can rest in peace there, far away from politics."

"I'm not sure how soundly his spirit rests these days," Naftali said. "I'm not sure he would recognize what's become of this country," he sighed wearily.

"What do you mean?" Lilah asked. She wanted to hear this, Naftali's take on what Israel had become.

Naftali turned down the music. He breathed deeply and then said, "Regrettably, today's Israel is not the labor commonwealth he and the other founders had in mind. I'm sure they would be outraged by how things are going: a paradise for capitalists, the clerical hold on the society and education. For three decades, the regime has been based on Revisionism, a distortion of Zionism infatuated more with land than people. The Right has been in power for more than a generation, and they have steered the country away from the values of social justice and tolerance that Ben-Gurion and the other founders believed in. The Old Man would simply be mortified," Naftali pronounced, stopped, then continued as though he could no longer contain his discontent.

"It's all become one great race for money and power, a society based on consumerism. Everything is for sale: protected lands released to build malls, natural resources – gas, oil, minerals – given away for a pittance to the Twenty Families. There's no commitment to reducing the country's carbon footprint; the marine life along the Mediterranean and near Eilat is dying. There's no coherent policy on migration, teachers are paid a shameful wage and the bankers and corporate executives keep milking everyone else with the government's blessing. The Knesset is full of jokesters, the cabinet is swollen with the minders of special interests, and writers and intellectuals are denounced as traitors and communists. In the void, octogenarian rabbis who wouldn't know how to write a check to the electrician, run cult-like political parties and issue policy pronouncements from on high. It's become a nightmare," Naftali said, his voice trailing off in sad realization, "a nightmare. I don't know where it will end."

Lilah looked at Naftali in his dismay. His eyes were staring outward beyond what was seen through the windshield to a future he dreaded.

"Why don't we pull over for a moment?" she advised. "Look, there's a place to stop, after the bend."

He stopped the car on a patch of gravel at the rest stop. He looked at her. In his eyes, she saw the punishment, the decades of long struggle. He closed his eyes and Lilah braced herself: Was he about to weep? she wondered. She waited.

When Naftali opened his eyes, from wherever he had gone those moments, from whatever he had recalled, he had recovered, his resolve was back. "Israel is part of the global civilization. We are no worse than most. But there is also an uncommon good here among our people. I truly think we can rise and recapture the night," he stated. "Lets have a look at the stars," he invited.

In the desert chill, Naftali and Lilah stood in the middle of the road hugging as they gazed into the endless heavens.

It was after eight when they awoke in the small, but comfortable room in a far corner of the hotel in Mitzpeh Ramon. They got up quickly and readied themselves. Naftali, was already attired in a sweat suit and sports shoes. He was standing next to Lilah as she put her earrings on and slipped his arm around her waist. She turned toward him and tucked his head into her breast, savoring being enveloped by him. She was surprised when he said, "We really should get going – the scenery around here is unbelievable," but was then promptly flattered when he said off-handedly: "Of course, if you prefer that we entertain each other under the sheets, I could be convinced that that's a worthwhile way to spend the day." His eyes sparkled with good humor. They decided to postpone the second possibility until after their outing.

They went down to breakfast. Lilah noticed that Naftali entered the lobby and dining room tentatively. He moved along the margins of the room where he was less likely to be spotted. "People don't leave me alone," he explained when she commented on the way he held his head low as if to hide his face, the way he avoided people looking directly at him. "Sometimes, like now, I just want to be anonymous, not a public figure," he added. In the busy dining room, no one seemed to recognize Naftali or his companion, Lilah, a personality of more recent prominence.

They were hungry and devoured the salads, thick omelets prepared to order, cheeses and fresh fruit. Rested and re-energized by the meal, they were ready to start the day. They had registered for a jeep tour of the canyon; their guide would pick them up at ten.

They used the hour before then to walk to the canyon rim in the bright yet chilly sunshine. Forty kilometers by nine, the canyon was a huge cavity stretching far into the distance beyond the Negev mountains on the western horizon. They walked first to the sculpture park, stark designs by human hands that were paled by the glorious natural surroundings. Naftali held Lilah close as they walked through the park, then peered out into the abyss, at the strata of rock in a palate of earth colors layered mountain high.

"I feel so out of scale," said Lilah as they looked out onto the northern expanse of the valley. "We really are puny aren't we?" she said to Naftali.

When Eran, the guide came to pick them up, he immediately recognized Naftali. "You're Knesset Member Kedem," he said approvingly, "you head the party, don't you?," he marveled as they stood in front of the front desk.

"Yes, but not so loudly," Naftali whispered self-consciously as he looked around the crowded room. "We've got only two days away from it all," he said.

"Don't worry professor. I've been a member of the party since you founded the New Democrats. I'll protect you." He then looked at Lilah. "And you," he said incredulously, "you're the woman from Na'aleh. Amazing," the tall, athletic, sun-baked man halfway between their age and Ido's enthused. "I identify with everything the two of you are doing." And then, struck by a realization he asked, "Say, weren't you assaulted at that little riot Epstein put on last night in Tel Aviv?"

"We were. We came here to recover," Lilah confirmed.

"I get it, some R&R after being in the trenches," Eran said. "Come on, I'll take you far away from all of that. I will show you things that are like nothing found anyplace else," he promised.

They piled into the jeep.

Eran shifted the vehicle into low gear. They crept down the steep road into the canyon passing towering walls, a tapestry of reddish and brown rock and sand that draped the vista as far as the eye could see.

"The Tethys Sea," Eran informed Lilah and Naftali as they drove on the valley floor five hundred meters beneath sea level. "We are on the bottom of the ocean, now," he said, casting his eyes over the landscape in frank assessment. "A few hundred million years ago, we would have needed scuba gear to see these sights."

The two-hour tour continued long past schedule. It was his privilege, Eran said, to escort the couple, leaders of a movement he believed in. He wanted to give them a respite from the hurly-burly lives they were leading. As they bantered, Eran steered the conversation away from politics. The closest they came to it was when he said, "I am not a sabra. My parents were, but I was born in Mombasa; I'm a native Kenyan. My father was an agronomist stationed by the International Cooperation Division of the Foreign Ministry in Africa, you know, when Israel was a progressive state interested in helping to lead Africa and Asia out of poverty," he said wistfully. "That was something to be proud of." Beyond that, they managed to talk only about nature and history for the rest of the tour.

They drove from Mount Ardon in the northeast of the canyon to Mount Ramon in the south. They visited the magmatic mount known as Ramon's Tooth and the pools of multi-colored sands nearby. The jeep lumbered up the two mesas, flattop summits on Mount Marpek and Mount Katom. As they stood on the windswept peaks and scoured the vistas in the brilliant midday sunlight, Lilah leaned into Naftali and he held her tightly.

They bought goat cheese and fresh tomatoes, peppers and cucumbers from a vendor the guide knew who peddled his wares at the southern edge of the canyon. Eran made a fire and baked fresh pita on the concave side of a pan he carried with him in the "work shed," the back of his jeep. They drank water, cold and pure, that he carried in jerry cans "drawn from a spring near my house at dawn this morning," he told them.

By the time he returned them to the hotel in the late afternoon, the sun had begun its descent. To Naftali's consternation, Eran refused payment, saying that being with them that day had been more than enough compensation. Lilah wrote out their phone numbers on a slip of paper and gave it to him. "I will phone," Eran promised, "I'm planning to come to Tel Aviv for the next demonstrations," he said. Lilah gave Eran a sweet kiss and Naftali embraced him, thanking him for a glorious day.

The couple returned to their room both exhilarated and exhausted. They showered and dressed for dinner. Lilah suggested that Naftali not turn on the evening news – "Why let anything ruin the mood? It's been such a great day and we only have one left." He concurred, "I'm too relaxed to voice opposition," he said.

It was Shabbat eve and as they descended into the lobby and entered the dining room, there was a subdued and refined peacefulness. Candles in a candelabrum were burning brightly. Most of the Israeli families had left and the other guests were mainly foreigners. Neither Naftali nor Lilah were recognized save by the hostess, who led them to a quiet table by a planter, obscured from the rest of the diners.

There was a bottle of wine on the table and a loaf of challah. Lilah was taken aback when Naftali placed a cloth napkin on his head and uttered the benediction: "Blessed are You O Lord our God, King of the Universe, for bringing forth bread from the earth." He tore a piece from the loaf, salted it and handed it to Lilah. "Shabbat Shalom," he said softly.

"I see Rabbi Ben-Yishai has had an influence on you" Lilah said, both amused and baffled by Naftali's display of devotion.

"In many ways, but not in terms of religion," Naftali was quick to state. "I've always believed that tradition – in proper measure – is important. At a time when the entire civilization is crashing, there's a message in that blessing: being thankful for the basics of bread and peace and rest. There're plenty of people on the planet who could use more of all three," he said.

What little they spoke over dinner consisted of acclaim for the dishes brought to them, classic cuisine from the Jewish Maghreb that they consumed with relish. By the end of the meal, they had finished a bottle-and-a-half of good wine. Lilah's cheeks were rosy and Naftali felt warm when they rose from the table to get some evening air.

They had intended to walk around the empty streets of the small settlement, but the wine had left them light-headed and they were exhausted from their tour of the canyon. They quickly returned to the hotel. There, a guitarist was serenading guests in the lobby. He was playing Israeli ballads, the music that Lilah and Naftali had grown up on in their parents' homes and in the youth movement. But nostalgia was the lesser of their moods and by ten-thirty they were back in their room.

They had no use for the oversized television in the hotel room that night, nor did they read the books they had brought with them. Instead, they disrobed and enveloped the other in a tangle of arms and legs. Their bodies pressed in high passion, welcoming the romance that had been displaced those many years. They slumbered peacefully.

They slept in and took their time returning northward. Neither wanted their holiday to end. They drove to Avdat, the ancient mountaintop desert city along the Spice Route that had been established by the Nabateans, traders from the East who had settled and brought agriculture to these parched lands. Following the Nabateans, the Romans had taken the city, then the Byzantines.

They parked near the summit and explored the ruins.

"What dramas took place here, in the middle of nowhere," said Naftali as he and Lilah walked through the Roman military encampment on the northern edge of the mount.

Then they walked through the churches on the southern end of the citadel. The pagan altars of the Romans, re-consecrated by the Byzantines as open-air Christian sanctuaries, were bathed by harsh sunlight. The stone works along the top and slopes of the mountain impressed them. Wine presses, tanneries, stables for camels and goats had been built here, high on a desert outcropping. Naftali was sobered by what he saw.

An experimental farm maintained at the foot of Avdat by the Hebrew University recreated Nabatean techniques for water husbandry and terrace cultivation. The farm was closed, Shabbat being the staff's day off. But a guard allowed Naftali and Lilah to enter and walk through the plots and vineyards. As they did so, gazing at the heights of the ancient city atop the mount, Naftali's chest puffed up a bit as he remarked to Lilah, "Great Rome and Byzantium came and went. Only the Jews have survived and returned," he said with satisfaction.

Naftali more than Avdat interested Lilah. She was delighted to see him revived.

They proceeded back along the main highway and stopped for lunch at a small restaurant run by a family who had emigrated from Chile in the 1990s. They maintained a goat farm and made cheese from their herd's milk. Lilah and Naftali enjoyed an *asado* lunch in the rough-hewn dining room.

"I'd like to visit Ben-Gurion," Naftali said as they walked holding hands back to the car afterwards. The Sde Boker compound where the great leader was laid to rest was just down the road.

"Then let's do it," said Lilah.

They drove fifteen minutes onward and entered the gateway into the national park on a promontory overlooking the Zin Wilderness. They parked in the deserted lot. "Jews are not supposed to enter a cemetery on Shabbat," Naftali said after they had gotten out of the car, "but Ben-Gurion's resting place isn't a burial ground. It's a monument to a titan," he said.

"I wish I had brought a real camera," Lilah said in frustration as she tinkered with the photo function of her cell phone. "This thing couldn't possibly capture the grandeur of this place."

They walked along the path through the immaculate grounds where olive trees had been planted and assiduously maintained. Lilah gasped when she turned a corner and spied deer meandering among the trees. In the quiet of this desolate place they appeared like an apparition, spotted darlings delicate as porcelain that gazed in innocence at the visitors to their abode. There were yearlings and their older kin with elaborate antlers held upright like statuettes. The larger ones huddled close to their young, protecting them and eying Naftali and Lilah with wonder.

There were tens of deer among the trees, some reclining, others ambling. As Lilah and Naftali walked deeper into the reserve, the deer they passed looked attentive – it was as if word of the humans' arrival had been passed on to them along the tree-lined arcade. When the path to the memorial ended, the deer remained behind as though they understood that there was something significant only to humans about the two stone slabs at the heart of the small reserve.

Naftali removed his handkerchief from his back pocket, folded it and placed it upon his head. In deference to the sanctity of this place Lilah zipped her sweater over her low-cut blouse. Naftali fetched pebbles from a bucket nearby. He gave Lilah several and kept a few in his own hand.

They held hands as they approached Paula and David Ben-Gurion's twin graves reverentially, in small steps. They placed the pebbles on the graves and read the inscription. Lilah watched as Naftali closed his eyes at the foot of Ben-Gurion's grave. He stayed that way in deep meditation. When he opened his eyes and looked at Lilah, it seemed to her that wherever his meditation had taken him, it had filled him like a vessel. For Naftali, this was a pilgrimage and he had been fortified by it.

They walked in silence back to the car, the deer again lining the path like some kind of peaceable guard sending off the visitors.

As they left the lot, there was a turn-off down further into the Zin canyon. It wound downward and Naftali drove the car slowly through it to an observation point that looked upon an open vista. The terrain was less arid here and the valley was furrowed into the rock walls. There were shrubs and small trees in the channels that wound laterally over the slopes of the hills to the east and south. The quiet was profound and Lilah's arm was in Naftali's, her head resting on his shoulder.

As they stood gazing, horns and then the large head of a beast, a bearded ibex, dramatically appeared from a terrace just below where they stood. The animal's muscular body was covered in shale-colored fur. Its thick but agile legs carefully negotiated the loose rocks along the slopes and kept the animal decorously balanced. There followed a smaller ibex, then another adult followed by second young one and a third.

The family of five mountain goats passed Lilah and Naftali undeterred by their presence. These were mighty creatures at home in this timeless domain, persistent and steadfast as they climbed from the depths of the canyon to feed on the vegetation of the park. They harmed no one – just sought what they needed on their land.

"Strong-necked creatures, they must be Jews," Naftali joked after the group resumed their trek further into the Wilderness of Zin.

The house where the Ben-Gurions had lived on Kibbutz Sde Boker was open to the public. When the Kedems arrived, the site was nearly devoid of other visitors and they wandered through the simple structure, a living room, dining room, kitchen and study. How simply the national leader had lived, Lilah commented as they walked through the rooms, modest and outfitted according to a laborer's sensibilities. It was here that the State's founder had retired, an agricultural commune on the desert frontier. It was, as all of Ben-Gurion's undertakings, a statement and a lesson he wanted to impart to his people.

"Look," Lilah called out to Naftali. He was examining the Old Man's shaving brush and razor in the bathroom. She was standing in the threshold of his bedroom and pointed to a slip of paper pinned next to the door.

"It's his medication schedule," Naftali said as he read the list. "Look, before bedtime he took a Numbon. I also take one whenever I have a hard time sleeping," he said, exalted by the knowledge that both he and the father of the State struggled with insomnia.

"All great men have trouble sleeping, that's widely known," Lilah said to Naftali. They left the site, silent but invigorated.

It was dusk when they reached Beersheva and took the highway toward Tel Aviv. It being a Saturday night and the Sabbath just concluded, traffic began picking up. As they drove, Lilah and Naftali briefed each other on what their weeks would be like. Each had a packed schedule.

Their weekend reverie faded as the conversation turned back to the events of Thursday night and from there to matters relating to the party, Na'aleh and the Sons of Gideon. They were relieved to hear on the eight o'clock radio news that there had been no major incidents during the forty-eight hours they had detached themselves from the tempest. But as their cell phones began ringing, their holiday was already fading into mere memories.

There was a huge traffic jam just as they entered Tel Aviv. Police sappers had been called to determine if a car that had been abandoned along the Ayalon Highway contained explosives. It was nearly midnight when they arrived at 3 HaGaon Street. Naftali carried Lilah's bags up to the apartment though he would not stay, as there was a Knesset plenum scheduled for the next morning. He wanted to get up bright and early in the capital to prepare for the session.

Neither he nor Lilah wanted to part from each other. It was difficult to say goodbye.

"I love you Naftali," Lilah said as he prepared to leave.

"I love you too," he assured her.

The two tightly hugged for several long minutes before they parted. The sense of expectancy that they shared was left unspoken.

◌ ❖ ◌

The past days had taken a different trajectory for Eli. He had not taken a break from the churning waters. After he had a talk with that woman, Lilah Kedem, the do-gooder with the tender eyes at the meeting in Rishon LeTzion, his pager had gone off as he started his car. He was signaled to call Retired Brigadier-General Dr. Ehud Shoresh, a former deputy chief of Military Intelligence. Eli wrote down the number, put the car in neutral, and called the general. "We've broken the code in the Ben-Avraham diary," Shoresh informed him. "You are going to want to see the contents as soon as possible. Where are you now?" he asked.

"Not far, in Rishon."

"Good," said Shoresh, who was also Sterling Distinguished Professor of Applied Mathematics at the Weizmann Institute. I did the deciphering and am at my office in Rehovot. That isn't more than fifteen minutes away from where you are now. Come see me, the sooner the better."

Eli rushed to Rehovot.

Prof. Ehud Shoresh, an Israel Prize recipient, was a national asset and access to the building where he had his offices was highly restricted. Without prior clearance, the security guards would not let Eli enter at that time of night. It took phone calls to Jerusalem, to Shoresh, back to Jerusalem and Rehovot before the security men would relent. It had taken twice as much time for Eli to be admitted through the security gate at the Weizmann Institute than it had taken him to drive from Rishon to Rehovot.

And there were conditions. Eli would have to deposit his firearms, both the pistol in his shoulder harness and the one in his ankle holster at the Institute's security office. He would have to leave his car at the lot outside the entry into the complex. A guard would escort him to the building where Prof. Shoresh worked in one of the Institute's security vehicles.

Eli had been to the Weizmann Institute several times before, years ago while a student. The imposing buildings bore impressive names, the "So and So Family Foundation Genome Project" and the "XYZ Corporation's Center for Bone Marrow Research." They were beacons on the heights the country's scientific community had achieved. Eli was proud of his nation's genius. Much of it was focused here, in the green island of pastoral Rehovot, where a great deal of national history had taken place. The home of Israel's first president, Prof. Chaim Weizmann was also situated on the campus. Eli remembered all of this as he was jostled on the ride in the security jitney that bounced over the speed bumps on the road to the Applied Mathematics building.

He and the guard entered the building. At this hour it was mostly abandoned, though an occasional graduate student or researcher scurried about. The lobby was large and full of encased artifacts, memorabilia of computer culture and thick framed portraits of the likes of Rene Descartes and Albert Einstein.

The guard conducted Eli through elevators, down hallways, through coded electronic gateways and into a hall where there were banks of mainframes. In one of the back offices sat Shoresh, an athletic-looking man with half-lens glasses wearing shorts, a sleeveless T-shirt and sandals. He looked more like a beachcomber than an army brigadier and renowned academic.

The guard departed and Eli and Prof. Shoresh quickly got down to business. They pored over a computer printout, a transcript of part of the Ma'ale Adumim codebook as if it was a battle plan.

"You don't have much time," the professor said. "The code employed in the diary was used by American commandos in Iraq in the early 1990s. I remember when I first saw it as an intelligence officer in 1993. Due to its ingenuity, we thought it an exceedingly good example of cryptology and taught it to our new analysts.

"Now, the log began on December 15th of last year, nearly a year ago," Shoresh deftly scrolled down the screen, nearly to the end of the file. "Here," he said, tapping the screen with a pen, "is the end of diary. This entry is from Tuesday of this week. Now, listen closely. In between the two entries are many others, some of which refer to dates in which specific events, violent events that I think you are investigating, were planned."

Eli was listening intently. He said nothing, though he took copious notes.

"What I am saying is that this diary was kept by someone intimately involved in the atrocities we have been experiencing. This material is rich in detail. I can tell you that this is an authentic log and planning document. I recommend that you send the original for graphological analysis as I imagine it could flesh out the psychological profile of the Sons of Gideon.

"Now, look here," Shoresh said commandingly. "Another attack has been planned. On line 22, where 12,200:12;19 appears. You see?"

"Yes. What do the numbers mean?"

"It means 00:12 in the morning on the 19th of December, which is to say tomorrow morning, just about two hours from now," he said gazing at the chronometer on his wrist. In the language of this code, it says, "Elimination of youngest daughter of Suliman ibn Musa, *mukhtar*, Lahat clan, in Bedouin township of Arka al-Khitab."

"There is an entry that the murder of this girl is going to take place tonight?" Eli said, half-stuttering.

"Correct."

Eli paused; he realized this might be his Rosetta Stone. "Is there an entry referring to plans on June 28?" he asked.

"I'll check," said Shoresh. He typed in a command and several keywords. "Yes. There is a reference reading 'Remove any old Arab lady in Jaffa. Make it clean and swift. Then issue press communiqué.' Do you want me to check another entry?" the general asked.

"Yes please," answered Eli. "The tenth of November."

"November 10th. Yes, it reads, 'Off Arab day workers. As many as possible. Pre-Dawn. Messubim Junction, Geha Road.'"

Eli grabbed his cell phone. He was routed through to the Lachish district police headquarters in Kiryat Gat, where Arka al-Khitab was located. Eli identified himself to the duty officer, making sure that the desk sergeant understood that this was a top priority request. The roads to Arka al-Khitab and its environs were to be blocked due to information about a murder attempt about to be undertaken. Shoresh called up a digital map on his monitor and located the village. Eli instructed the sergeant to mobilize as many policemen as possible to meet him at the gas station at an intersection near the village.

Within minutes of leaving Shoresh's sanctum, Eli was in his car racing down Highway 3 toward Arka al-Khitab. He had left without signing out from the Institute's security office. He could not afford being delayed by over-wrought security guards.

He arrived at the gas station and waited for what seemed to be an interminably long time. At 11:53 – according to the Ben-Avraham log, just nineteen minutes before the planned attack – there were still no roadblocks and no police presence in the vicinity of Arka al-Khitab. Eli was both angry that backup hadn't arrived and fearful about his prospects: He had no idea who or what he would encounter in the village.

Midnight was fast approaching and there still was no sign of police reinforcements. It was a kilometer from here to the one-lane blacktop that led to the town, and probably another kilometer or so to the first houses. Eli reached for his phone and redialed Lachish police headquarters. The duty officer he had spoken with earlier answered the phone.

"Where are the men I requested? I'm here and I see no one."

"There aren't any," the officer admitted.

"Where the hell are they, out riding camels?" Eli shouted.

"There will not be any police reinforcements," said the officer.

"What do you mean by that?" Eli shouted. "I made an explicit request concerning a homicide attempt in progress and you willfully disobeyed my instructions? We have intelligence that the Sons of Gideon are out here tonight and are targeting a little girl. I don't care if you have to send units here with sirens screaming, but I need them right now. Do whatever you need to get me at least fifteen or twenty officers. Now!"

"I can't," said the duty officer, his voice full of regret. "I acted immediately on your orders. I began mobilizing men for roadblocks. But according to regulations, an operation of the kind you requested, if not issued in advance and in writing, requires the approval of a second police or security commander. I contacted my superior and he went up the chain of command to the national center. Chief Inspector Mordechai Carmi is in charge this evening. My superior spoke with him and told him the request came from you. Commander Carmi countermanded the order."

"He what?" Eli asked incredulously.

"You have my deepest regret, really. But the rules are what they are and I don't have the authority to override them. There isn't a thing I can do. Normally, there is someone else in Carmi's place and I wouldn't have any problem getting approval. But tonight, he is at the top of the chain of command. And from the way he carried on when I tried to reason with him, I'm already concerned about my job."

It was then that Eli decided he would take this all the way to the top, to the Prime Minister himself if he had to, possibly even the media: evidence of a cover-up.

Eli realized that he was on his own.

It was 00:03. Eli drove his car along the road to the settlement. He parked just outside it and made his way in on foot. Not a single light was on in any of the homes. As he lumbered up the steep road into the village, he was conscious of his own furious breathing. His blood was racing, his temples throbbing. He was overcome with rage. How he would have liked to wring Carmi's neck just then.

Eli felt a curious mixture of desperation and anticipation. He did not know how many assailants he would be facing or whether he was up against explosives, guns, or knives. Then there was the lack of information – he didn't even know where Suliman ibn Musa lived.

He paused to catch his breath. He looked at his watch. If the Gideons struck with the same exactitude as they had in the past, there were five minutes to go. He eyed the village. Its hovels and shacks hugged a few adjoining hillocks that were separated by shallow gullies and ravines. Many had tents in their yards and small livestock herds.

Eli banged on the door of the first house he came to. He

continued pounding until a youth in his early teens sleepily answered the door.

"Where does Suliman ibn Musa live?" Eli barked in Arabic.

"Speak to my father. He sleeps in the tent in the backyard," the boy said, anxious to return to bed as he began shutting the door.

Eli pushed the door open and slapped the boy's face hard. "I am the government. Do you want me to take you and your father and mother to jail? Tell me right now where the Mukhtar Suliman ibn Musa lives or you will go straight to the prison in Beersheva."

The boy quickly became alert. "That is his house, the big one on the hill over there," he pointed.

Eli darted in the direction indicated by the boy. The most direct route to ibn Musa's house was through a gully. To go that way would leave him exposed in open terrain. There were some boulders along the path but he would still be a clear target, especially in the moonlight. The alternative route, through groves, would take him much longer.

Eli opted for the gully. Steeling himself for the perilous run, he reached for a gun.

There were none in his holsters. In his rush from the Weizmann Institute, he had left them behind.

Eli froze, petrified by his vulnerability. Even if he could cross the ravine and elude the notice of a gunman, even if there were no wild dogs and no snakes, how was he going to face the attackers without a weapon? For what? To save the life of an Arab?

Yes, he concluded, to save the life of a human being, a citizen of the State – and snare a Gideon.

Eli dashed to a nearby pile of tangled metal, what had been an automobile in another incarnation. A sharp piece of the metal chassis had been sheared nearly free and could serve as a dagger. Eli bent the piece back and forth until it gave way and broke off; the new edge was good and sharp. He ripped a piece of fabric from a nearby rag and wrapped it around the blunt end to serve as a handle, and then tied it to his leg. He took a deep breath and then tore off for the first ravine, aware of the sound of a motorcycle on the main road.

Eli reached the low point of the gully and threw himself against a boulder, grateful not to hear the report of a gun. Gazing upward, the angle of the slope favored him. He was out of sight to anyone looking down from the crest of the hill. In the bright moonlight, he saw no one. If he moved quietly and no dogs were near enough to catch his scent and start barking, there was a chance he could make it up the rise.

He heard the sound of the motorcycle approach, then stop.

Eli ran through the first gully. There was a stone ledge at the end of the ravine, half a meter above him. He leapt for it. His hands caught and held. It took complete exertion but his arms dragged him up the rest of the way. He was sweating and the perspiration dripping off his brow burned his eyes. His arms were scratched. Winded, he needed to take a break. "My God, my God," he uttered under his breath, until he was able to push forward once more.

He crawled along the ledge to the far side. It ended abruptly at a second chasm that was two-and-a-half meters deep, which lay between Eli and the last third of the way up to the mukhtar's house. If he took a running jump, he had a chance of making it across. And if he landed quietly, there would be no more than a hundred meters between him and the house. But if his jump was short, it would all be over, with him wedged into the narrow chasm.

Eli heaved his body as he never had before. For a split-second, when his back leg wavered on landing, he almost toppled backward into the emptiness. His balance held. Barely, but it held.

Eli recited a prayer of thanksgiving and crawled on hands

and knees to the top of the hill. His heart was thumping wildly, a choke of fear wrapped around his throat.

He continued on.

He reached the back end of a car. Peeking over the edge, he made out a silhouette in the shadows. Eli looked at his watch. It was exactly 00:12 on the night of December 19th and there, a stone's throw away from him, was the figure of a Gideon.

Eli heard a noisy truck storming down the distant highway and when it was at its closest, he took advantage of the roar to make a run for a tractor parked near the house. He crawled under the tractor, not twenty meters away from the man in the shadows.

The Gideon was garbed in dark, tight-fitting clothes. He was a very large man, much taller and heavier than Eli. In the moonlight, Eli discerned that the man was wearing a shoulder harness under his left arm with a large pistol in the holster. Strapped to his lower right leg was a large hunting knife in a sheath. The man wore a beret. His face, the back of his hands and his neck were dark, Eli presumed, with camouflage paint – unless the Gideons had black recruits.

The man removed something from his waist. Using his teeth, he ripped off a piece of tape from a roll that was around his left wrist. He taped a penlight to the door, with the strong, thin beam aimed at the lock. The man reached up to his beret and pulled something small and slender from it. Eli watched him use it to soundlessly pick the lock.

Eli had to make his move, just then or not at all.

He slipped out from under the tractor. Once he was out and up, he saw that the Gideon had succeeded. The door was unlocked and stood ajar. Eli picked up a rock and hurled it at the far side of the house. It did what it was supposed to do – distract the man.

The assailant had been about to cross the threshold. He withdrew and, with feline grace, pulled his gun from its shoulder harness. He held the weapon chest-high and straight out, gripping it in both hands, combat-style. He turned slowly to one side, then turned around and looked in Eli's direction. He did not see Eli crouching next to a pickup truck in the yard. The Gideon began to walk around to the far side of house, searching for the source of the noise.

Eli made a quick run for the house. He tripped on a half-buried pipe and fell hard, his face smacking the ground. He picked himself up, blew dirt out of his mouth and pressed forward until he was flat against the exterior wall of the house.

Kneeling low by the wall, he heard nothing save for the crickets. He edged himself toward the corner of the house and ventured a quick glance down the side wall. There was the Gideon, his back to Eli, coming back around to where he had been before.

Eli stooped low. He could hear the attacker inching his way around the back of the house. Two meters away, one meter. Eli could hear him breathing. The gun appeared, blindly held in one hand now, high off the ground.

Eli took the opportunity. He swept his arm out and slammed the Gideon's wrist with all his strength. The pistol went sailing into the ravine. Eli heard it tumble down into the chasm a split-second after he thrust a swift kick into the would-be assassin's groin. The man was on his knees, at Eli's feet.

Eli flung himself over the Gideon, pulled out the makeshift knife, and pressed it up against under the man's jawbone, at the jugular vein. "That's it," Eli wheezed. "It's over. Don't make a …"

The bear of a man did not surrender. He tossed Eli off of him faster than Eli could think. Eli lay face down, behind the man, who was getting up slowly. Like a yoga master, the man controlled his breathing into a cool, deliberate pattern. He reached for his leg and unsheathed the knife. Glinting in the moonlight, the blade seemed enormous to

Eli. The man seemed huge, too.

Eli rose to his feet and gripped the makeshift dagger in his right hand. Get a hold of yourself, steady yourself, he thought. Remember your commando training: slash horizontally, don't stab, or he'll have a chance to take your knife. Be cool, be slow. Be ferocious.

The man collected himself, too. Towering a head over Eli, he was calm, deliberate and rapacious. Looking into the man's steel-blue eyes, Eli could see he was an animal, a killer. Eli observed this in a moment, as he and the Gideon faced off against one another. Both men clutched their knives with great care. He's a professional. Oh so professional, Eli thought.

He was more than that. The man was a ferocious human cougar. His hand was a paw, his knife an extended claw. And he's not going to make himself vulnerable with sloppy, convoluted moves either, Eli concluded.

Eli studied the man's movements. They were sculpted in the air, measured and weighed. The man shifted his weight, muscle by muscle, in movements that were studied and smooth. They seemed effortless.

I'm thinking too much, Eli thought. He was right. His opponent had read Eli's look and took advantage of it to pitch toward him. Eli felt cold steel cut thinly across his chest. It wasn't deep, but it grazed his skin and Eli was infuriated. He let out a high-pitched shriek, simultaneously sweeping his foot behind the man's ankle, bringing him down quickly and heavily. The man's knife stuck flat on the ground under his massive weight.

Instantly, they collided and wrapped each other in a devil's embrace. They grunted as they wrestled, cursing and sweating. Eli held the advantage of being topside but with the man's incredible strength and giant's hand clamped around his throat and neck, Eli couldn't breathe. He saw black for a moment. He gasped, then slammed his elbow into the man's ribcage. He could feel the shift of mass and the bones cracking in the man's chest. With his other hand the Gideon had pulled free his knife from under him and held it high, directly over Eli's Adam's apple. Despite Eli's blow to the man's ribs, the knife remained suspended, though the pain on his side momentarily paralyzed him. Eli was intent on taking advantage of the man's pain, and jammed his elbow even deeper into the man's side.

Eli's adversary howled in pain like a beast, yet this seemed also to give him strength. The attacker dropped the knife, and with his now free hand grabbed Eli's thumb and bent it backward. Eli heard the bone crack and then felt a snap, the stem breaking off from the ball joint at its base. The pain was blinding. Eli screamed, though he somehow managed to keep the man locked in a grip.

Eli caught sight of the discarded hunting knife and considered reaching for it. He knew, though, that the Gideon wouldn't let him get it and even if he did, he doubted he could hold it long enough to stab. But he could also keep his attacker from being able to use the weapon against him. Pushing himself onto his haunches, Eli seized the hunting knife with his good hand and threw it as far as he could.

The raider exacted a price for Eli's success. He whirled around him in an about-face and flung Eli to the ground with terrible force. He threw his body across Eli's – Eli felt as if a pile of rocks collapsed on him – and immobilized him.

They both needed a respite to catch their breaths, overcome the pain, and plan their next moves. Suddenly, a light went on inside the house and the Gideon was distracted long enough for Eli to take hold of his makeshift knife and drag it across the nape of his neck. The man screamed as hot drops of blood dripped from the gash on his neck onto Eli's face.

The door to the house opened and a man in a long Arab *galabia* walked out. He gazed in shock at the two bleeding and tattered fighters, not knowing what to think. The Gideon rose to his feet, spat out blood and – Eli could not fathom where he found the strength to do so – swiftly dragged himself away. It was as if the he wanted to avoid being seen at all costs, as though he were shamed by his performance: first by his failure to kill Suliman ibn-Musa's daughter and then by his inability to decisively defeat Eli.

Eli wiped the blood from his eyes and saw that he had a clump of the man's hair in his hand. The Gideon was a blond.

"State security officer," Eli squeezed out in Arabic from deep in his throat. "Phone for help," he called out.

Lying on the ground, his strength ebbing away, Eli could hear the revving of a motorcycle – the Gideon's motorcycle, he was certain – as it sped away from Arka al-Khitab. The shrill whir of the engine, like Eli's consciousness, soon faded.

Chapter Sixteen

Eli had no idea how he had reached the hospital and he had only a faint recollection of the debriefing. Amos had arrived with the Shin Bet chief of operations and a police artist shortly after he had been rushed to the medical center from Arka al-Khitab. They spoke in an ER treatment room after the various contusions Eli had sustained on his trunk and extremities had been dressed, before he was taken for surgery on his left hand. The Son of Gideon had torn the flexor and extensors of the thumb and crushed several carpal joints of the adjoining fingers. Eli had been badly pummeled in the battle. He had saved the life of the Bedouin girl, nearly at the expense of his own.

The assailant had also taken a rough beating in the combat with Eli. The Gideon had left behind a rivulet of blood from where he and Eli had fought to where he had mounted his motorcycle. Hospital emergency rooms and first aid clinics around the country had been alerted to be on the lookout for a large and powerfully built man with blond hair who had sustained trauma to his body and had been cut on his neck. Despite the painkillers, Eli had given the police sketch artist a good description of his facial features – the man's countenance had been seared into Eli's mind. He appeared in the darkness whenever Eli closed his eyes.

The laparoscopic surgery only grossly reassembled the musculature of Eli's hand. He would have to undergo additional surgeries and extensive rehabilitation. He left the operating room with his hand encased in a heavy plastic cast. It would be weeks before he could begin physical therapy.

As Eli lay in bed or sat on the recliner next to it on the day after his surgery, all he could think about was the entanglement with the Son of Gideon. Eli had nearly caught him. By now, the police artist had surely finished the suspect's portrait and it was imperative to circulate it as widely as possible. It would certainly bring in a wave of new information. With the drugs deadening the pain that pulsed low in his arm, Eli worried that his computer was filling with emails requiring his immediate attention. Being stuck on his back with only the view of a sprawling shopping complex outside the window to occupy his attention did little to improve his mood. Instead, he desperately coveted another encounter with his attacker, a decisive one.

By noon, Eli decided that staying in the hospital was an indulgence he could ill-afford. He persuaded the overworked resident in charge of the ward that the wonders of laparoscopic surgery had left him feeling quite capable and since no further treatments were scheduled, he could convalesce more easily at home. By four that afternoon, discharge papers in hand, he was in a cab heading for his office in Holon.

Once there, Eli was surprised by how exhausted he felt. He had intended to rest for only a few minutes but slumbered heavily on the couch throughout the afternoon. When he awoke, he found a plate of sandwiches and a pot of strong coffee that his secretary had left him. "Good hunting," she had written on a note slipped between the rows of his keyboard. "Bring them down!"

Eli logged onto the computer. The first order of business was the police sketch. Eli found the drawing hauntingly accurate as it slowly appeared on screen. The melancholic face with strong cheekbones and jutting chin had slit-like eyes locked in a far-away gaze. At first, Eli bristled with disgust at the image, but as he gazed at it, it became clear to him that there were long years of pain in the Gideon's troubled eyes. Something in them said that he had seen a lifetime of horrors.

Eli disseminated the police sketch along with Lilah Kedem's photo of the woman at Ramat Zion to every arm of the defense establishment, the police and Border Police and the security community. He contacted the prison service, customs authorities and numerous other agencies and directed that their warders and inspectors be on watch for the person depicted. The security offices of regional, district and local authorities and every public institution in the country received the flyer by fax or email with a request to display the picture prominently and to distribute it by every means available. Then Eli forwarded the portrait to the government press office with immediate authorization to release it to the media. He knew the press would devour and immediately regurgitate it on the cover of every newspaper in the country.

Eli received an email concerning the DNA analysis of several strands of the man's hair. Results would be forthcoming within the day. Another message reported that fingerprints found on the scene were being checked against every possible national and Interpol database. Also, there was now concrete evidence of a connection between the incident at Arka al-Khitab and a previous attack by the Sons of Gideon: The police had recovered the gun that Eli had knocked out of the assailant's hand from the ravine near the sheik's home. Initial ballistics testing indicated that the weapon was likely the same gun that killed Fatima Abed.

There was now a cascade of evidence concerning the identity of the attacker at the Bedouin village. With the photographs and files missing from government agencies much on his mind and gnawed by concerns that there might be official complicity in the case, Eli feared that the material exhibits could be compromised. He wanted the original forensic materials kept off limits to Mordechai Carmi. He would request that the blood and hair samples and the gun be safeguarded where they could not be tampered with, and the experts reports on them placed somewhere out of Carmi's reach.

When Eli phoned Amos to discuss the matter, he did not expect the volley of rebuke he received. Amos was furious with Eli for leaving the hospital.

"I should have had you chained to the bed. Do you know

how badly you were hurt? You're damn lucky you are not on a pathologist's slab right now."

Eli offered an apology and explanation. After Amos had fully exhausted his invective, Eli felt it safe to make his appeal.

"Amos, listen. We are making progress. I don't want anything to happen to the evidence. Mordechai Carmi's conduct in this entire matter has been unusual; I would say even suspect. Aside from his lack of cooperation, he set me up to go into the lion's den with no shield last night. I'll describe the details in the report I am filing. I want the physical evidence kept away from him."

"What do you suggest I do?" Amos asked. "Deny the head of police investigations access to evidence? That's a tall order. Officially, he has the same right to inspect the material that you do."

"If you ask me, officially he should be behind bars," Eli exploded, the mounting pain in his hand having eroded his patience.

"I could order you to take time off, you know. In any case, the field is off limits to you until one of our doctors examines you tomorrow. We'll schedule you an appointment."

"Alright, I'll be there," Eli agreed. He then asked, "Will you keep Carmi away from the evidence?"

There was a pause. Eli could almost hear the wheels turning in Amos' head as he devised a solution. "I'll issue a directive to have the materials and reports released only to you or me. But if Carmi wants it badly enough and finds out about the restrictions, he can go to the internal security minister. They're sweethearts and the evidence would surely have to be released. I don't think though that Carmi is interested in the evidence. I think that man is well aware of his incompetence and that the only thing he's really interested in is covering it up. There's no real proof of anything conspiratorial. If I'm wrong and he does go after the evidence, we'll hear about it before he can gain access to it. We'll make a decision at that time on whether to make a stink out of it or not. Okay?"

"Thanks, Amos," Eli said appreciatively. He continued: "There's something else I want to discuss with you. I don't know if I told you when we spoke at the hospital that the professor at Weizmann, Shoresh, the reserve general from military intelligence who cracked the Ben-Avraham diary, knew the origin of the code."

"Really? What is it, something used in MI?"

"Not our military. Shoresh says he's sure it is a code that was used by American troops in the Gulf War in the early nineties."

"Don't tell me you suspect the Americans of being behind this?" Amos protested.

"No, of course not. But that block of stone, the guy I tangled with at Arka al-Khitab used hand-to-hand fighting techniques that he didn't pick up pilfering candy shops. He was very professional and practiced and fought differently than the way we are trained. They're first-rate combatants and I'll bet that at least one of them had advanced Special Forces training in somebody's army. Somebody in this case could be the Americans."

"You want to talk with someone at the American Embassy?"

"Yes. I don't care if it's me or you who meets with them. But we should speak to them soon. They may have an angle on the identity of the assassin I met last night."

"I'll arrange a meeting with their intelligence attaché," Amos agreed.

"I think it is warranted – as soon as possible."

"As soon as possible," Amos concurred.

After the call with Amos, Eli phoned Ehud Shoresh and arranged to have the decrypted version of the Ben-Avraham diary retrieved and brought to him. He then lay down on the couch and began dictating his report on Carmi's actions into a recorder. His words slurred and then he crashed into unconsciousness, from the pain, from the drugs and in advance of further battle.

03 ❖ 80

The tranquility of Lilah and Naftali's weekend away quickly dissipated the next morning. Just before Michal arrived at 3 HaGaon Street around eleven, Lilah had received the call: Lucian had suffered a stroke.

"Do you think I should go?" Lilah asked, crestfallen.

Michal wasn't sure what she should answer. She barely knew who Lucian was.

"They say he's in critical condition, touch and go," Lilah said as she rose from the chair at the kitchen table. "Fly to Boston?" she wondered out loud, "it all seems so far away – a different existence."

"From what you've told me, Lucian was a major figure in your life for a long time."

"He was," Lilah answered, her tone nostalgic, as she rinsed dishes in the sink.

Ido entered the kitchen. He had been home over the weekend, two days of relief time between duty in the North. He was in uniform, about to return to his base. He pecked Michal on the cheek as he passed her and then hugged his mother.

"What's wrong?" he asked, "Something is. I can see it in your face and in the way your shoulders are all hunched up," he said.

"Lucian's in the Brigham and Women's," Lilah answered in English.

She and Ido filled Michal in on who exactly Lucian had

been to them. Ido recounted how when he had lived with his mother in Cambridge during middle school, "the venerable oak" had been like an uncle to him. He had deep feelings for the man, a strong influence in the important years he had spent growing up, and who had always been dear to his mother. As they spoke about those years, it came up that the relationship had later cooled as a result of Naftali's discomfort with Lucian's role in Lilah and his son's life. As Naftali saw it, Lucian was another alpha male, his relationship with Lilah had been an intimate one, and his son cared too strongly for him. Still, Lucian had been an anchor in Lilah's life for over three decades. With time, Naftali made peace with that.

Ido had a friend, somebody he went to school with in Cambridge who was a resident at the Boston hospital. He would call him in a few hours, once it was morning there and ask him to find out more on Lucian's condition. In the meantime, Michal phoned the airlines about a flight that night or the next day to Boston – if that's what Lilah decided to do.

They agreed that pending news about Lucian, Lilah should go about her day as planned. She would go to a salon meeting of the Na'aleh's branch in Carmiel.

Lilah did plan to do that, attend the salon meeting. But she had a more preponderant agenda planned before that – visiting a neighborhood rally that Na'aleh was supporting in Kiryat Zebulon, Haifa's poorest district. She did not tell her son or Michal that she was going to look for the Sons of Gideon. She was aching to unmask the phantoms, to catch them on film in whatever incarnation they assumed.

It had become an obsession.

03 ❖ 80

The respite that Naftali and Lilah had enjoyed over the weekend had come to a resounding end for Naftali as well. After returning to Jerusalem, during the Knesset session held on Sunday morning, he found that the release of the Sons of Gideon photo at the press conference had raised a storm. The entire country was abuzz with speculation about the bomb-bearing woman the photo depicted.

Over the weekend, the Nationalist leadership decided that the exposé, the release of Lilah's photo at the Na'aleh-New Democratic Party press conference could profitably be turned into a political club to be employed against the opposition. During the various radio and television interview shows on Friday and Saturday, Nationalist partisans criticized Naftali Kedem for his part in releasing the photo and questioning the government's efforts to capture the extremists.

The matter came to a head during the Knesset plenum on Sunday at noon in a session that had been scheduled to debate an educational reform bill. The Rightists had seized the occasion with particular zeal to skewer their chief nemesis, Naftali Kedem.

"Censure this man who incites the nation against its elected government," said one right-winger, Rabbi Epstein's closest ally in the parliament, as he waived the weekend newspaper bearing the headline, "Kedem implies government duplicity."

"Let's see what this communist has to say for himself," said a Nationalist member of the chamber as Naftali went to the podium to rebut the last half hour of vilification leveled against him.

Ido was behind the wheel of Lilah's car when the radio went live from the Knesset to report on the uproar. He and Lilah had just passed under the Rehavam "Gandhi" Ze'evi Bridge – named after the ultra-nationalist gunned down in 2001 by Palestinian terrorists – in Hod HaSharon when news of the ruckus was reported.

"You are a quisling. You give comfort to the Arab enemy!" shouted one of the extreme right-wing Knesset members, "Naftali Kedem walks hand in hand with Arabs to undermine the State," he continued.

The radio report then spliced in Naftali's remarks to the forum.

"For more than thirty years, your movement has imposed an ideology based on force and discrimination. You have taken the national assets and divided it among the super-rich. You have created divisions within the people and between Israel and the nations. You have made every effort to leave the accords with the Palestinians unconsummated and pave the way to another war...

"Now the people are determined to rise up and the tide is turning against you. I cannot say – at least for now – that the Gideons are your sons – that they somehow receive support from people in the government or the security services or the police. But the Right has created an atmosphere where such terrorists can thrive. In this, the twilight of your rule, the people have seen the arrogance, the ineptitude and the dangers of the Right's vision. The people of Israel are on the rise, we will continue to rise. You will not stop us!"

Ido looked over at Lilah, a broad grin, proud and approving stretching across his face. "Dad still has the same problem he always has. He's tried to reason with morons, his Knesset buddies. They haven't got a clue of how right he is."

As they drove, Ido and Lilah noted the Na'aleh bumper stickers, which were if not ubiquitous at least abundant on vehicles all along the highway.

"Neighbors United – Na'aleh," read the hand-lettered banner hanging over the main entrance of the dilapidated Kiryat Zebulon Youth Center. Activists had succeeded in wresting approval from the city for a community rally on the site.

There had been newspaper articles on Kiryat Zebulon, where volunteers had started a local food cooperative that had become popular in the neighborhood. The co-op had extended its services to include a time bank where services were traded among the neighbors – across the ethnic divide. It was emerging as a model for coexistence between Jews and Arabs for the advancement of all the local residents. Against this promising backdrop, the co-op's board decided that an open-air rally celebrating the neighborhood's achievements was in order. There would be speakers, refreshments, and the music of an up-and-coming rock band composed of Arab and Jewish musicians originally from the neighborhood.

It was both the right and the wrong place for Na'aleh to sponsor an event. The Movement had only begun discussing the possibility of expanding its activities to support social and economic change on the community level. Primarily, Na'aleh had gotten involved in Kiryat Zebulon because one of Rabbi Ben-Yishai's students had founded a synagogue there. He was among those that had started the co-op and urged his mentor to convince the national movement to support their work.

Kiryat Zebulon was plagued by social and economic maladies. The majority of its residents were the children or grandchildren of Jewish refugees from Arab lands who arrived in Israel in a massive wave of immigration in the early 1950s. What had been temporary housing for the new arrivals had become permanent and was now a low-income neighborhood inhabited by the descendants of the original settlers. Israeli Arabs had also moved in over the years and had come to represent a third of the local population.

The unemployment rate among local males hovered at nearly 30 percent. Many people had been out of work for so long they had all but forgotten what a paycheck looked like.

Most households survived on National Insurance stipends. During the day, the two busiest addresses in Kiryat Zebulon were the besieged unemployment bureau and the badly understaffed drug treatment center. At night, the turf belonged to drug dealers and other bottom dwellers who stole whatever meager pickings they could cull from the overcrowded apartments in the district.

Schoolteachers, social workers and others in the helping professions would make every attempt not to be assigned to Kiryat Zebulon. The very real prospect of violence against them was a distinct deterrent. The local grocer conducted business with a large pistol strapped to his hip and the HMO clinic had armed guards to escort the doctors and nurses to their cars parked in a lot surrounded by barbed wire. So many soldiers from the neighborhood had been dismissed from the army for unbecoming conduct that a dishonorable discharge had been become known in the northern command as a "Kiryat Zebulon." The first food riot to break out in Israel in forty years occurred in the neighborhood after the government removed subsidies on bread, oil and eggs.

Lilah had looked up Kiriat Zebulon on the Internet before driving there and her knees felt rubbery as she got out of her car. She hadn't told anyone of her plan to attend the rally – she covered for herself by saying she would visit a museum in Haifa before going to the salon meeting in Carmiel. Michal and Issam and certainly Naftali and Ido would have been appalled by her visit to Kiryat Zebulon – especially since she aimed to ferret out the Sons of Gideon.

Lilah had dropped Ido off at Binyamina, where he caught a ride to his base – he promised to let her know about Lucian as soon as he heard from his friend, the doctor in Boston. She arrived at Kiryat Zebulon as she had hoped, early enough to scout out the scene.

Little by little, her fears were eclipsed by nervous

anticipation and then by the excitement of being behind a camera. Kiryat Zebulon was eminently photogenic. Its sad sights spoke volumes about a community with its own smells, rhythms, sounds and scenes. She began walking the streets, taking aim, focusing, adjusting, re-gauging, shooting, aiming again, reshooting. No one seemed to mind her taking photos. In fact, some people seemed to walk a little taller when they saw Lilah at work.

Lilah made her way to the rally site. She had not gone to the organizers and introduced herself, and no one seemed to recognize her. Her eyes scoured the attendees as the speakers addressed the crowd. Everyone, yet no one seemed suspect. As the audience threw their souls into the music, Lilah stayed along the edge of the crowd and watched.

Lilah had taken dozens of photos from the margins of the stage and at a distance from the surrounding streets. After she had withdrawn as far back as she could to the furthest point from which the stage was still visible, someone caught her attention and her arm. "Hello, beautiful lady," said a rail-thin man with a face worn by furrows and eyes full of an addict's cravings. Before Lilah knew it, he had boxed her into the entryway of the abandoned building. Even as the music echoed from the rally site just across the street, Lilah was completely isolated, cornered. She was terrified.

"Excuse me," Lilah said, trying to push past him.

"Why do you fear me, beautiful lady?" the man hissed as he blocked Lilah's path. "Here, let me take that heavy bag for you." He grabbed the equipment bag roughly and began walking away.

"Hey, give it back. I'll scream!" Lilah panicked, as she started after him.

"Oh, so you want to get to know me? That's very nice," he said.

"I just want my bag back."

"Come here and get it, madam. Come," the man beckoned and then moved toward Lilah.

"I'm going to get help," Lilah cried, as she tried to leave the vestibule. But the man was faster than she.

"Now, miss, we are going to get to know one another." He cupped his hand over her mouth, "I saw you taking pictures of us here, of our places and our people. You took from us, and now I am going to take from you. We'll see who's in control." He tried to push Lilah to the ground but she squirmed and resisted. He slapped her once, then again. He stooped down and was trying to pull her to the ground when someone called out, "Hey, what's going on there?" In a flash, the mugger got to his feet, fled the building and vanished down the street.

The rescuer stopped next to Lilah and knelt over her. "Are you okay?" he asked. Lilah nodded. She recognized her rescuer, Eli.

"Are you alright?"

"Yes, I'm alright. Just shaken."

Eli then tore out of the foyer after the assailant. Lilah slowly got to her feet and adjusted her clothes. She picked up the equipment bag and stumbled out onto the street. She leaned against a parked car, numb.

Eli returned moments later. Lilah's attacker had eluded him. He paused to catch his breath. He then took Lilah's bag in his good hand. "Come," he said. "Let's go to a police station. Let's get his description out."

"No, Eli – that is your name, isn't it? – I'd rather forget about it."

"But why? That guy just assaulted you. You've got nothing to be afraid of – he does."

"No. Please. Let's just leave it alone. I want to forget about it."

"But what about the next victim...," he began, then reconsidered. "I'm sorry," he said, "you've got a right to deal with this however you like."

"Please, just get me away from here."

"Sure, of course," said Eli.

Lilah leaned on him. They walked without exchanging a word, Eli silent as Lilah began to weep softly.

Eli led her to his car. He opened the passenger door and helped her get in, went around to the driver's side and got in beside her. He stole a glance at Lilah. Again, he was taken by her eyes, his mother Deborah's eyes, their innocence, their goodness.

"You're very pale and your lips are blue. Maybe you'd like to go to the hospital?" he said.

"No, I'm okay. Just shaken up."

"Right," said Eli awkwardly. "I'm terribly sorry that this happened, really."

Lilah nodded in acknowledgement. She stopped crying.

"I have cousins who live not far from here, just across town. It's a nice place, quiet and safe. Would you like to go and rest there a while? You wouldn't have to talk about what happened."

"No, thank you. I'm beginning to feel better. You've been very kind."

Eli changed his tone. "You came alone?" he asked, incredulous and disapproving.

Lilah nodded.

"Why the hell did you do that? Don't you know where you are? It's a war zone out here. It's no place for someone like you!"

"I'm here for the same reason you are. I'm hunting them," she admitted decisively. "It's no coincidence that you're the one who found me. It seems we're both looking for these monsters, each in his own way."

"Who? Who do you think you are going after?"

"The Sons of Gideon. Except that instead of using weapons

like yours, I am using my camera. I want to identify them, to capture them on film."

"I'm doing what I am supposed to be doing. I've already asked you not to try to tangle with these people. They're killers – and damn good ones."

Now it was Lilah who changed her tone, more assertive.

"What happened to your face?" she challenged, "and that thing on your hand what's that all about?"

"An accident."

"What kind of accident?" Lilah asked suspiciously.

"I had a little run-in with a Gideon member – if you must know."

"My God! You mean you were in a fight with one?"

"Yes."

"When?"

"Some days ago."

"You look like you were badly hurt. What are you doing back on the streets?"

"I'm alright," Eli insisted.

"So I guess we're both martyrs for the same cause. So why are you so committed to getting them? I'm sure it's not because you like getting beaten up."

"I'm not in this to further Arab-Jewish brotherhood. That's Na'aleh's department."

"Then why do you risk your life for them? After all, it's just Arabs they're after."

"First of all, it's my job. Secondly, these people are enemies of the State. As if that isn't enough, they are hitting Jews pretty hard, too."

"You must have a hard time referring to Jews as terrorists."

"I'm not too keen on going after Jews."

"So why not leave it to someone else?"

"I told you, they're enemies of the State. They are destroying my country."

"So you are a patriot," Lilah baited.

"Yes. That's how I see myself."

Lilah let the subject fade. They rode in silence for a while. "Where are you taking me?" Lilah asked. She wasn't at all concerned that he had ill intentions. Somehow, she felt safe in his presence.

"Home, I am taking you home. You are in no shape to drive and I'll see to it that your car gets to Tel Aviv. Is there somewhere else you would prefer that I take you?"

"No, home is fine. Although it's interesting that you haven't asked me where home is. Obviously, you already know."

"Yes, I do," Eli said frankly. Lilah noticed him wince in pain.

"Are you taking something for that? It seems to be hurting a lot."

"You can't drive and take painkillers. I'm alright."

"Your wife or girlfriend can't be too happy about the shape you're in."

"I live alone."

"Don't tell me you're gay." They both laughed, a release.

"No, I just don't have much time for someone else in my life right now."

"You're pretty committed. But work isn't all there is to life."

"So they tell me."

They drove onto the Coastal Highway in silence. As they left the city limits of Haifa and passed near Zichron Ya'akov, Lilah asked Eli to pull over. He did so. She got out of the car and stared at the roadway, then at the sea, and then up and down the road again.

"Memories?" Eli asked. He had gotten out of the car.

"Not good ones, I'm afraid. Remember the bus bombing last summer? This is where it happened," she said sadly.

"You knew someone involved?"

"Me. Not on the bus. I was driving several kilometers behind it. I was there for the second explosion." Lilah said, staring off for a few more moments. She shuddered, then got back into the car. Eli followed and they drove off.

"So you've seen what they can do," Eli said, his face stormy. "You've seen what the Arabs can do, how they are willing to kill innocent people to supposedly further their cause. But still you reach out to them. Are you Christian? You just turn the other cheek?"

"I'm as good a Jew as you are. And that's why I believe in justice for them and for us."

"I don't understand you gentle souls. How many times do you have to get smacked in the face before the reality finally sinks in?"

"There's not so much to understand. I just have faith in humanity."

"But the situation doesn't improve. They still want to put us there," he said, pointing to the sea.

"That attitude won't get us anywhere. Yes, there are Arab leaders who won't settle for peace – and they have begun to fall. I believe there are many Arab people, the ones simply trying to get by in places like Al-Bakr and in Old Jaffa and in Haifa who will come through if they see that we're willing to treat them with basic human respect."

"I don't believe it," said Eli. "There's too much bad blood."

Again there was silence in the car. Eli coped with his physical pain, Lilah with her memories.

"What was he like?" Lilah finally asked. "The Gideon who attacked you."

"We didn't exactly have a conversation."

"Was he what you expected?"

"More or less. A savage."

"Where did you find him?"

"He was going to murder someone."

"Really."

"Yes, but I shouldn't be talking about this."

"What happened? Did you track him down?"

"I received a tip that he would be at a certain place at a certain time. The diary entry read that he would attack the sheik's..." Eli stopped short. "You really are asking me things you shouldn't. I've told you too much."

"Sorry, I don't mean to pry," Lilah let the conversation trail off before resuming. "So he was going to kill the head of the Arab village," she went on. Eli was deep in memory, recalling the encounter.

"No, he was after the sheik's daughter. A little girl."

"So you saved the life of a little Arab girl. She's going to give birth to Arabs one day, you know, and according to your reasoning, one of her sons just might turn around and kill a Jew."

"I was doing my job. I protect the State."

"Chief Inspector Carmi says he is doing his job, too. Except that, even if he's not behind any of this, he certainly hasn't done much to solve the case – especially compared to what you have been doing, not to mention the physical wounds you've gotten. So why are you taking the fall for him?"

"I don't work for Carmi. He's irrelevant to all this."

Lilah egged Eli on. "All the work has been yours, hasn't it?"

"Look, my friend. If you think I am going to give you ammunition for your war on the establishment, guess again."

Lilah looked at Eli's casted hand and his bruised face. She thought of her fallen brother, and of Ido. She was flushed with a mélange of feelings.

Eli said nothing. Neither of them did for the rest of the way, forty minutes, while Eli drove Lilah home.

As he pulled up in front of her building, Eli broke the silence.

"Lilah, I don't want to find you again at one of these gatherings or in a place like Kiryat Zebulon," he admonished.

"Your movement needs you in one piece, so don't take anymore foolish risks," he warned tenderly.

She was touched. "I appreciate your caring," Lilah said, peering into his earnest eyes: kind, intelligent, warm. "Thanks for helping me. I hate to think what would have happened if you hadn't come when you did."

He walked her to the entryway of the building. "It's pretty clear to me that the investigation wouldn't be going anywhere without you. You seem to be the one who it all depends on," Lilah said. "Take care," she said in a whisper, low and emotion-filled. "You take care. I mean it. Watch out for yourself," she said.

As Lilah climbed the stairs and thought about Eli, she felt quite strongly that in life there are people you are meant to meet.

Later that evening, Eli drove to the US Embassy. Amos had arranged a meeting with someone in the military attaché's office. The man confirmed what Professor Shoresh had stated: The code used in the Ben-Avraham diary had been used by American Special Forces troops in the Gulf War during the early 1990s. Clearly, the Sons of Gideon included someone who had experience with that code.

As he was about to step outside the fortified bastion of the U.S. Embassy, in the night air aglow with Tel Aviv's neon lights and as hot in February as it generally was in June, Eli recalled a man he had once met, maybe eight, nine years ago.

The man was a moshavnik who worked as a vice squad detective in the Beersheva area. He was a strange, tough little guy with a spare, patchy beard and shrapnel scars on his face. He was an American veteran of some special outfit that served in Iraq and Kuwait during the Gulf War. Eli wasn't sure about the nature of his service there, only that he had mentioned that he was in contact with American veterans, expats and military types who lived in or passed through Israel. Maybe, Eli thought, he might have heard some talk on the street.

Eli went to his office and instructed his secretary to find out the identity of the moshavnik, contact him and arrange for Eli to see him as soon as possible.

CHAPTER SEVENTEEN

Lilah would have been grateful had Michal been out of the apartment, at a meeting or running an errand. That would have given her time to catch her breath and settle her nerves after the assault, to come up with a proper explanation about why she wasn't in Carmiel and to process the odd assortment of feelings she had about Eli.

Michal was in the apartment. So was Ido. He had come back all the way from the Golan to bring her the news.

"Hi Mom," he said, his voice tender and sorrowful. His uniform was dusty from a day in the field, he smelled of sweat and his hair was tousled. He steadied his mother between his hands. "Lucian isn't going to make it. It's a matter of days, maybe less."

The El Al flights were booked up and the quickest route Michal could find was with Air France via Paris on an expensive business class ticket. If Lilah made the slim connections, she would arrive in Boston by mid-morning the next day.

Lilah felt as though she was being uprooted as she boarded the airliner in Tel Aviv. The sudden passage from Kiryat Zebulon to Boston via the French capital seemed so out of place, so out of time.

Lilah read two pages of the Isabella Allende novel she had brought with her, but as soon as the lights dimmed, she fell asleep. She woke up just before the plane landed, hurriedly refreshed herself in the lavatory and bolted off the plane destined for the gate across the terminal where she would catch the flight to Boston.

As the airplane propelled out of the Parisian dawn back into the darkness of the prevailing Atlantic night, Lilah's mood tumbled. While Israel was in ferment, it felt wrong to be cruising away from it, nine kilometers in the sky. It was as though she was somehow traveling backward rather than forward.

She had been dozing when she felt a sudden tug at her breast and breaths of harsh cold around her. There was a mournful whistle – one that did not seem to come from the mechanical systems of the aircraft but from another source, elsewhere in the cosmos. Then she felt a terrible sense of grief wash over her. She anxiously asked the steward if everything was all right with the plane. Assured it was, she fell into deep sleep.

Lucian's son, Edgar, picked Lilah up at Logan International.

Lilah knew Edgar well from Thanksgiving dinners at Lucian's home and weekends spent at the beach house on the Cape. The slight and bashful boy with a lisp had become his own man, an editor at a prominent literary publishing house.

When Lilah spotted Edgar as she exited the gate, his eyes were as rose-colored as his wind-blown cheeks. He looked bereft and Lilah understood that Lucian had died. Lilah took him into her arms and Edgar, a few years older than her own son and whose straw-colored hair was also balding at the crown, cried like a baby. Another man, Antonio, a look of deep sympathy on his dark, pockmarked face hovered about Edgar and placed his hand lovingly on his back.

"Just after midnight," Antonio said to Lilah after she asked when Lucian had died. He wheeled her valise behind him.

Lilah calculated the differences in time zone and trembled. She recalled the bursts of cold she had felt on the plane, the whistle she thought she had heard and realized that the sorrow that had overcome her coincided with Lucian's passage from this earth.

"Dad never really came out of it. He did open his eyes several times when he heard my voice or Elyse's though," Edgar said.

"How is she handling this?" Lilah inquired, the Israeli inflection on her English sounding much more pronounced than she had remembered. Edgar said his sister had been holding her own, that she was alright.

"Tell Lilah about when your father opened his eyes, the smile," Antonio urged Edgar.

"Yes, yes. Last night he opened his eyes and saw me. It was the one time he seemed alert. He looked at Antonio then back at me and with this really small nod, you could barely detect it, I think he finally gave us his approval. Then he looked at me and if you can talk about someone smiling through his eyes, that's what he did. I felt like a little boy again, like my daddy had given me a kiss," Edgar recalled before crumbling into another torrent of tears.

It was late December, between Christmas and New Year's Eve, and the Boston air was cold and wet. The road from Logan Airport through the Callahan Tunnel was backed-up by some mishap midway through. Antonio was driving, and Edgar rubbed his neck.

"We had quite a snowstorm a couple of days ago, Lilah," he informed her.

"Yes, like you get all the time in Tel Aviv," Antonio joked.

The comment elicited an image. In her mind's eye, Lilah saw 3 HaGaon Street awash in Mediterranean sunlight. She found herself woefully nostalgic and missing Ido, Naftali and Michal deeply. She felt a sudden desire to get on the first flight back home.

Once they were out of the tunnel, the traffic was sparse. Lilah, Edgar and Antonio conversed, updating each other about their lives. In the late model Volvo, the two well-dressed gentlemen and the lady would have struck all observers as Boston vintage, high-brows or well-heeled members of the urban elite. But as they passed over the Charles River and Lilah caught sight of the Boston skyline, she realized that though she once could have been counted among that select group, she no longer was. She was an Israeli who was now very connected with her country.

Edgar related that he had started arranging his father's funeral after the senior neurologist who examined Lucian in the ER predicted a rapid decline and demise. Lucian had long ago issued instructions on how his remains were to be disposed. His body had already been taken from the hospital for cremation. Edgar and Elyse were to take his ashes to Norway. They were to be sprinkled along the seacoast near the village from which Lucian's parents had emigrated.

A memorial service would take place on Monday evening in the lobby of Camera Distincta House. The institute's staff was attending to those arrangements. In the meantime, callers could pay their respects to the family at Lucian's apartment on Beacon Street.

Storrow Drive was closed due to repairs and traffic was directed through the city. As they traveled along the eastern fringe of Boston Common down Tremont Street, Lilah noticed a large throng of people, demonstrators it seemed, huddling on the green. They were shadowy figures, round-shouldered and brooding. Their winter-pale faces were masklike. Lilah thought of Edvard Munch's works, his paintings of the despondent.

"What's that about?" Lilah asked.

"That, that's a Tea Party rally."

Lilah watched the scene as the traffic slowed to let a stream of people, many families, cross the road and enter the growing mass of attendees on the Common. Many carried placards: "Demolish the Global Warming Myth," "Get the Feds out of My Pocketbook," "Family America: Banish the Illegals." Lilah found other signs seemed particularly menacing, "New York Special Interests Bleed Christian America," "American Taxpayer: Don't Subsidize Israeli Aggressors."

"The movement of American idiots," said Edgar.

"Oh look," said Antonio, "there's one especially for us," he continued, pointing to one sign that read, "Homosexuals: An

American Disgrace."

Later, once they arrived at Lucian's apartment and settled in and congregated in the living room, the Tea Partiers were discussed. "Oh yes, they're right-wing," said Edgar, as he poured Lilah a glass of orange juice. "Right-wing and raw."

"And growing. They've become a political and social force," Elyse said with a dose of alarm.

They were sitting in the large wood-paneled room filled with thick-cushioned sofas and recliners. Lucian's large oversized desk and wooden file cabinets and bookshelves encased the room. The apartment had a foyer and large formal living room with picture windows overlooking the Charles River. The home was elegantly furnished. It exuded affluence.

Lucian had grown up in modest circumstances, but after his father made a fortune in transatlantic shipping later in life, Lucian inherited his wealth. It afforded him the means to devote himself to the pursuit of photographic art and build a portfolio and reputation. The acclaim he had won landed him the post of Camera Distincta's founding director. Ensconced there, he became the guru of American photography and visual design for a generation.

Lucian's presence was strongly present within these walls, though other souls had left their impress here as well. Lucian's first wife, his children's mother, had died when Edgar was three and Elyse not yet two. The subsequent women he had brought here, a second wife and later a girlfriend had left accusing Lucian of domestic tyranny and insensitivity – charges he countered by dismissing his second wife as a floozy and her successor as certifiable. Lucian's children had no easy time with their single-parent, his women and the various nannies he had engaged to rear them here. He had been stern, at times aloof, and it had cost him a small mountain of therapist bills to finally achieve a livable order in this house for his small family.

There were Christmas wreaths on the front door and on the

mantle of the marble fireplace in the living room. A fire was blazing in the fireplace of the sitting room where Lucian's children, their partners and Lilah were gathered. There, Edgar and Antonio, and Elyse and her lover Jane, sat with Lilah reminiscing about "the venerable oak," while they waited for condolence callers. They would certainly begin arriving after the news of Lucian's death had filtered through to the various communities of which he had been a part.

"He loved you Lilah," Elyse said, "in a special way. I can't easily characterize your relationship, father-daughter, mentor-disciple. I don't know if you were ever lovers – but he had a place in his heart where only you resided."

"I'll say," said Edgar.

Over wine and cheese, they spoke about Lucian, his propensity to be tight-fisted and the nagging suspicion that he had really been a closet conservative who had grudgingly accepted liberal values as the fashion of the circles in which he traveled. "If he secretly was of that persuasion, he got his just desserts," Elyse said laughingly when the matter of both his children being homosexual came up.

"I knew his progressive side," Lilah countered. As the relative oldster in the crowd, she sought to set the record straight. "I remember how when I first met him in 1974, he was a veteran of anti-war rallies and marched against racial discrimination. Of course, he would always go to such events in style, dressed to the hilt and duly liquored," she conceded, "and with some female peacock on his arm."

"Yes he did like his drink," Edgar recalled.

"And his ladies," Antonio added.

The crowds began arriving around four and continued visiting until nearly midnight. Lilah had been given Elyse's room with a private bath to stay in. Elyse and Jane would stay in the guestroom down the hall.

Before the condolence callers arrived, as Lilah unpacked her bags in Elyse's room, she felt mixed emotions. Boston seemed so familiar – yet at the same time foreign. Lilah wondered how she had spent three decades living in this place – and thriving. As she peered out of the window onto the Charles and beyond it into Cambridge, she could see the balcony of her apartment, now on long-term lease. Does that place really belong to me? she asked herself. Did I, myself, reside there?

How very different things had been just a relatively short time ago. How very different she had been, thought Lilah.

The people who filed into Lucian's home to pay their respects were an elite group: Lucian's banker and the man's wife, trustees of the institute, photographers and art critics, editors, artists, academics. They were a bouquet of colors and types, spinsters and hipsters dressed in everything from pinstripes to jeans. There were Hispanics and WASPs, African-Americans and Asian-Americans. Lilah spotted a man with a knitted *kipah*, a professor at Wellesley College.

Gradually, the atmosphere changed from mournful and solemn to cordial and convivial. The apartment bloomed with flower settings and trays of food sent by friends; liquor flowed freely. The house filled with loving energy toward Lucian. The visitors mourned and celebrated him. But none, Lilah averred, could possibly feel the loss she did. The way he was a part of her was hers alone.

After the crowd had departed, as she undressed in Elyse's room and readied for bed, it occurred to Lilah that the bulk of her adult life had taken place in these environs, Boston, Cambridge. Here, without expectation or plan, she embarked on her life's work and had arrived at the pinnacle of her profession. As one acquaintance after another came up to her throughout the afternoon and evening and lavished praise on her work, she had felt a certain pride. She blushed when acclaimed as a "photographer's photographer," by a critic for the *Phoenix*. "No one holds a candle to Lilah Kedem," said another visitor, a museum curator to his companion. "She is the rightful inheritor of Lucian's place," he declared.

Someone keenly asked Lilah what she was working on now. The question required a creative response, thought Lilah, evasive yet tenable – these people couldn't possibly understand what was going on in her country, that she was tracking an evil pack, called The Sons of Gideon, who were wreaking havoc on her society. "A project aimed at creating a visual portrait of changes in our national landscape," she replied. The interlocutor was satisfied with that and did not press for details.

In the cushiony bed with thick pillows in Elyse's room, amidst the posters of Anaïs Nin and Simone Signoret, Lilah pondered whether she had made a mistake in leaving all this existence and returning to Israel. Here she had gained entry into the cosmopolis and had built a life that was rewarding, untroubled. Why had she given it up?

Then, she recalled the less congenial aspects of her life in America. The hassles she had faced getting her residency visa; after thirty years of paying taxes, she still hadn't been granted citizenship. The struggle she had faced raising Ido by herself in a society that had little patience for single mothers. The difficulties keeping a secular Jewish identity in their home which in America meant synagogue attendance on the High Holidays, lox and bagels on Sundays and a vague sense of ethnicity. She recalled having no one among her American friends to share her anxiety with during the Lebanon Wars and after terrorist attacks in Israel. And there were the cultural discomfiture and the conflict of values: American materialism, the society's insularity and detachments from global realities, the prevalence of handguns and the specter of drugs that she endeavored so feverishly to keep away from her son.

Her life here had had the feel of velvet, perhaps. Soft and smooth. But beneath the surface, it had not all been glad and welcoming. Why had she given up America? The biggest part was to be with Ido and Naftali in her own land. But also, Lilah now realized, because she had tried to set root on alien ground and had never quite been allowed to do so. She did not quite belong.

Lilah dreamt of being at Mitzpeh Ramon with Naftali, two days of unbridled being. In the morning light after she awoke, it was clear to her why she had returned to Israel: a return to belonging.

Edgar and Elyse had errands to run during the morning before the memorial service that evening. Lilah asked them if they would be offended by her taking a flight back to Tel Aviv after the service, late that night.

"Of course you should get right back home," said Elyse.

"We are so touched and grateful that you flew all the way over to be with us," Edgar assured her.

Lilah phoned the airlines and booked her return. Seeing the Tea Party discontents had roused her anxieties about the Sons of Gideon. She was keen to get home.

Lilah spent the morning at Camera Distincta. She worked with the photo editor preparing the final proofs of *Women of the Ports*. "How fortuitous it is that you are here," exclaimed the older woman, "despite the sad circumstances of your visit," she added.

Lilah grabbed a sandwich for lunch and visited the Museum of Fine Arts, just down the street from Camera Distincta. She went straight to the landing where Monet's *Morning on the Seine, near Giverny,* was displayed. It was the painting she had thought of when she sat by Naftali as they drove to Mitzpeh Ramon on Thursday, just a few days before. She thought of her love for Naftali, of the majesty of the landscape they had witnessed together, of the herd of deer that made their home where the Ben-Gurions rested. And again there arose in her an aching nostalgia. Her heart beat strongest there, in Zion and while to know the world and to be a citizen of it was a grand thing, she was a daughter of Israel and she yearned to restore herself there, with Naftali, Ido, Michal and Issam, her comrades in Na'aleh – with the whole blasted society, now so sundered and discordant.

As Lilah meandered through the museum collection, a song she adored, *Into the Mystic*, came to her. She could almost hear Van Morrison singing gently into her ear. As she passed the paintings in the permanent collection, she felt as though she was viewing signposts of moods and awakenings that she had experienced during the thirty years when she lived a subway ride away from here. She saw them anew now. They had a different function. Then she held them in different regard; they were just as beautiful but had assumed different hues.

How she had grown, thought Lilah.

Lucian's memorial service was to begin at six and Lilah, one of the remaining stragglers when the museum closed at a quarter to the hour, hastened to make her way back to Camera Distincta.

As she walked at dusk down the long city block, the Christmas lights along the avenue shone brightly. Lilah had always loved the felicity of the lights, the message of good cheer that they carried. As she hurried along the boulevard in the rising cold and whipping wind, she spied a woman and two children huddled together in the entryway of a closed flower shop. There was something in the woman's eyes, some kind of hopelessness and despair. Lilah thought she saw bruise marks on the woman's face but wasn't sure.

What a terrible thing despair was, thought Lilah. Don't give up, Lilah strived to say with an empathic smile. She hoped that the woman would garner some strength from that. What more could Lilah give her?

The institute's lobby was brimming with people. Lilah sat in the front row with Elyse, Jane and Antonio. Edgar would preside over the service and stood behind the podium. Confusion swept over Lilah for a moment, her memory turning back to the press conference where her photo of the bomb-bearer at Ramat Zion had been divulged five nights earlier in Tel Aviv. She turned around, rising a little from the seat half-expecting to see Epstein's thugs lumber up the aisle. She remembered that things were different here. The anxiety passed.

A cellist and flautist were playing fugues. The flowers, the music – how foreign it was, thought Lilah. How very different from the way we bury our dead back home. She did not begrudge their rites. They just affirmed to her that people have their place in the world and hers was not here.

A large portrait of Lucian framed with black fabric, rested on an easel next to the podium. "It makes him look pompous," Antonio whispered disapprovingly to Lilah, "not to say that he wasn't," he teased.

"Not pompous, just grand," Lilah offered.

Antonio laughed and pressed Lilah's hand.

Lilah looked at the sea of faces in the audience, a sea of colors. It was as though light had been cast through a prism and the resulting hues painted on the faces.

The music stopped and Edgar began the memorial service. He called to the podium five speakers who had known Lucian long and well. They recounted bittersweet memories and comical anecdotes in their emotion-laden remarks. His ex-brother-in-law, an insurance company executive who had remained a close friend of Lucian's even after his sister had divorced him, lampooned the venerable oak – nothing was spared. Bill McGluggan, a politician from Southie with gubernatorial ambitions, had known Lucian since they served together on the Bay State Little League Commission. He described Lucian's shenanigans as a coach. Concerning the McGluggans, Edgar confided to Lilah later, "I was such a pansy, the McGluggan kid would just knock the shit out of me for the sport of it," he said. "Then Dad would call Bill to make sure that Liam got the licking he had coming and that would get me a couple months of grace," he recalled.

The dean of the school of fine arts from one of the local universities gave a high-brow academic eulogy "for Lucian, my master." Elyse scoffed at that over dinner later near Faneuil Hall. "I think Dad got his master's degree by trading it for a box of Havanas. He was smart, well-read but no academic master."

At the end of the speeches, Edgar led the audience in the reading of psalms. Lilah read the English translation of her favorite one, *Shir HaMa'alot*, psalm 121:

> *A song of ascents*
> *I lift up my eyes to the hills—*
> *where does my help come from?*
> *My help comes from the LORD,*
> *the Maker of heaven and earth.*
> *He will not let your foot slip—*
> *he who watches over you will not slumber;*
> *indeed, he who watches over Israel*
> *will neither slumber nor sleep.*
> *The LORD watches over you—*
> *the LORD is your shade at your right hand;*
> *the sun will not harm you by day,*
> *nor the moon by night.*
> *The LORD will keep you from all harm—*
> *he will watch over your life;*
> *the LORD will watch over your coming and going*
> *both now and forevermore.*

The scripture filled Lilah with emotion.

"I hope they're true, those words," she said to Elyse.

"You really take it to heart?" Elyse asked.

"Yes," said Lilah, "I do. That faith is my people's shield; it's our spiritual lodestone."

The two couples, Lucian's children, drove Lilah to the airport. The parting at the curbside was difficult. They realized that with Lucian gone, it would be up to them to maintain their relationship. Elaborating on how they would do so almost made Lilah miss her flight.

As Lilah hurried to the gate, her eye caught the headline on the cover of *The Boston Globe*. She scooped up the paper and paid for it. After she boarded, even before she stowed her bag in the overhead compartment, she read the article: "Twenty-three killed in Palestinian school. Jewish Extremists take blame."

Lilah calculated how long it would take to get home. She was impatient.

Sixty-nine hours out of time and out of place had been long enough.

Eli had just finished the Carmi report when his secretary buzzed him over the intercom and told him he had an urgent phone call. Her tone was ominous.

"Who is it?" Eli asked and when she answered that it was the team at Ma'ale Adumim, where nothing eventful had taken place since they began their surveillance, he took the call.

"It's Eli, what's going on?"

"This is HaCohen. My team came on a little while ago."

"What have you got?"

"We don't know exactly. But the apartment we have been monitoring has been destroyed, apparently by a small missile."

"Repeat that."

HaCohen repeated the message and added, "the blast originated from outside the building. Whoever is responsible scored a direct hit, from a distance."

"What makes you think it was a missile? It could have been

a remote-controlled bomb."

"We heard a whistle that grew louder. Then there was the sound of the impact and then the blast."

Eli did not wait to hear the details. He wanted to check them with his own eyes. "I'm on my way," he said, and hung up.

Just as Eli finished the call, a message flashed on the screen of his computer:

> "Following recvd 07:51 at Natl Police Hdqtrs:
>
> 'To the Head Headhunter', Mordechai Carmi, you traitor. You danced well with our fighter at Arka al-Khitab. Are you feeling better? Poor you, you got bloodied. You were pretty impressive though, bruising our man pretty good. That's alright. We're giving the country two presents in his honor. Got that, Carmi? Two presents.
>
> 'Sons of Gideon'"

Eli was stunned: The group believed that Carmi was calling the shots, that he was directing the investigation aimed at them.

Carmi, then, was no confederate of the Sons of Gideon.

The second part of the message was enraging, demonic. The Gideons were promising two "presents," which Eli took to mean two attacks. One presumably had already happened at Ma'ale Adumim. That left a second attack – somewhere in Israel or the Territories – and there wasn't the slightest clue of where it would take place. That left no chance of preventing it, no possibility of issuing a warning to the potential victims. Everybody and every place was at risk – echoes of the same sheer terror that had afflicted the country during the Second Intifada when Palestinian suicide bombers reigned on Israel's streets.

Eli fretted as he and his men picked through the debris in Ma'ale Adumim. Anticipating news of the second attack, he flinched at every squelch of the field radios and each ring of his cell phone. At least no one had been injured at Ma'ale Adumim. Would that also be the case for the second assault?

The vacant apartment building tottered on three pilings. With the concrete and steel supports of its fourth corner having collapsed, the Ben-Abraham apartment was buried, exactly as intended.

Units of the IDF Engineering Corps had been called to autopsy the structure. After its casing had been found, the munitions specialist concluded that a missile had indeed been fired, deployed from the southeast. Based on his calculations, a launcher was soon found near Nebi Musa, southeast of Ma'ale Adumim. The Sons of Gideon had precisely calibrated the pinpoint attack on the Ben-Abraham apartment from nearly five kilometers away.

Why decimate an apartment belonging to one of your members? Eli wondered. They must have concluded that the diary had already been discovered. Eli's confrontation of the attacker at Arka al-Khitab proved that. What then had they accomplished by destroying the empty apartment? As he foraged through the ruins of what had been a bedroom, Eli decided to contact the Shin Bet psych profiler. How would he explain the act? What were the Sons of Gideon trying to convey?

"Vengeance," the psychologist texted Eli in reply. "And that they're still in the game," he added.

Eli had just found part of the projectile in the ruins when the call he had been anticipating came. Ninety minutes after the missile was fired at Ma'ale Adumim, there had been some kind of attack about 50 kilometers away, in Nablus.

What were the Sons of Gideon trying to show by executing two very different attacks far from one another within fairly short order? That there were at least two operational cells brazenly operating in Israel and the PA? Eli contemplated the questions as he drove to Nablus, a three-quarters-of-an-hour drive north and a world apart from Ma'ale Adumim.

A Palestinian intelligence officer Eli knew from liaison work met Eli at one of the check posts between the Israeli and Palestinian positions and escorted him into Nablus. There he briefed Eli on what had occurred. Shortly before 9:00 a.m., five or six rocket-propelled grenades were fired into the main courtyard of the Bustani School for Girls, a respected finishing school for the daughters of wealthy West Bank residents. The courtyard had been filled with students about to enter the main building. The carnage left twenty-three lifeless bodies strewn on the ground. Forty-seven students and three teachers were injured, twelve of them seriously and two in life-threatening condition.

Detailed reports on the massacre immediately filtered out from local hospitals and infirmaries. Eyewitnesses gave their accounts as the media swarmed into the Palestinian city. Once the news of the attack spread, youths throughout the West Bank began throwing stones and burning tires in furious protest.

By late morning, the embers of rage and unrest flared throughout the West Bank, East Jerusalem and Gaza. The violence was spreading like wildfire. A Jewish settler from a settlement east of Bethlehem was shot dead by a roadside sniper. Two other Jews were killed when their car was firebombed by militants. In response to a raging mob in one refugee camp near Jenin, Border Police fired on a crowd of demonstrators, killing three protestors and injuring twelve others.

From the intensity of the rioting and the way it rippled out from Nablus, Eli worried that both the Israeli government and the Palestinian Authority could lose control of the populations under their respective control. After he left Nablus and drove south toward Jerusalem, he half expected to encounter a firestorm hurling down the road. The air itself, so dry and hot, seemed on the verge of combusting.

Passions spread like a contagion over the Green Line into Israel. In Israeli Arab towns, heated demonstrations began in mid-afternoon and proliferated dramatically after the evening news reported on the Sons of Gideon's second declaration of the day:

> *Arabs of the Land of Israel, take note! You have seen the extent of our reach. None of you can evade it – as long as you remain on Jewish land. Leave the Land of Israel immediately or the events that occurred today in Nablus will be repeated time and again, wherever you are. You have been warned.*
>
> *Sons of Gideon*

Following the broadcast of the communiqué, the police were hard-pressed to maintain control of Arab towns and villages within Israel. Fires burned throughout the night across the Galilee. Roads were blockaded in the region of Israel known as the Little Triangle that skirted the border with the Palestinian Authority. Nasty graffiti appeared everywhere. An ugly spirit gripped the Israeli Arab sector fed by intense fear, rumor-mongering and the stirring of passions by Islamic radicals who promoted panic and hysteria. Some villages closed in on themselves entirely, their inhabitants too frightened to venture outside their homes.

The Sons of Gideon had set off a tinderbox.

☙ ❖ ❧

Lilah arrived home from the airport just as the emergency meeting began. Michal had convened the Na'aleh Board. They would want to respond to the Nablus bombing.

The Board members gathered in her living room were, like

Lilah, outraged, aghast and scared. The Sons of Gideon had the country in convulsions and the Board unanimously agreed that "interventions" – massive and unequivocal – had to take place and rouse people to action.

The meeting began with Issam describing the feelings of isolation and vulnerability felt by the Arabs on both sides of the Green Line. The Board decided on a direct people-to-people response: Na'aleh would send condolence delegations to call upon the families of the deceased. A fund for the rehabilitation of the injured girls would be established. It was further resolved that teams of Na'aleh members, Arabs and Jews, would also visit Israeli Arab villages and neighborhoods in an attempt to defuse tensions there.

Not enough, the Board members agreed after further discussion. The situation was incendiary. The Sons of Gideon were succeeding and whether that was because the government could not or would not stop them was quite beside the point. The government's policies provided a substrate for malignancy. They created the social conditions in which such extremists thrived.

The consensus among the Board members was that more needed to be done. The situation was perilous and the outcome could be fateful for Israel. Israel's future was at stake and in that Na'aleh would find its patriotism. The future of Jewish people everywhere required an Israel at peace – with the Palestinians, with the other nations of the world, and with itself.

The Board member representing the New Democrats briefed the group on the political prospects. The pervasive belief held by the party's leadership was that the Nationalist government was too beholden to the Twenty Families and entangled in the tentacles of the extreme Right to engage in real reform. There was a sense that only a massive show of popular dissent could sway things and bring a bloc of Nationalist moderates to defect to the opposition. Were they to do so, he reasoned, the government would fall and recent polls showed that were elections to be held soon, the New Democrats and their allies stood a good chance of winning.

The second resolution passed by the Board derived naturally from the briefing: Demonstrate the popular will. A candlelight vigil would take place in Jerusalem near the Knesset after the close of the next Sabbath. A call would be issued for all citizens who "reject the hatred and violence, injustice and malaise," to "rise out of the darkness and help restore Israel to the path of light."

The goal was to bring out masses of people from all walks of life to express the people's demand for change. "Rise this Saturday evening" was the call that would be texted, Facebooked and Twittered, e-mailed and published in ads summoning the masses to the vigil.

Still, the people meeting in Lilah's salon at 3 HaGaon Street were disconsolate. What could be done, they asked themselves? Lilah thought of the words in the psalm, *A Song of Ascents*:

> *I lift up my eyes to the hills—*
> *where does my help come from?*

From people like us, Lilah concluded as she surveyed the people in the room, their voices somber but determined and resolved that the battle had to be taken to a higher order: Asserting the popular will and demanding new elections to end the rightist stranglehold on the minds and body politic of Israel.

Rabbi Ben-Yishai then asked for the floor. Lilah had been watching him with worry. His eyes were glassy, his skin pasty. He didn't seem well. He had been silent and detached throughout the meeting.

Once he was recognized by the meeting chair, he closed his eyes as if retracting into the deepest part of himself. He then began speaking.

"I agree with all that we have done up to now. I agree with what we have decided: the condolence calls, the delegations, the vigil. But we now have come to a juncture. The violence grows rather than lessens. The struggle has to be waged on all fronts.

"There are ways to create change in the world that do not involve physical force. They begin with a new consciousness: that change is possible, that the world can be repaired. We have to do everything we can to awaken people to the dangers posed by the fanatics and the pathetic men who rule the House of Israel. We must offer an alternative vision of the society. And that, in large part, is a spiritual matter.

"Whoever the Sons of Gideon are, they are a byproduct of a process that began well before them. It started when this society abandoned the progressive vision of the founders of the State. A new ideology arose, one based on the belief that our historical rights to all of the Land of Israel precede those of the people living there today. And that's wrong. Those people have their rights too."

The rabbi paused, closed his palms against his face for a moment, then looked up and announced. "Changing values means changing consciousness. I have instructed my students and the students of my students to take that message to the people, the entire House of Israel, Jews, Arabs and all others. They will walk the length and breadth of the land, they will travel along every highway of this country and awaken those..."

"Rabbi, the secular majority is hardly going to respond to a group of religious..." one of the Board members began to protest.

The rabbi asked for patience. He continued.

"I know what too many of my colleagues preach: narrowly-interpreted doctrines and ritualism, much of it custom and superstition that pays little heed to Jewish ethics and the reality of the world today. Those are things we will not preach. My students will plead that Israel's salvation won't be found in how much land we hold, but in the quality of the society we build on it. We have to hold on to our place on this earth with all our might, but that does not mean continuing to rule another people. We are citizens of Israel, but also of the world. We must continue to build a better society here while also turning our face toward the other nations, offering our hand to the peoples around us and to the rest of humanity.

"That is the message my students will carry and as they move across Israel and they will seek to mobilize the spiritual power that comes from this realization. Their mission is not to call for greater conformity to the letter of the Law but to its spirit, which has been lost for too long by small-minded people, including rabbis who support the extremists and serve the current powers ruling the land.

"My students share more with enlightened people who do not observe the *mitzvot* than with the wrong-minded men who divide the world between us and them, Jews and Amalekites. Spiritual warriors, both yeshiva students and secular believers in the power of good, peace and justice can together move the people to cast out those who sow hatred or close their eyes to it.

"Also, I have decided to go on a hunger strike, beginning this evening," the rabbi announced. "I will take no food until the Chief Rabbinate expresses its support for change. I will establish myself in the plaza in front of the seat of the chief rabbinate at Hechal Shlomo, and I will demand that it clearly condemns the Sons of Gideon and calls for their isolation by the people. As for the government, it is clear to us and great numbers of our people that it does not represent the people, but only the interests of the few. It has no interest in justice or peace. The chief rabbis must call on it to go, to surrender power to the will of the people.

"We are in a war of wills. Either the priests of hatred will win or the prophets of justice will," said the rabbi. He paused and then, as if drawing from some inner fountain, his trembling finger pointing slowly at all those in the room, "We absolutely must win. We cannot rest until justice triumphs. We must resist the forces of darkness. We must banish them."

The third resolution approved by the Na'aleh executive Board that night was sponsorship of the "Sackcloth Marchers." The doctrine of "Spiritual Engagement" was added to the Movement's arsenal.

"A turning point" is how Michal summed up the meeting as she, Issam and Lilah sat drinking tea after the meeting.

"An awakening," said Issam as a volley of rain struck the kitchen window. It startled the three of them. Mid-winter, the rains had finally come.

Lilah said little. She sat in contemplation. Over the course of a week, the photo she had captured of the bomb-bearing woman at the kibbutz had intensified the manhunt for the Sons of Gideon. Then, during 48 hours alone with Naftali at the edge of a gulch, she had found deeper communion with him than she had since their relationship began. She had ventured to Kiryat Zebulon, had been assaulted and then rescued by Eli Zedek, whose path has crossed hers over and over these past months. After that, Lucian had died and she had reencountered America – and knew better why she had returned home. Once home, she found flames licking at the threshold.

Spiritual resistance. It sounded Gandhi-like – yet at the same time, quintessentially Jewish, she thought.

Against the drumming of the rain, so dearly needed and so long in coming, Lilah had the sense that nothing would ever be the same again. The person she had been was gone. She was stronger now, she realized, far stronger than she had ever been.

She also had the eerie sense she would need to be.

Chapter Eighteen

Rabbi Ben-Yishai led the first group of marchers that set out from their yeshiva near the Cardo in the Jewish Quarter of the Old City. They had finished their prayers and in the early morning light, the group of bearded men garbed in sackcloth made their way through the alleyways of the souk.

The marchers left the Old City and walked along Jaffa Road. Chanting, beating drums and blowing shofars, they commanded the attention of everyone who saw or heard them as they proceeded along the avenue.

The initial group passed the main post office near Safra Square and, as planned, met a second bevy of marchers, Na'aleh activists who awaited them in City Hall plaza. The latter had been busy distributing flyers to municipal employees arriving for work. The growing company of marchers continued toward Zion Square and along the Ben-Yehuda pedestrian mall, where they attracted stares from the café patrons. Shoppers and shopkeepers suspended their exchanges and stepped out onto the street to watch the procession, now a mixed group of Sackcloth Marchers and secular Na'aleh activists reciting verses from Isaiah and Hosea, and a kind of anthem that had first been heard at Kibbutz Ramat Zion after Rabbi Epstein and his coterie arrived to spew their venom:

Move me, move me,
From the depths
We shall rise

Move me, move me,
Out of the fire
We shall rise

Move me, move me,
We will redeem ourselves,
Israel will rise.

Na'aleh volunteers were waiting on King George Street in a van equipped with speakers and bedecked with banners announcing the candlelight vigil on Friday evening. The van led the way for the marchers as the streets began to fill with traffic. The marcher's tone became more affirmative and confident.

By the time those walking behind the van reached the Mahane Yehuda market, there were enough of them to walk five abreast in seven rows parallel to the light rail train tracks. Amid the catcalls of toughs, the group maintained its order. Several jeep-loads of Border Police drove slowly alongside them and a police car, its roof lights pulsing caution, led the procession toward the city exit at Romema.

As prearranged, a third and fourth group of marchers were waiting at the International Conference Center and the Central Bus Station. These included groups of young people from the Scouts and youth movements and students from various campus groups at the university and local colleges.

In the glorious sunlight, a fair-like atmosphere pervaded in the conference center's parking lot where the newcomers were welcomed by Rabbi Ben-Yishai. By the time the column reached the edge of the city to continue its trek along the highway to Tel Aviv, television and radio crews began to arrive and follow them.

Under the Chords Bridge, Rabbi Ben-Yishai addressed the marchers. His remarks were brief: "March on, Lions of Judah, restore justice to this Land," he exhorted. Assuring them that they would meet again soon and that their numbers would swell, he bade them farewell. The marchers, now well over a hundred people, continued their march northward along the shoulders of Highway One.

The rabbi who had maintained a complete fast since the previous evening, boarded a bus to the city center. He got off the bus in front of the old Knesset building along King George Street and walked to Hechal Shlomo, where several of his students were waiting for him. They reverentially led him to a cot that they had set up under a large canopy in the plaza fronting the seat of the chief rabbinate.

The rabbi took a copy of a tractate of Talmud and began a study session on Honi the Circlemaker. He had chosen the subject of his lesson deliberately. Honi, an ancient Galilean sage, was renowned for his miraculous works – and tenacity. According to lore, he once drew a circle in the dust on the drought-ridden ground, sat down and threatened to remain there until God agreed to the coming of winter rains. Legend has it that his efforts were successful.

One of the rabbi's students was dispatched to the suites of the chief rabbis to inform them that his master was giving a class dealing with Honi the Circlemaker just outside the building and that perhaps they would like to participate. This followed the letters that had been brought that morning to the two chief rabbis informing them of Rabbi Ben-Yishai's intention to continue his hunger strike until the rabbinate condemned the Sons of Gideon and called for government reform.

"It is forbidden to abuse one's body," was the official reply of the Ashkenazi Chief Rabbi.

Rabbi Ben-Yishai smiled when a news reporter asked him on live TV about the Chief Rabbi's response. "I am not abusing my body," the rabbi explained, "I am strengthening my soul."

By the time they reached Latrun, the Spiritual Warriors, as the media had dubbed them, comprised two hundred people of Rabbi Ben-Yishai's Sackcloth Marchers and a mélange of youth-movement members, students and ordinary citizens of sundry ages. They encamped in the fields near the Latrun Monastery. By dawn the next morning, several busloads of students from yeshivas in Yavne, Rehovot, Beit Shemesh and Lod, and youth movement members from as far south as Arad and from Metula in the north joined the marchers. At noon, several bus loads of students from colleges in Kiryat Shmona and Safed joined a group of kibbutz and moshav members from throughout the Galilee. More groups arrived from Tiberias and Haifa and further bolstered the number of participants. At daybreak on the third day, close to one thousand Spiritual Warriors from all around the country were on the move, blowing ram's horns, singing songs and reciting both poetry and psalms. Their chant grew in popularity and became a kind of anthem on the radio, both army and civilian:

Move me, move me,
From the depths
We shall rise

Move me, move me,
Out of the fire
We shall rise

Move me, move me,
We will redeem ourselves,
Israel will rise.

By the time they had reached Modi'in, the planned city built midway between the capital and Tel Aviv on the ancient site of the Maccabean revolt, the teachers' and nurses' unions had declared their solidarity with the Spiritual Warriors and urged their members to join the march.

Their numbers grew by the hour.

A stiff cold wind coughed dustily over Jerusalem on the third day of his fast and with Rabbi Ben-Yishai accepting only water, his students and the myriad others who had joined his circle were concerned about his well-being. Still, his senior students were firm in their support for his actions and five of them, all rabbis, had joined him in the fast. A paramedic was on the scene and volunteer physicians visited the hunger strikers throughout the day.

While negotiations were held with the Chief Rabbinate over a formula for ending the strike, the rabbi and his group had become a focus of media attention. Journalists from abroad asked for and received interviews with him. He offered his opinions freely and proved himself a lively raconteur with deep knowledge of both Israeli and world affairs. He charmed various interlocutors who took to his kindly image and began branding him in the mold of a liberation theologian.

A police barricade and officers had been stationed at the Hechal Shlomo plaza to keep knots of Nationalist youth, Keepers of the Faith and Hebrew Fighters at a distance from the rabbi and his camp. The epithets they flung at him were deflected as his group, bolstered by Na'aleh members who had formed a periphery around them countered the jeers through songs and the chant:

From the depths
We shall rise

Out of the fire
We shall rise

We will redeem ourselves,
Israel will rise.

Throughout the day and into the evening, when he was not conversing with well-wishers, answering the questions of journalists or deliberating strategy with Na'aleh leaders, the rabbi led his students in Torah study. He waited resolutely for the Chief Rabbinate to meet his seemingly simple demand: Denounce the Sons of Gideon and the evil spirit roving over the land.

☙ ❖ ❧

In the government precinct of the capital, in the vicinity where the vigil would take place, a dozen bomb-sniffing police dogs tugged at their leashes as they searched the Givat Ram sports stadium. Thousands of regular and special police from throughout country had been called to duty in Jerusalem. In view of credible fears of an attack by the Sons of Gideon, the security forces were on full alert.

With the bomb squad on site and sharpshooters positioned on the roof of the Knesset, the Prime Minister's Office and the Finance Ministry building, nervous police commanders continually reviewed the detailed plan for containing threats to public order. Along Museum Boulevard, Border Police combed the district, looking for anything that might be used to disrupt the vigil that evening. The parking lots of the Israel and Bible Lands Museums and the entire length of Herzl Boulevard had been cleared of all but emergency vehicles. Traffic around Neveh Sha'anan, Na'ot and Givat Ram was rerouted far from the area.

The march would begin under the Chords Bridge at the entrance to Jerusalem. Buses would drop off their passengers at the Sakharov Gardens and they would walk from there to the assembly site under the bridge.

Many thousands of people were expected to come, though no one could predict how large a crowd there would be. The vigil was scheduled to begin at 9:00 p.m. At ten, buses were still unloading passengers at Sakharov Gardens. Thousands of people had been discharged from a caravan of vehicles meeting from the south and north and backed-up past the Harel Junction. By 10:40, the estimated number of people congregating in the Capital now well exceeded the 300,000 that had been at the Rally of Hope in Rabin Square. More people were streaming in.

The first rows of marchers included Lilah, Naftali, Michal and Issam. Dignitaries from academia, entertainment personalities, judges and civil servants, business people, literati and cultural figures assembled alongside them. Behind them were masses of citizens from all sectors of the society, a phalanx demanding change and justice that spilled along the boulevard.

The march and vigil was conducted in silence. Marchers filled the width of Herzl Boulevard and walked southward to Givat Ram. There they turned toward the capital precinct past the university campus and onto Museum Boulevard. Above them, churned two police helicopters scrutinizing events below. The gendarmerie was everywhere.

An army of domestic and foreign journalists covered the event and the proceedings were aired live. By eleven, estimates of the number of participants were between 650,000 and 750,000. As one Scandinavian broadcaster put it, "Proportionate to Israel's population, this is one of the greatest, perhaps *the* greatest single outpouring of public sentiment in modern history."

It was close to midnight when the last marchers arrived and the vigil commenced. The light of nearly a million candles shone bright and observers as far away as Mevasseret Zion, twelve kilometers away, said that it had formed a lustrous glow hovering over Jerusalem.

Remarks were kept to a minimum. Nachum Rashumi, considered the greatest Hebrew poet since Bialik, addressed the "great gathering, all the Tents of Israel assembled," and read verse he had composed for the occasion that concluded "Ascend, ascend, Oh Israel, cast off the dark mantle and rise." Naftali then read the People's Petition, a document posted on the Internet and already signed electronically by well over 500,000 citizens from all sectors of Israeli society demanding that the government call for elections within sixty days.

As the vigil disbanded, the ambassador of the Netherlands, a Jew, described the vigil as a "spiritual experience unlike anything I have ever known. I felt like I was one of the Israelites crossing the Red Sea. It was a passage, a shifting of moral weight, an awakening." The elderly leader of the country's most influential secularist organizations told a reporter, "It was a communion. We were touched by a great Spirit. The nation will never be the same."

As Lilah held Naftali's hand and clutched her candle like a flag, she looked behind her at the multitude and felt exalted. Finally, the light had begun to drown out the darkness.

At three in the morning, after they had gotten back from Jerusalem the two couples, Lilah and Naftali, Issam and Michal were in a celebratory mood. They were hungry and decided that a meal of Middle Eastern salads and pita with baked cheese and *za'atar* from al-Salim's, the all night eatery in Old Jaffa was just the thing. They phoned in their order and Naftali and Issam headed out to retrieve it.

Naftali had sent his driver home in his official vehicle. In high spirits, the two men left 3 HaGaon Street and headed down the block toward Lilah's car. It had been returned some days earlier from Kiryat Zebulon by one of Eli's men, and she had parked it outside her building just before she left for the vigil.

Naftali and Issam squeezed into Lilah's car and once they were belted, Naftali put the key in the ignition and turned it.

The ensuing blast was deafening.

CHAPTER NINETEEN

By dawn, the police had cordoned off three blocks in radius around Lilah's apartment building. There, units of the bomb-sniffing dogs and their handlers who had been deployed at the vigil that same evening had been rushed back on duty to Lilah's neighborhood. Explosive experts were on the scene along with two companies of firefighters who were hosing down the remains of what had been Lilah's automobile. Municipal workers were beginning to sweep up the glass and debris left by the explosion up and down HaGaon Street. The police were interviewing local residents to determine if anyone or anything unusual had been seen in the area prior to the bombing.

Eli entered the apartment and approached Lilah.

"You have my deepest sympathy," he offered.

"Thank you," she responded in a whisper, her head bent in grief. She could not raise her eyes.

Ido arrived a few moments later and sat next to his mother on the couch. He removed his beret and buried his face in her breast and sobbed. She embraced him, silently crying and running her fingers through his hair.

Eli found it difficult to watch their grief, Lilah's and that of her son, the young colonel he had read about in the background reports. He thought it right to give them privacy, leave them to their sorrow. Also, with the ante having been upped by the Sons of Gideon, there were things he must now attend to. He spent a few minutes getting briefed by the police detectives who had established themselves in Lilah's kitchen. All that could be done on the scene was being done he assured Lilah and Ido. They were safe for now. He would return, he promised.

The irony, of course, was that Naftali and Issam weren't slated to be slain. The person that had been targeted was Lilah and only by chance had she lived and they died.

The shock of the nation at the death of parliamentarian and

New Democratic Party chairman, Prof. Naftali Kedem, along with his friend and comrade, heart surgeon Dr. Issam Halaby, was deepened by the murder that same evening of another prominent Israeli. The Sons of Gideon claimed responsibility for all three of the slayings.

The statement that was phoned into the Voice of Israel minutes after Lilah's car exploded stated:

> *What we did tonight to the traitor Lilah Kedem and to Police Commander Mordechai Carmi should serve as a warning to all Jews. We have been divinely directed to render the Land of Israel pure of all alien presence. The Arabs must be cast out, and any Jew who interferes with our mission will be included in the body count.*
> *Don't try to stop us. We are unstoppable.*
>
> *Abide by us,*
> *Sons of Gideon*

For all their bluster and vaunting, the Sons of Gideon had now suffered a series of blunders – their lairs in Romema and Ma'ale Adumim had been discovered, their code had been interpreted and the attack at Arka al-Khitab foiled. Now they had bungled the attempt on Lilah's life and persisted in believing that Carmi was directing the search for them. Eli, of course, knew that was false and given the group's sophistication, he thought they would have known as well. The man they wanted was him, Eli.

Were they growing weary? Eli wondered. Had they been worn thin?

Eli returned to his office and found his email inbox bursting with messages. He had just begun to review them when a call came in from the ballistics unit. The serial number of the shoulder-fired missile that had wrecked the Ben-Abraham apartment had been identified. It was part of an ordnance lot missing from an army base near Arad. As for the explosives that had ripped through Lilah's car, they were traced to a shipment hijacked the previous week from a truck belonging to a Negev mining concern, also near Arad.

Eli assigned an investigator to follow the trail of the stolen materiel. The military police were asked to examine the records of all soldiers who had at any time come into contact with the missing items. Names were gathered, fed into the computer and cross-referenced.

There was also new information in the form of an account of the attack on Carmi given by his girlfriend. She had seen a woman straddling a motorcycle near Carmi's car. As the couple approached, the rider made a sudden U-turn so tightly that the motorcycle brushed against them. The woman on the motorcycle stared at Carmi with a look of horror on her face. "But you're not the one," she muttered in a panicked voice that sounded surprisingly deep to Carmi's girlfriend. The motorcyclist then sped away, leaving a black trail of rubber down the entire block.

Carmi told his girlfriend to wait where she was and then ran to his car, evidently intent on chasing the motorcycle. He got in and put the key in the ignition and started the engine. That set off the explosion that killed him.

The meaning of the comment, "but you're not the one," was clear to Eli, as he was the one the assassins were targeting. The assailant he had fought with at Arka al-Khitab had come back to finish him off, believing he was Carmi. But he had fought a man at the Bedouin hamlet, of that he was sure. No one else had been at the village when they fought that night. How did the motorcyclist know what he did or didn't look like? Was Carmi's killer and the man he had fought with the same guy in drag? Were they the brother and sister Ya'akovi?

As Eli shuttled between the various security agencies throughout the afternoon, he had the feeling that things were moving toward resolution, that he would soon be able to make sense of the puzzle. He was grateful for that. He would deliver up the Sons of Gideon soon. Once and for all. He could feel it.

Throughout the meetings he held that day and the paperwork that followed, Lilah was very much on Eli's mind. One of the emails he had received had been from the Shin Bet profiler who warned that the Gideons "share a syndrome of past guilt and shame and can't tolerate criticism or the humiliation of failure. They will likely seek revenge." He suggested that they might – probably would – try to correct their most recent failure, the botched attempt on the Na'aleh spokeswoman, Lilah Kedem.

He must protect her, Eli concluded. He must make right what he had been unable to do when he was a boy. Then, he had been unable to save his mother before she was swept away by the churning waters of the river in his dream. This time, he would shield the woman with his mother's eyes.

It was, though, nearly eleven o'clock that night before Eli could return to Lilah's apartment. There had been so much to do.

A sheet covered the mirror in the front hallway. Lilah's eyes were puffy, veined in bright red and ringed in black. She looked as though she was crying, without tears, without sound. Her blouse had been cut with scissors at the collar. Lilah sat low on the couch, the cushions had been removed. She was in stocking feet. A Jewish house of mourning.

Through the crowd of condolence callers, Lilah spotted Eli as he entered the room. She walked over to him and embraced him.

Eli had not anticipated such a welcome, nor had he expected her hospitality and concern. "Eli, go into the kitchen and get yourself something to eat. You probably haven't eaten all day," she said to him.

"I'm fine, really," Eli said. "How are you holding up?"

"As well as can be expected, I guess," she sighed sadly. Lilah was then swallowed up by visitors who vied for her attention. Eli withdrew to the kitchen.

Twenty minutes later, Eli had just finished eating from a plate of food an elderly woman had served him when Lilah appeared in the kitchen looking for him. "I'm sorry we were interrupted," she said. "You're probably here for information," she said solicitously. "How can I help you?"

"No, that's not why I am here. I'm…" he hesitated for a moment, then declared, "I'm here because the ones who killed Naftali may very well seek a second chance against you. It's best that I remain here and supervise the guards posted to protect you."

"You mean you want to stay here to guard me? Aren't those men outside the door and downstairs enough?"

"Who knows what is enough? I would like to be here, personally," said Eli. "I assure you that I will be discreet and that your privacy will be respected."

"That's not the issue. I trust you. Michal is sleeping in one room, and my son is using the other. Can you make yourself comfortable in the living room?"

"I won't be sleeping. Just a place for me to put my feet up and rest is sufficient. The living room is fine."

It was well after midnight when the apartment finally emptied of visitors. Exhausted beyond words, Lilah brought Eli a towel and some linens and told him to help himself to anything else he needed. Before she entered her bedroom, the room that had been her safest haven since she had been a girl, Eli insisted on inspecting it. He assessed the line of sight through the window and only after he was satisfied that there were enough obstacles to a sniper's shots and that there was no ledge for an intruder to stand on, he nodded his approval and wished Lilah good night.

Once Lilah locked her bedroom door, Eli reconnoitered the

rest of the apartment. Concluding there was little else he could do to make things more secure, he established himself on an easy chair and lay his pistol on a small table within easy reach.

Eli kept the room darkened, switching off all the lights but a solitary lamplight. He nursed a cup of coffee. And then another.

At first, he sat stiffly in the chair scrutinizing the darkness, but when it became clear that the evening would in all likelihood be long, boring and uneventful, Eli relaxed. He had his own men stationed downstairs along with the police. He removed his shoes, loosened his trousers and propped himself in semi-repose on the couch.

There was a feel, an ambiance about this place that Eli found calming. It was strange, he thought, that he felt at ease in Lilah's apartment. Munching on the food she had left out for him, he picked up a picture book – one of Lilah's – and thumbed through it, fascinated by the contents: Carnival in Brazil, Oktoberfest in Germany, crowded back streets and alleys of Hong Kong, an African tribal celebration. Suddenly, he felt a hunger to see the world, the world as Lilah knew it.

As he peered at her photographs, he concluded that Lilah was extraordinarily sensitive from the way she had recorded these places. He gazed into the eyes of a Zulu child in Soweto and understood what Lilah had meant for the viewer to find there: the ravages of apartheid. Her picture of a Dutch female construction worker, robust in her hard hat, cradling a baby in one arm, holding a bottle of beer in the other, made Eli laugh. Then he came to photos of Somali women and children, refugees precariously adrift on a rickety raft tossed on turbulent waves with looks of terror on their faces. The message – that human cruelty knows no bounds – was abundantly clear.

This was the work of a special person, Eli thought. He felt admiration for Lilah, whose eyes were like Deborah's, his mother, a woman of valor.

His reverie was disrupted when he heard the door to Lilah's

room opening. In the darkness he made out her silhouette.

"Hello Eli," she said. She smiled softly, sadly.

"Can't you sleep?" he asked. "It's only four."

"No, I'm completely awake," she replied. She walked into the kitchen with him trailing behind her. She filled a kettle with water and placed it on the stove.

"Don't you have any sleeping pills or something to ease your nerves?" Eli asked.

"The doctor left me something, but I want to be as much myself tomorrow as possible."

"Yes, of course, I understand," Eli said. He felt he wanted to say something supportive, comforting. "You are a very strong person, obviously. Still, you must accept help if you need it."

Lilah sat down at the table and invited him to join her. "And you? Are you ever off-duty? Do you have a life other than chasing terrorists?"

"Once I have the Sons of Gideon in a secure cage, I'll take it easier."

She nodded. She put out some salads and breads. They ate quietly. Conversation came slowly.

"I was looking at some of your photographs in the living room. They are impressive. I was really touched," Eli said.

"Thank you," said Lilah.

"How long have you been working as a photographer?"

"Forever, I think sometimes. As a professional, over thirty years."

"It must be satisfying to do that kind of work. It's an art, it seems."

"It is gratifying – most of the time."

"You've traveled a lot."

"Too much, perhaps."

"You're very fortunate to have seen the world."

"Fortunate? Yes, in many ways very, very fortunate and lucky that my work has been received as well as it has. But, as I said, I was away from home a lot and my family paid the price. I spent much more time out of the country than I should have." Eli watched Lilah well up with emotion, an upsurge of grief and regret that flowed from her heart into her shoulders, her neck, then into her face and eyes. She held it at first, only droplets brimmed onto her lashes. But then, a moment later, she said with infinite sorrow, "I lost many, many years when Naftali and I could have been together. And Ido might have had a normal family rather than the gypsy life I forced on him," she said, her lips trembling. Then the dam gave way and Lilah began crying.

Eli reached out across the table and took her hand, holding it as gently as he could. He wanted to get up and hug her but did not. He meant to respect her, not burden her with anything that might be misconstrued. Lilah seemed to sense that. She stopped crying, allowed only quiet tears, then slowly stanched those away.

"Yes, I've seen the world. And the people I have met and photographed made it worth it."

"People dream of that all their lives. How many Israelis travel abroad and do not return."

"Would you?" Lilah asked.

"Me? Of course I'd come back home. I mean it's always nice to see different parts of the world and experience them for short periods of time. But to live? No, Israel is where a Jew belongs."

"I think so, too," said Lilah.

"You do?" Eli asked, surprised.

"Of course," Lilah said as she sliced a bread roll.

"Then why do you dwell on our problems? The picture that you and your friends paint certainly isn't going to attract Israelis to return or Jews from abroad to come and live here."

"Knowing that there are Israelis here who share their values might be the only way to get many of those who left to return."

"Tell me, there's something I don't understand. Why are

you people so worried about the way that Arabs get treated here? Why is it such a major issue?"

"Because I am a Jew and Jews are interested in justice."

"Then you should worry about Jews first. No one else gives a damn about us. Your criticism gives comfort to our enemies, to people who don't share your values and want only to hurt us."

"Anti-Semites and enemies of Israel don't wait around looking for excuses to hate us," Lilah said sharply.

This line of conversation elapsed as Lilah brewed coffee.

"You've really got a handle on the world, don't you? You've got it all figured out," Eli said. It was an odd comment of admiration that seemed to come out of nowhere.

"I'm not sure I know what you mean. Is that an insult or a compliment?"

"I mean I admire your commitment to your principles. A woman like you could easily keep her head in the sand, lead the good life and not give a damn about what's going on outside of her bubble."

"What good is a life like that? It ends with you. Nothing survives. Besides, for the better part of the last thirty years, I did just as you said, at least as far as Israel was concerned."

"It seems to me that you were busy trying to help the people whose pictures you were taking."

"That's true, but taking care of your own people takes precedence."

"So that's what you think of yourself as doing now, taking care of your own? You know something, Lilah? There's one thing our enemies could never accuse you of. They could never say that you don't care. But enough is enough. You've made your contribution to the cause. It's time for you to stop making yourself a target for a bunch of raving, violent madmen like the Sons of Gideon."

"Do you think they could possibly stop me from following

my conscience?"

"Surely after what's happened, you're going to stop now."

"Not on your life. I don't turn on and off like that."

"Lilah, they tried to murder you last night. Next time, you probably won't be lucky enough to survive."

"No, the fanatics are the ones who should be worried. Did you see what happened in this land at the vigil yesterday night? Close to a million Israelis – Arabs and Jews – came together in Jerusalem to reject the hate mongers. The government is about to fall to people power. Don't you see the young people on the rise, marching all over the country for justice? Naftali worked his entire life for this, and we have done what he told us to do: Rise. Don't wait for the politicians to lead, he urged us, lead them. Put power in the hands of the people. We've accomplished this and now the majority is about to take back control over our collective lives," Lilah declared. Her tone was a mixture of regret, anger and triumph.

"Why do you want to keep tempting fate? What more do you want?" Eli challenged.

"The people want a new era, and that means putting an end to the Sons of Gideon and this visionless, incompetent, self-interested government. I want it so that none of their ilk ever finds fertile ground in my country, not in my lifetime nor that of my son and of his children after him."

"You keep this up and you'll never know your son's children. You are on their list. They want you dead, don't you understand?" Eli hurled the words. He rose from his seat and walked out of the kitchen burning with worry about this woman.

"Look who's talking," Lilah shouted after him, following him into the living room. "Barely two weeks ago, you went after them and almost didn't make it back. But you still spend night and day pursuing them. So why don't you throw in the towel before they get you?"

"Because I won't put up with filth like that on my turf, not in my country. They are beasts," he spat out, "who will destroy this one chance in two thousand years for us to be masters of our own destiny. There's no going back for us. This is our last stand."

"I guess the difference between us is that I don't think the country is so fragile. I don't think it needs to be coddled. You do. I think Israel is strong enough to fix whatever's wrong and recover, improve without limit. You think it needs to be protected and spared any challenges. Any way you look at it, the extremists are a plague. We agree on that. For the sake of what we both hold dear, the Sons of Gideon have to be stopped."

"I won't let you walk through the lion's den alone," said Eli.

Lilah nodded, acknowledging what he said. Moments passed in silence as if some kind of understanding between them had been reached.

The funeral had been scheduled for Sunday afternoon. It had taken that long for Naftali's brother to return home from Perth, where he was on sabbatical.

Dawn had broken that morning to thunderous rain.

"Not all at once," said Ido as Eli drove them through the downpour to Kibbutz Ramat Zion, where the men, Naftali and Issam would be buried together. The kibbutz was the only place where the martyrs who had died together could be buried alongside each other. The gatekeepers, both the Jewish and Moslem clerics would not have their respective graveyards compromised by the presence of an unbeliever. "Just let us get them into their resting place," Ido said almost as a prayer, "don't wash them away."

Ido rode in the passenger seat next to Eli, occasionally trading small talk, but mainly just peering into the grim, steady rain. Lilah and Michal took turns crying. They held each other in the back seat of the car, huddled under their raiment of sorrow en route to bury their men.

The government, trying to find ways to forestall the mandate delivered in the People's Petition calling for it to resign, sought to appease. They had agreed to the New Democrats demand that Naftali and Issam be given a state funeral. They had enough sense to realize that it was not only what the Party wanted. The people would have it no other way.

After they arrived, as they walked toward the kibbutz burial grounds, Eli hovered over Lilah. He held the large umbrella over her with one hand, his right placed softly on her back. A "guardian angel" is how Lilah described him to any friends or family who asked about Lilah's attentive shadow.

The prayer leader was intoning the *El Ma'ale Rachamim* prayer and Naftali was being lowered into his grave when a Shin Bet man tapped Eli on the shoulder and handed him a piece of paper. The message was short and straightforward. The moshavnik – the veteran of US special services in Iraq he had been seeking – had something to tell Eli, something important that might help.

Chapter Twenty

"I came as soon as I heard you called," said Eli, leaning against a rail in the moshavnik's milking shed. He had raced the three hours from Ramat Zion to the desert moshav in the afternoon heat.

"There's some beer in the refrigerator by the desk, back there in the office," said the former detective. "Help yourself," he added, as he adjusted the milking tubes under the udder of one of his cows. His movements were quick and jerky. He seemed to be constantly scanning his surroundings in a paranoid manner.

"Thanks," said Eli as he wiped the perspiration from his face with a paper towel the moshavnik had handed him. "It may be February, but it feels more like August to me," he commented. "I just came from the Kedem and Halaby funerals in the North. It was pouring up there. The air was chilly," Eli added.

The moshavnik seemed disinterested in small talk.

"So you have something for me?" Eli asked.

"Maybe," said the moshavnik. He activated a switch on the control panel and a vacuum swooshed loudly in response. He shouted above the din as he continued to work. "For the record, I only heard that you've been looking for me yesterday. That's when my wife got around to telling me that you phoned," he said.

"When I spoke with your secretary," he continued, "she told me a little about what this is about, told me how I might be of help. She made sure I understood about this being urgent and the connection to, you know, the Sons of Gideon. This being of national importance and all, I decided to do my part, and see if I could get some information off the street. That's something I am experienced at and that's why you contacted me," he said, his eye cocked at Eli, awaiting affirmation.

Eli nodded.

"So I got someone to cover my milkings yesterday and went to some bars in Tel Aviv, places that not many Israelis hang out, but certain foreigners do: UN troops, soldiers of fortune, arms dealers and others who are engaged in, shall we say, military pursuits.

"When I first came to Israel," he continued as he rolled up and disengaged the hoses, "I used to spend a lot of time in those dives. Sometimes, I'd come across someone like me who had done a tour in the Gulf," he said distantly, morosely. "Anyway, I went to this one place late last night. I didn't recognize anyone there except for this sleazy cracker-asshole from Alabama who moved here and has managed to leech off the Welfare Ministry for the past who knows how many years."

The moshavnik stopped working for a moment. He untwisted a pack of cigarettes from the upturned sleeve of his T-shirt. He lit a cigarette and sucked in the smoke as if it were marijuana. An anxious vigilance pervaded his pockmarked, thick-mustached face as if he were continuously on watch, on the lookout for some peril lurking in the desert darkness. The cigarette calmed the man. He went on talking. "So this guy and I share a table and throw back a few beers last night. We're bullshitting, reminiscing. He's having chasers with his beers, and I could see he was pretty wasted. I start making some vague comments about there not being very many U.S. vets around Israel these days. He tells me about a few he knows, including one who might be of interest to you," he said, gazing at Eli.

"I'm listening," Eli said.

"Well, he starts telling me about this guy who's been in the country off and on for the past couple of years. A real tumbleweed, a lost soul. The fellow I'm drinking with starts telling me how weird this other guy is."

"What do you mean by weird?" Eli asked.

"I'm getting to it," the moshavnik snapped sharply. Eli

recalled he had read something about the man, some kind of a personality problem mentioned in his file.

The moshavnik calmed himself, then continued. "He meant that the other guy's a loner, a big tank of a man who's shy and withdrawn – most of the time. He said this other vet would come to the pub now and then, once every few weeks or so, and would be real tame, sitting at the bar all by himself, barely speaking to anybody. But a couple of times, he'd come in real self-possessed, in a cocksure mood, pleased as punch with himself and ready to roll. He'd have a few drinks and then start shooting off his mouth, bragging about this or that fight he'd gotten into, stuff like that. Then he'd go on about all the ragheads he had blown away on the road to Kuwait City and all the Africans and Asians he had popped off in other places. He'd be all full of bravado – but only sometimes. Most of the time, as the other guy tells the story, this vet is a pussycat."

"Interesting," said Eli, "so what do you think the story is?"

"That's what I was wondering. Don't know, can't say for sure, but the guy sounds like a real live wire. My drinking partner was getting pretty ripped and he was wagging his tongue something fierce. He tells me that this other guy, the psycho case, had talked about how Israeli Arabs and the leftie Jews ought to be blown away, that he couldn't stand them, and that he had already taken care of a few anyway."

"When was this, supposedly?" Eli asked, hungry for any information.

"Hold your horses, my friend," the moshavnik shot angrily."I used to be a cop, remember? That's why you came to see me in the first place. So trust me, okay? If you don't, well, hell – just decide if you want my help or not."

"Sorry," Eli apologized, taken aback. He remembered details he had read in the ex-detective's personnel file, something about the man "being quick to anger" and "lashes out," and that he "constantly seeks validation and expressions of confidence from colleagues and superiors" – those being the reasons he had been given a disability discharge from the Israel Police.

"I'm sorry I interrupted you," Eli said apologetically. "The tension of this case, you know, I guess it's just getting to me. Please go on, the intelligence you have collected could be pivotal to our breaking it."

The man was pacified. He continued. "This cat I'm drinking with tells me on the sly, in a real low voice, that this other character and some of his friends were behind things that were driving the security services crazy. As you can imagine, I wanted him to get specific but I needed to do everything I could to keep from blowing the lead. It was pretty clear to me that I was on to something that was relevant."

Eli nodded that he concurred. The moshavnik lit yet another cigarette. Then continued.

"This loser across the table from me starts telling me that the other guy had come to the bar a few weeks before, real high and maniacal, bragging about how he and his buddies were doing some pretty grand wasting of the enemy, meaning lefty sorts and Arabs. He said that they would be even more productive if they hadn't run into problems getting guns and explosives."

The moshavnik stopped talking for a few moments. He drew on his cigarette, looking as if he was drifting away to some other place, some other time. Eli waited patiently for him to come back to himself. Finally, he resumed.

"I took a chance," he confessed to Eli. "I don't know if you'll think it a good idea or not, but I felt like I was on to something and that I had to nail it down. I told my drinking buddy that I knew where this guy we were talking about could get supplies. I said that I had a friend who was in the business of selling guns and military hardware. I went on to tell my drinking partner that he stood to make some bucks for introducing me to the psycho killer. He was real hot about that, asking me what a 'few bucks' meant. I said that my friend usually paid a finder's fee of $500 in cash for someone referring potential clients. When I asked him if he could set up a meeting, he said he could try but that he didn't know very much about the guy he had been talking to except that he was a loner, that he lived in Jerusalem and that he was known as the Walrus. Now, does that name mean anything to you?" the moshavnik asked Eli.

"A sea mammal, right?"

"Yeah, but there's more to it than that," the moshavnik said. "When I spoke with your assistant, she asked me if I had heard about an operation called 'Magical Mystery Tour.' Something about a code the Gideons used."

"Yes," Eli confirmed, recalling the name for a military operation that the attaché at the American Embassy had mentioned, a campaign in Kuwait where the code used by the Sons of Gideon had also been used in the early 1990s.

"Well, *Magical Mystery Tour* is an album by the Beatles. It's a real psychedelic record, with all these bizarre symbols and lyrics. On one song, there is a character who proclaims that he's the Walrus, whatever that's supposed to mean. I'm thinking this has got to be more than just a coincidence, the people you are looking for being involved in an operation called 'Magical Mystery Tour' and someone who sounds like he has plenty to do with the Gideons' attacks is nicknamed the Walrus. Do you see what I mean?"

"Yes, I follow you," Eli said.

"So that's the score," the moshavnik concluded. "I arranged it so that if the guy I drank with gets in touch with the Walrus, and if he's still interested in buying guns, then he can meet me at the bar tomorrow around ten in the morning," he said, as he sprayed down the cows and milking pens with a high pressure hose. "So how do you want to handle this?" he asked Eli.

"You think this is a viable lead, don't you?" Eli asked rhetorically.

"I don't waste my time," said the moshavnik. "I'm busy enough with Daisy and Holly and all the other girls here," he said, patting a cow on the head.

"This could be dangerous. Are you willing to meet with him?"

"These bastards have to get caught, don't they? And I am a sworn lawman, or at least I was," he laughed a hollow, self-deprecating cackle. "Besides, I've been in dangerous places before."

"About this bar, would someone, say the health authorities or the income tax people, be likely to find violations of standing regulations or some other such violation?" Eli asked.

"The place is about as raunchy as they come, if that's what you mean. The owner is running craps or prostitution, or both from rooms in the back. The furnishings are beaten up and when I go there, I drink only directly from a closed factory bottle. The glasses and everything else are filthy. They must be paying off someone to turn a blind eye."

"Good, it's always easier to enlist a proprietor's cooperation under those conditions." Eli said. "Just give me the name and address of the place and we'll set up for your rendezvous. We'll wire you – if that's alright with you," Eli quickly added, "and I'll be outside in a van listening in on your conversation. When we hear enough to justify an arrest, we'll move in and take the Walrus. I'll be there with plenty of backup, but he won't even feel that we're around. I am going to want to have a nice long talk with him afterward, so we'll be very careful that no one gets hurt."

"Sounds good to me," said the moshavnik.

"Can you meet me here at nine in the morning?" Eli asked, writing out the address of his office on a slip of paper.

The moshavnik took the paper and nodded.

"I think we're seeing some light at the end of the tunnel in this case. I can't tell you what a help you've been."

The moshavnik had already withdrawn, retreating to a fortress within himself.

Eli didn't rush back to Tel Aviv. The Sons of Gideon were within reach, their invincibility was cracking and Eli wanted to carefully prepare the final coup. He was also hungry, the first genuine hunger he'd felt in a long time. He stopped at a roadside grill and ordered a steak. Then he ordered another.

The heat of the day had broken and suddenly the air felt cool and moist and cleansing. It added to Eli's sense, embraced with caution, that he would soon have the Sons of Gideon in hand. Eli dared to imagine the relief that would come with closure.

As he drove northbound through the dusk and into the darkness on his way to Tel Aviv, Eli thought of Lilah. He was thinking of all that Lilah had seen in the world and that she had returned home to Israel and was committed to making it a better place. Eli also wanted to make Israel a better place, rid it once and for all of twisted souls like the Sons of Gideon.

Gradually, as Eli drove on, drops of rain began gently tapping on the windshield. As he got on the main highway, the rain increased and there was faint lightning and low thunder in the distance.

As he continued north, the flashes of light in the darkening sky came faster and fiercer, and the roar of the thunder grew louder. Something came to mind, something he had memorized in the past:

> *When you marched from the field of Edom,*
> *The earth trembled and the heavens poured,*
> *The clouds also poured water.*
> *The mountains gushed before the Lord,*
> *This Sinai, because the presence of the Lord.*

It was a verse from the Book of Judges, the Song of

Deborah. He had committed the entire book, Judges 5, to memory. It is what he had chosen as the subject for his Bible class project in high school. He chose it because of the connection to his mother, Deborah.

As the rain grew heavier and the traffic backed up, Eli began remembering more of the Book:

> *The open cities ceased,*
> *In Israel they ceased,*
> *Until I Deborah arose;*
> *I arose as a mother in Israel.*

The rain became torrential and there was little visibility through the drops splattering against the windshield. The flashes of light fractured the sky and thunder boomed. On the approach to Route Six just north of Beersheva, drivers began pulling their cars off the road onto the shoulder. Eli decided to pull over as well.

In the darkness, with the rain drumming on the roof, Eli turned off the windshield wipers and closed his eyes. He recalled more from the Book of Deborah and began reciting the verses, feeling as he had felt then, imagining his mother's countenance before him, a woman of valor, her eyes, Lilah's eyes: true, full of love and caring – and determination:

> *When they chose new gods, then*
> *There were wars in the cities...*
>
> *My heart is toward the lawgivers of Israel,*
> *That offered themselves willingly among the people...*
> *Instead of the noise of the adversaries,*
> *Between the places of drawing water,*
> *There they will tell the righteous acts of the Lord,*
> *The righteous acts of restoring open cities in Israel.*
> *Then the people of the Lord went down to the cities,*
> *Praise! Deborah. Praise! Praise!*

He recited the verses again. Then again, the words dropping from his lips likes leaves from a tree. It calmed him, a respite, intimations of tranquility.

Eli remained parked along the shoulder until the rain tapered off and the other drivers began returning onto the highway.

He resumed the trip, anxious to bring the battle to its end.

Redemption he hoped. Redemption.

Eli arrived at his office and systematically arranged the logistics of the meeting with the Walrus. He would leave nothing to chance. He contacted Amos, explained the operation and asked for a squad of select Shin Bet agents to work with his own team. He needed the best people, people who could handle the operation adroitly and with expertise. Amos agreed to Eli's request. The agents would convene at Eli's office during the next few hours.

Eli found the name and home address of the bar owner. He and his team would pay him a visit by sunrise and insure his cooperation.

The knock at the door came just as the night slipped away. "Go away," a husky male voice shouted sleepily from inside the decrepit south Tel Aviv apartment. Eli and his agents pulled their guns – more for effect than defense – and knocked heavily a second time. "Security forces!" Eli yelled. "Open the door now!"

"What's this about?" an obese, middle-aged man wrapped in a towel nervously asked as he opened the door.

"Keep your hands where I can see them," Eli said harshly as he pushed his pistol into the man's flank. "On your head, both hands. Come on!" Eli shouted. The man obeyed and the towel fell down, adding just the right amount of humiliation to secure submission. Eli pushed him back into the apartment and had him sit in a living room chair, guarded by one of his men.

The agent who had been covering the back door was

admitted into the apartment, and he and other security men fanned out, searching for any illegalities they could pin on the bar owner.

"There's a hash pipe and powder, looks like cocaine, in here, Eli. The pipe's been used very recently, the embers are still warm," one of the men shouted from the dining room.

Another agent barged into the bedroom; a young girl screamed as he did so. "I think our friend is looking at a statutory rape charge," he shouted to Eli. "This girl's no more than fourteen." The girl grabbed her clothes and fled the room.

"There are all sorts of foreign currency under the mattress and a pistol," the agent continued. "Make that two guns. No, three."

"Okay," Eli said, staring coldly at the man. "We've got you on guns, drugs and statutory rape. That in itself should keep you locked away for quite some time. Add to that certain activities that we've heard take place at your little entertainment establishment and you're looking at being jammed up for an awfully long time," Eli said gravely.

"I'm not saying a word until I talk to my lawyer..."

Eli cut him off. "You're damn right you're not saying a word. I'm doing all the talking. In return for us not immediately tossing you into prison, you're going to cooperate with us, aren't you?" The man said nothing. Eli went on. "You're a smart guy and that's why you are going to do exactly what I say."

Fifteen minutes later, they were at the crumbling neighborhood near the beach, not far from the Carmel market. The sun was just rising.

While the bar owner, covered by an agent, opened the tavern, Eli and his technical crew scouted the street and determined the deployment of personnel and equipment. They planned where each of the agents would be positioned and where the monitoring equipment and video cameras would be placed. The tables and chairs were moved so that they could quickly hustle the suspect out of the bar.

By 7:45, all the plans were finalized and all of Eli's team members were assembled. The field agents were briefed inside the bar while the technicians, working out of a bogus building contractor's truck, began installing the monitoring equipment. The equipment was in place and tested. The agents had two run-throughs of the stakeout.

Satisfied that everything was in order, Eli returned to his office to work the phones and to arrange a secure holding place in the Prisons Service or Shin Bet facilities to take the suspect after his arrest. He dispatched one of his men to sign out $500 in marked bills, along with a cloth hood from Police Central Investigations – the latter so that neither the press nor anyone else would get a glimpse of the suspect before Eli was ready to publicly identify him. Eli visited the office of a Shin Bet doctor who provided him with a syringe containing a fast-acting sedative in case the suspect had to be restrained before transport.

Eli arrived back at his office ten minutes later than the appointed meeting time with the moshavnik. The moshavnik was already there, on edge and angry that he had been kept waiting.

"If this is how you are going to run the operation, I want out," the moshavnik barked.

"We were just making the final preparations," Eli said, his tone expiatory. He couldn't afford to lose the man's cooperation now as things were peaking. Within minutes, a technician had wired the moshavnik with a microphone taped under his shirt. He was also given the cash that he would in turn give the go-between for making the arms deal referral.

The moshavnik was driven to the area of the stakeout in an unmarked truck. Eli and the technician took a cab to the bar and entered the contractor's truck, the operation's forward command post.

At 9:50, from inside the van, Eli watched as the moshavnik walked eastward down the street, pausing in front of the bar and lighting a cigarette as planned. Eli checked with the agents inside the bar. They signaled that they were ready. The operatives took their assigned places at tables and at the counter.

The moshavnik entered the café at 9:58.

The first twelve minutes of waiting seemed to last forever. From his cramped position in the truck, Eli was thinking about the moshavnik's unusual, almost belligerent behavior in the dairy the day before and then again at the office this morning. Feeling the exhaustion of another night with little sleep, Eli's thoughts became vulnerable to doubts about the informant and the operation, all sorts of "What ifs?" Not the least of these was the possibility that the moshavnik himself was a member of the Sons of Gideon.

The prospect was eclipsed when at 10:13 the monitor inside the truck showed a large woman walking toward the bar. The woman looked hauntingly familiar to Eli, and he had the technician focus the image of her. She was dressed in a skirt and long-sleeved blouse and her hair was covered with a scarf. Eli couldn't be certain, but at this distance she resembled the woman in Lilah's photograph who had planted the bomb in the bleachers at Kibbutz Ramat Zion. Suddenly, the rendezvous seemed bona fide; a member of the terror group had arrived.

On the screen showing the view from the other direction, Eli saw a man walking up from the other, shorter end of the street. The woman stopped him. With no microphone near where they stood, Eli couldn't hear the conversation between them. He had the technician focus and enlarge the image. The man seemed not to know the woman, though she appeared to have been looking for him. Walking toward the bar, they had a short exchange of words.

The man seemed jarred, irritated as he conversed with the woman. He seemed reluctant to walk into the bar. Finally he did so while the woman waited outside.

"Hey, my friend," the moshavnik said as the man entered from the street. He waited for him to take a seat at his table. "I thought you might have forgotten our appointment."

"No, I didn't forget," the man said.

"So did you find your friend?"

"Yes, we spoke last night. He said he'd be here this morning."

"Is he one of the creeps in here?" the moshavnik asked quietly of the other people, Eli's men, interspersed in the bar.

"No," said the man, without looking at the agents. "The Walrus isn't coming."

"He isn't coming? I thought he told you he would be here this morning."

"Well he isn't. He's sent some Jew-bitch – damn if she doesn't look like a female version of him – who just stopped me on my way in and said that the Walrus sent her with a message. She says she represents the Walrus and that he wants you to go ahead with the meeting, that she'll take the Walrus' place. I can't vouch for her – for all I know, she's a cop. So it's up to you to decide if you want her to come in for a meeting."

Eli watched as the moshavnik fell silent, obviously trying to decide what to do. The ex-detective slid his key chain off the table and leaned down, looking for guidance from the security men seated nearby.

"Signal him to go ahead and meet the woman," Eli directed one of the operatives through his in-ear speaker. The agent discreetly nodded affirmatively to the moshavnik.

"Alright, what do I have to lose? Sure, bring her in," he said to the man seated across from him.

"I'll send her in, but I won't come with her. You're on your own."

"I didn't know you were the nervous type," the moshavnik said acidly to the intermediary. "Send her in," he added.

"What about my broker's fee? Where is it?"

"I've got it, but you haven't exactly held up your end of the deal."

"I sure as hell have," the man said angrily, jumping nervously to his feet. "Give it up or I'll trash the meeting."

"Hey, hey, my man, take it easy," said the moshavnik. He reached into his shirt pocket and withdrew the cash. "Here it is," he said, begrudgingly handing over the money.

The man counted the bills, grunted goodbye and began exiting the bar.

"Make sure she comes in," the moshavnik hollered after him.

Outside, the man approached the woman. He spoke hurriedly to her, then rushed off. The woman then entered the bar.

"She's the one we want to take, but don't move until I give you the go-ahead," he instructed his the agents.

Despite her gawky appearance and the oddity of a religious woman in a dingy bar at 10:00 a.m., the woman was grinning affably as she sat down at the moshavnik's table.

"Hi! The Walrus sent me," she said with an unmistakably American inflection.

"Oh yeah?" the moshavnik said coolly. "What about?"

"About a transfer of technology, you could say." The woman smiled coyly. Eli asked the technician if he was getting all of this on tape. He was.

"What kind of technology are we talking about?" asked the moshavnik. "I want to make sure we are talking about the same thing." he said.

"Don't fuck with me," the woman said. Her tone suddenly changed. It became more natural – deep and masculine. "I'm looking for explosives and fuses – American military issue –

and ammunition."

"What would you need that kind of stuff for? I've got to know the nature of the enterprise if I am going to get you the right stuff."

The woman said nothing.

"Well?" the moshavnik pressed. "What kind of operation will you be pulling off?"

"Scorched earth," she seethed. "Scorched earth."

Eli recognized the phrase from several of the Sons of Gideon's communiqués. He concluded that the moshavnik was face to face with Shoshana Ya'akov nee Sandra Jacoby. "Alright, we're going to take her," Eli instructed his agents. "Give me half a minute to cross the street. In the meantime, split up and block the exits. Leave it to me to approach the woman, but be prepared to subdue her right away. Remember, don't hurt her, we need her to sing."

Eli got out of the truck and walked into the fresh air. He took a few seconds to steady his cramped legs and adjust his eyes to the bright sunlight. He crossed the street and entered the bar.

Eli walked to the counter, then slowly moved toward the suspect. The woman recognized him and rose abruptly to her feet. Two agents grabbed her, struggling to hold the massive, muscular woman, while the agent with the syringe stood poised, awaiting Eli's instructions. Another agent readied handcuffs and ankle restraints.

Within three seconds, the suspect was belly down on the floor, hands immobilized and feet in chains, her body pinned by five security agents. Eli knelt down and frisked the prisoner, the first of the Sons of Gideon he had captured. He withdrew a Magnum pistol from the suspect's shoulder holster and a hunting knife harnessed to her thigh beneath her skirt.

Eli and his men raised the stone-faced suspect to her feet. So far, she was under control and Eli motioned away the agent with the syringe. As he raised the hood over the prisoner's head, he saw the features of the man he had fought at Arka al-Khitab. He looked past the makeup deep into the suspect's face and saw dark bruises, and on more careful inspection, stitches. Under the blouse collar, a bandage covered a wound on her neck.

Eli's mind was swimming, and his knees buckled. He caught himself on the chair and steadied his legs. Eli tugged the skirt upward and felt over the underwear.

The woman was a man, the attacker he had fought at Arka al-Khitab.

ೞ ❖ ೞ

"These aren't matters one can quickly and definitively diagnose with a thermometer and stethoscope," said Professor Evyatar, one of the two expert psychiatrists sitting in the cubicle-like interrogation room close to where the Son of Gideon was being held. He and several colleagues had just spent three hours interviewing the suspect. Amos and Eli had been watching through a two-way mirror, incredulous about what they had heard and seen.

"We need more time to make a thorough observation of the patient," the professor stated. This was not the answer the two security men wanted to hear.

"The suspect," Amos emphasized, "is responsible for the death of many, many people. Other homicides could be in preparation right now. All I want is a simple yes or no. Is this character to be believed?"

"That's precisely the problem, the question of character," offered the psychiatrist. "He's been detained for less than ten hours and we've seen him for a fraction of that. It's far too early to say anything conclusive, though it appears that the detainee suffers from some kind of multiple personality syndrome including that of at least one man and one woman. You are dealing with a person who appears to have more than one ego, more than one self. Unless we have ample opportunity to observe him in a clinical setting, it is impossible to precisely determine who this person is."

"Could he be bluffing?" Eli asked, leaning in exhaustion against a wall. The room itself seemed to perspire as the two psychiatric experts and two security men debated what exactly it was that they were encountering – a patient or a prisoner. "Could this guy be taking us for a ride? The Sons of Gideon have proven to be very clever, so maybe this is just an elaborate fraud?"

"It could be, though I'd stake my reputation, even on the basis of the brief talk we've had with the prisoner, that he is seriously ill," said Dr. Leora Almog, who, though no more than thirty-five, had already earned a reputation as one of the country's foremost forensic psychiatrists. "He wasn't capable of sustaining a coherent line of thought for more than a few sentences over the course of my interview with him. Granted, in a detention center surrounded by hostile people, he's under tremendous stress and that could be producing a temporary psychotic episode in an already weak, fractured personality. But earlier, when he started screaming and nearly broke loose from his restraints, I assure you he wasn't playing games. He was given a high dose of a powerful tranquilizer over ninety minutes ago and he's still, as you can hear, terribly agitated," she said. She was referring to the shouts emanating from a room down the hall from where they sat. The doctor was so well-reasoned that Amos and Eli had no choice but to take her seriously.

"Now," she continued, "we just administered a heavy dose of another type of tranquilizer, an anti-psychotic that acts with greater subtlety. If he is, as we suspect, psychotic or in the midst of a psychotic episode, this drug will calm him and clear his thinking a bit, at least to the point where he'll be more comprehensible than he has been up to now. If he's faking, we'll know that soon too, since anti-psychotic drugs produce extremely disturbing, one could say painful effects, when taken by a non-psychotic. Now that the medication has been administered, we will soon have either a more lucid patient or a bluffer in plenty of discomfort. At that point, things should be clearer to us."

"If he is mentally ill, if he is, in effect, more than one person, could he be as crafty and effective as the Sons of Gideon have been?" Amos asked.

"Absolutely. He can be both deranged and resourceful beyond what we see in so-called normal people. A mad genius, if you will," explained Professor Evyatar. "But there's only one way to confirm that, as I have said from the start, and that's by our carefully observing him in a hospital setting, not a place like this, a prison. I can make arrangements to have him admitted to my department at the hospital and we can keep things quiet, out of the public eye and away from the press. We could have him transported by ambulance..."

"Professor," Amos interrupted, straining to control himself, "we are dealing with someone who may be the most dangerous man in the history of the country. There are major security considerations that have to be taken into account, not the least of which is his own safety. Can you imagine how many people would like to take a shot at this fellow? No, I'm sorry. I cannot authorize his being placed in a regular hospital. Whatever medical facilities you need can be provided at this institution. It's the most secure one we have, and it will have to do."

"If you insist on those conditions, then I cannot justify my continued participation," Evyatar said, as he stood to leave.

"Itamar, please wait," appealed Dr. Almog, reaching out and halting her colleague. "Could you excuse us for a few moments?" she asked Amos and Eli.

"Yes, alright," Amos said as he took Eli by the arm and led him out of the room.

They went into the nurses' room, and had a cup of coffee. "It sounds as if our friend is settling down," said Eli. The Son of Gideon's screams had turned into grunts alternating with utterances too incoherent and ill-formed to understand.

"Is it possible," asked Amos, still disbelieving as he removed a cigarette from the pack, "for one psychopath to do all this to the country? Israel has been held hostage by a single lunatic? I don't buy it and neither will anyone else."

"We might not have a choice," said Eli. "I don't know very much about psychiatry but we can't dismiss what the doctors are saying. They're tops in their field. Psychosis can do terrible things to people. Given the right conditions, those diseases can turn men into monsters."

"Even if we accept that, how are we going to put together all the pieces? As Dr. Almog said, the prisoner can't even get his names, his name, straight. How are we going to figure out whether there are any other attacks planned and how they are going to pull them off? How are we going to get him to cough up all the details of past incidents and who his accomplices are? The attack at Al-Bakr, the attack in Nablus. How could those major operations be pulled off by one person?" Amos asked, his voice quavering.

"I know it sounds outrageous, but it may be possible," Eli said faintly. He too was still far from convinced that there was only one "Son" of Gideon.

"So what are we supposed to do?" Amos asked rhetorically. "Wait forever and a day for them to confirm their diagnosis and begin to get to the bottom of who this guy really is and the personalities he's used? It might take forever. We can't wait. What if we're wrong and he isn't the only group member?"

Eli thought of Lilah and the peril she would face were the Sons of Gideon – whoever he or they were – still pursuing her.

Now that the spotlight was on the one man in custody, what if there were others lurking in the shadows, waiting for an opportunity to finish her off? Eli would not leave Lilah – and himself – vulnerable. They were both still prey for any of the assailants that remained.

Eli paused, thought deeply, seeking a course of action that would cover all the bases.

"What I propose is this: We ask our computer people to take all the data we have about the Sons of Gideon and work on modeling different scenarios to see how one man *might* have done all this – to see if it is at all possible. We can program the computers to recreate scenarios matching the reality that was created and we'll see if it can be done, physically, by one person. At the same time, we'll wait for a clearer picture from the prisoner."

Amos asked Eli to elaborate.

"We have the programmers gather all we know about the various attacks. Then try to simulate how the attacks could have been committed by a single person. For example, could one man, Moshe Ben-Avraham, possibly have had enough time and resources to carry out the assault at the Nablus school after blowing up his apartment in Ma'ale Adumim, tens of kilometers away? What would have been involved in doing so? In the bombing at Al-Bakr or Rabin Square, how could one man working alone manage to plant explosives that would go off as precisely as they did? How did he get the materials in place without anyone catching on? What is the American dimension, the connection to the Gulf War? There are thousands of pieces of data we have collected that we can now try to have the computers piece together."

They were summoned back into the meeting with the psychiatrists.

As they walked back toward the room where the doctors waited, Amos took Eli by the arm and whispered, "I'm skeptical, but we don't have an alternative. You work on modeling the scenarios while the doctors work on the prisoner," Amos said.

Professor Evyatar had been persuaded to stay on the case – under the condition that special quarters be set aside for the detainee at the prison. Amos agreed to the stipulation and ordered the Israel Prisons Service to have part of the hospital wing vacated of other prisoners and isolated. The prisoner would be seen only by the medical team handpicked by Prof. Evyatar and Dr. Almog. Security would be handled exclusively by Eli and his men.

This being Israel, word that a suspect had been arrested had gotten out within hours of the suspected terrorist being taken into custody.

When Eli left the facility late that evening, he dodged the reporters who had laid siege to the prison since the late afternoon. The news had leaked out somewhere between the Prime Minister's Office and the Israel Prison Service. The press, government officials and the public were clamoring for information. With one day without sleep rapidly turning into another, Eli was grateful that Amos, and not he, had to contend with the media.

Eli left the prison with a jumble of thoughts and feelings, his wounded hand throbbing. Even though at least one of the "Gideons" was being held, it was neither elation nor relief that Eli felt: that "they" were one individual, who alone had been responsible for the bloodshed defied his and everyone else's expectations. It was hard to comprehend, difficult to accept.

Eli got in his car, departed the prison parking lot and headed down a service road.

As he got on the highway, Eli kept wondering: How was it, how could it be that the spate of murder and terror that began with the slaying of Fatima Abed and ended – at least to date –

with the car bombings that killed Naftali, Issam and Carmi really be the doing of one man?

Eli was still contemplating how a single individual might have pulled this all off as he drove off the ramp on his way to his apartment in Holon. Suddenly, he saw something dart out into his field of vision. With a steady stream of pain pulsing through his left hand, Eli had only his right hand on the steering wheel. He couldn't steer sharply enough to avoid a cat, which froze in the beam of his headlights before his bumper struck it.

Eli felt the ghastly thump as the car rolled over the cat. The blood and viscera formed a lubricant under his tires and in a split second the car had shot around, the headlights of oncoming vehicles blinding Eli. Horns started honking furiously. A car somehow maneuvered around Eli's car just in time to avoid hitting it. A van right behind it screeched to a halt to keep from colliding with both cars. Then, a tractor-trailer further back nearly jackknifed as it attempted to avoid crashing into all three vehicles.

Eli got out to see if the people in the other vehicles were hurt. Aside from frayed nerves, everyone and their vehicles were intact.

Eli slowly calmed himself. He thought: a single cat scampering onto the road and who knows how many people could have been killed or injured.

All for a single, wayward cat.

CHAPTER TWENTY-ONE

Eli had intended to come to 3 HaGaon Street much sooner. It was late evening on the day after the Son of Gideon's arrest before he could finally free up the time to visit Lilah. He wanted to explain why he had left Naftali's funeral so abruptly, that he had been summoned to a meeting that set the stage for the terrorist's capture.

He wanted to assure Lilah that her life was no longer in danger, that after two days of questioning, he was certain that they had landed the people, the person, responsible for the perdition that had ravaged the country for the past nine months. Na'aleh no longer had to divert its efforts to demanding that the government capture the Sons of Gideon. He thought that Lilah would want to know that, too.

"One man," Lilah said shaking her head incredulously, "no one is going to believe that."

Yes, one man. Eli explained. He described how Shoshana Ya'akov, Shimon Ya'akov, Moshe Ben-Avraham and several other identities had their origins in the muddled brain chemistry of a man named William Connely Ferguson, Jr., a deranged veteran of the United States Special Forces who had fought in Kuwait and Iraq during the Gulf War. Later, it would be discovered that Ferguson had run a few minor confederates, cronies who had done his bidding in return for the affections and gifts he accorded them. The role played by the three lowly government clerks and a derelict soldier – marginals on the fringe lured by promises of glory or professions of love – paled in comparison to Ferguson's. Their involvement had been confined to spiriting away ministry files, rummaging through offices and creating diversions that enabled Ferguson to prepare for and commit his atrocities. The harsh prison sentences they would undoubtedly be meted would adequately punish them for their wrongdoings. None of them, though, knew the whole picture of what Ferguson had been undertaking. It would be confirmed that he had been the architect and executioner of all that had been done in the name of the Sons of Gideon. The infamy belonged to him.

"It's got to be part of a government cover-up," Lilah insisted.

"Are you accusing me of making this up?" Eli asked Lilah. He was exhausted, having slept little since he had taken down the suspect, but with the little stamina he had left, he revealed details about the man in custody to Lilah. With his voice scratchy and his eyes looking as they would shut from the sheer weight of fatigue, Eli explained that he too had been rattled by the macabre account the psychiatrist had retrieved from Ferguson and his derivative personalities. Still, when checked against the facts, what the man in detention told his interlocutors held water.

Eli sipped the broth Lilah had prepared for him. The hot steam against his face and the robust flavor of the beverage revived him a bit. "I am telling you that we have ample reason to believe that he unleashed the entire rampage alone. It's hard to accept, I know, but that's what the facts point to."

"You say that he is sick. What if he's a pathological liar? What if it is all fantasy and fairy tales?" Lilah challenged.

With greater patience than he thought he had in him at the time, Eli told Lilah that defense ministry computer modelers had been able to take the information that Ferguson had provided and shown how several of the crimes could have been committed by a single individual. Further, Ferguson had revealed details that only the perpetrator of the attacks could have known. It had also become apparent how he had slipped up and committed the errors – believing that Carmi was behind the search for them, the botched assassination on Lilah that had resulted in Naftali and Issam's deaths and the meeting with the moshavnik to resupply his weapons stores. The man in detention also revealed plans for a final assault, one in which he planned to take his own life in the course of an attack in East Jerusalem that, Eli stated, "would have been heinous beyond belief," had it taken place.

"You think the world is going to believe that one person, however insane he might be, did all this to us? The government and the right-wingers will gladly welcome hearing that. It lets them off the hook," Lilah stated tersely.

"Believe me – even the agent I've got posted downstairs is no longer necessary. It's over. We have them – him – in custody and the details of how he did it all are pouring out. The more we hear, the more convinced we become. I wouldn't leave you exposed for a minute if I thought anyone was still out there," Eli said.

Lilah didn't doubt that he felt that way. But accepting what he was saying, that all the devastation had been the doings of one man, defied belief.

Only after Eli brought Lilah to the facility where Ferguson was being held did she begin to accept that it was true.

"This isn't going to be pleasant. Places like this are never nice and the man we are holding is a very, very sick individual. You can still change your mind about going in," Eli offered after he had parked the car in the prison parking lot.

"He'll certainly be asleep now, won't he?" she asked timorously.

"Don't count on it. They're having a hard time getting him to sleep at all."

Still, Lilah did want to see Ferguson, the man who had killed Naftali and Issam while stalking her.

It took nearly an hour to complete the identity checks before the warders at the gate of the prison would admit Lilah. There had never in the history of the State been a prisoner so well guarded. Lilah got a glimpse of the regular prison wings as they passed through several corridors to the special suite of rooms where the alleged terrorist was being held, a different world from the cellblocks. It seemed much more civilized than the regular prison. The doors and gates opened electronically, and the well-mannered Shin Bet agents who secured the immaculate, high-tech suite were in civilian dress, not uniforms. Yet the security and medical teams surrounding Ferguson were determined to keep him at bay and safe until a full accounting of what he had done could be obtained.

A young man came out of the doctors' lounge after one of the agents summoned him to meet the visitors.

"I am Dr. Bruzonsky. What can I do for you?" He had just come on staff and had not yet met Eli.

Eli introduced himself and Lilah Kedem, "an associate," he told the doctor.

"I know that you were the one who broke the case and arrested Ferguson and I am familiar with your instructions concerning the security arrangements," said the doctor, offering his hand to Eli, then politely shaking Lilah's as well.

"How is he doing now?"

"Well, why don't we sit down? Help yourself to some coffee or tea," he said as he directed them into a staff room. Eli and Lilah made themselves something to drink and then sat down.

The doctor began. "His parents are with him now. They arrived from the United States this afternoon and have been with him since then. He's calmed down and we've been able to lower the dose of chemical restraints that we had to administer when he first saw them. We would have preferred not to have given him what we did, as he'll be almost vegetative tomorrow. But given his state when he first saw his parents, the team on duty didn't have a choice."

"I was here. I saw it all," said Eli. "He was completely out of control. The orderlies couldn't subdue him. You heard what he did to that nurse I'm sure."

"Yes, I did," said Bruzonsky. "It took fifteen stitches to close her cheek. Anyway, before he became agitated today, he was

Bill, which is his core identity. As far as he was concerned, he was in southern Iraq when everything happened. The recordings are being transcribed now. Let me warn you, it's very ugly stuff. What those soldiers did, and what they had done to them, was one nightmare after another. Around noon, before his parents arrived, he became delusional and adopted his Shimshon Ya'akov identity. He spilled out a lot of information you'll be interested in. I think you'll have a better idea of how the bombs were planted at Al-Bakr as a result of that session."

The doctor and Eli spoke for a few more minutes discussing the prisoner. Then Eli said he and Lilah wanted to observe him.

Eli and Bruzonsky entered an adjoining room, darkened and aflicker with the light of several large monitors showing various angles of the room where the prisoner-patient was contained. Lilah diffidently entered the observation room. "He can't see us, right?" Lilah asked nervously. Eli affirmed that he could not.

Lilah had not expected the man to look the way he did. He was fair-skinned with straight blond hair graying at the sides and hanging close to his sad, aqueous blue eyes. Lilah had expected to see some kind of warlock, yet the man lying in the bed could have been described as handsome. He was no youngster though, and from what she had been told certainly no innocent.

Next to his bed sat an elderly couple with porcelain complexions and Yankee countenances that reminded Lilah of some of the people who had been at Lucian's memorial service in Boston. The man wore a pinstripe suit and tie; the woman was well-appointed in a blouse, skirt and pearl necklace. They looked terribly drained. Rivulets of tears had streaked the woman's makeup. The man, his head bowed, looked absolutely despondent. The couple was holding hands tightly, subdued and disconsolate.

"It's so sad," said Lilah under her breath, her eyes welling up. "It is so, so sad."

"What's your opinion, doctor? He's not going to be able to appear in court, is he?" Eli asked Bruzonsky.

"I don't believe any competent psychiatrist in the world would pronounce him fit for trial. He's a very sick man. My belief is that he'll spend the rest of his life in a high security institution. He remains very dangerous to society – and to himself."

"Can't he be cured?" asked Lilah. "Surely with medication and therapy he could get better."

"We have no cure for such severe psychosis. His has been shattered by his past and I doubt that any amount of therapy can piece him back together," the doctor stated, his tone authoritative, definitive. "If it is punishment anyone's after, believe me, this man's life has been punishing enough. He isn't responsible for what he did. We may want him to be, but he's not."

"I can't stand this anymore," Lilah said tearfully, rushing from the room.

Eli made some notations in the log and escorted Lilah quickly out of the suite and out of the prison. They walked silently in the cold night air, Lilah's muffled weeping being the only audible sound in the lot at two in the morning. Eli started the car. In the stillness, her breath vaporous from the damp cold, Lilah composed herself and in a steadied voice said, "Alright, let's say that I accept that it was one man. It's what I heard and saw here that convinced me. But what are you going to do? The public isn't going to easily accept this. It is simply too implausible. Are you going to parade him in front of the media? Take him in a cage from one end of the country to the other? And what about the widespread belief abroad that this is just an official cover-up? That the government is just trying to conceal the truth by pinning it all on one crazed man?"

Eli's response surprised her.

"People have to understand that the Sons of Gideon weren't the problem, only a symptom, a germ that grew and grew, feeding off the rot that has set into the society. That's what we have to be concerned with, getting rid of the disease that you people, Na'aleh, have been talking about. That's what this is all about. That's what should concern us."

"My, aren't we sounding progressive."

"It's not a question of progressive or conservative, Left or Right. It boils down to people living and letting others live. Hating the other side, whether it's Jews against Arabs or Arabs against Jews, doesn't solve our problems. Society has to recognize that. Hatred is a drug that both sides in the conflict have gotten hooked on. This was the growth hormone in this case, the main accomplice."

"When did you come to this realization?"

"That night at Arka al-Khitab when I fought Ferguson. He was ready to kill a little girl for no other reason than her being an Arab. She was totally innocent of any crime. No, I can't live with such sickness. It feeds off the craziness, the hatred that we have been given to swallow. I can't understand how Jewish values have been turned around to justify all sorts of things in the society: that a greater Israel is a stronger one, that there is only one way to be a Jew, that the rich and powerful should run things for the rest of us, that our historical rights mean that we can run roughshod over another people. The terror that the Sons of Gideon inflicted was just a product of the times, a disaster waiting to happen. Ferguson should be seen as a red flag, a wakeup call before we drive ourselves into extinction. What happened here is not about him. It's about us, Israel, the fight for our soul."

Four cars in convoy traveled to the broadcasting studios at

Neveh Ilan, fifteen kilometers northwest of the capital.

The Shin Bet men had picked up Amos and the military censor at the prime minister's office in the capital district. The unmarked vehicle drove evasively, crossing routes, reversing direction until any journalists that might be trailing were shaken off. As planned, it joined three other vehicles filled with security men near the Sultan's Pool across from Jaffa Gate. Eli was there waiting for them, drawing nervously on a cigarette and impatient to get the business started and done. He was directed to the car where Amos and the censor were waiting.

They rode without speaking. The driver deftly negotiated the traffic and the crowds of pedestrians that marked the close of another business day. What was it like to have a workday end? Eli wondered. He had all but forgotten.

When they reached the intersection of King George and Agron streets, the military censor, a wiry, grim-looking man, handed Eli a hood, similar to the one he had placed on Ferguson when he arrested him five days earlier. "Put it on now," he instructed Eli.

"Already?"

The censor nodded.

"Go ahead," Amos said, "in the long run, it's for your own safety," he added. Eli was unsure if that was a comradely recommendation or an order. He placed the hood over his head.

"Now," the censor began, "there is a green light and a red light atop the teleprompter. When the green light appears that's me letting you know that you are permitted to answer that question. If the red light goes on, then you answer 'no comment' in English. You are to briefly answer the questions without volunteering any more information than required. Your words will be delayed for a few seconds to give me the opportunity to squelch any confidential information you might disclose. Understood?" the censor asked gruffly.

Eli nodded without looking at him. He was staring through the windshield. A light drizzle had begun to fall.

Eli did not relish the role into which he had been cast – the front man, whose job it would be to explain to the country and the world who the "Sons of Gideon" were and how they, he, had pulled off the reign of terror. The government was counting on the media show, the press conference, to prevent its fall, or at least cushion it, in the wake of the public's call for its demise.

"I know how aggravating all this must be for you," Amos said to Eli as they waited for the traffic to clear near the Chords Bridge, where Na'aleh activists were holding a demonstration under the banner "Let Israel Rise." A moment passed before Amos, his voice flat, resumed. "It will take time before your personal role in breaking the case can be acknowledged. But know that the public will eventually learn of it, and I am sure the nation will find a way to express its gratitude." He sounded as if he were reciting from a prepared text. His words did not comfort Eli.

"You know what I found out before I left Tel Aviv this morning?" Eli said, ignoring Amos' little speech.

"What's that?"

"You know the former police detective who helped us trap Ferguson?"

"The moshavnik? The American immigrant who had fought in the Gulf War?"

"Right. I got a call from his wife."

"I had the check requisitioned yesterday...." Amos interjected.

"Their son found him hanging from a pipe in the milking shed. He killed himself after the dawn milking."

The words hovered like black crows against a winter sky.

"I'm sorry," Amos said earnestly, his tone muted. "What happened?"

"Well, he didn't leave a suicide note. He wasn't the most

communicative man in the world."

"The man is something of a hero. Why would he take his life?"

"He had a history of depression. He had been treated off and on in the past for post-traumatic stress disorder."

"I'll see to it that he is posthumously decorated," said Amos, keen to make things easier for Eli in any way he could. "I'll see to it that the defense ministry extends full bereavement benefits to his family." Amos was sincere, but for all his good intentions, Eli was skeptical about whether they could lead anywhere. He had come to doubt whether anything of worth could come from this government.

"It's not your fault," Amos said, trying to buttress Eli. His performance at the press conference had to be convincing. "He was a big boy. Nothing was imposed on him. He knew the score before he was asked to take action. We cannot be held responsible for his fragile state of mind."

"I guess not," Eli muttered as they swept past the sign "Go in Peace" and departed the city limits of Jerusalem.

The first car in the convoy pulled up to the television complex. The Shin Bet men got out and surveyed the waiting crowd of journalists and photographers who were jockeying for position at the police barricades. Intent on protecting one of their own, the security men took no chances. Once Eli exited the car, he was buried in a tight cordon that moved like a steamroller through the mob of reporters.

Eli was conducted into the studio and then to the chair and table at which he would be sitting under the lights at center stage. Behind the heavy curtains, a group of men in suits and ties, cabinet ministers, stood talking. They had come to claim credit for an investigation they hadn't aided. Why were they so calm and self-possessed? Eli wondered. Certainly they had taken note that masses of citizens attending the vigil in

Jerusalem last Saturday night had called for their ouster. Since then Opposition leader Naftali Kedem, Chief Inspector Mordechai Carmi and prominent physician, Dr. Issam Halaby had been slain, yet these insolent politicos were basking in the splendor of the Sons of Gideon case coming to a close. What a joke, Eli thought. They had done nothing to stop the madness.

Amos led Eli by the arm to where the men were standing. "This is Agent Aleph," he informed them. Eli was conscious that the agents who had delivered him were now withdrawing from the room. He felt forsaken, abandoned to the sharks.

"Good," said the minister for internal security. "Now Amos," he continued, "I think that the public would expect me to be the first speaker."

"No," said the defense minister, throwing his heavy arm over Eli's shoulders. "Eli, I mean Agent Aleph, works under my auspices," he declared – a dubious assertion, even if formally true – "I should make the introduction."

What a jerk, Eli thought to himself. I never exchanged more than two words with this buffoon, he recalled.

The Justice Minister was more concerned with substance – electoral considerations. His party's dismal showing in a recent public survey was weighing heavily on the anxious conservative, especially in light of the vigil and the slayings. "You realize," he said gravely to Eli, "that the fate of the government is in the balance tonight. It is up to you to convince the public that we were in no way responsible for the reprehensible developments that have transpired."

What a stinking bunch of fools, Eli thought as the ministers fought over the limelight. They had allowed the climate of hatred to spread in the first place. Now they think I will clean up their mess. What am I to them? A puppet? A poster boy? He wasn't about to be tied to anyone's whipping post, he decided.

The ministers were seated at center stage behind a long table, with Amos slightly behind them and Eli to his side. Dr. Leora

Almog, who would be called on to describe Ferguson's mental illness had been seated next to Eli. She touched his hand empathically, rolling her eyes in shared disdain as the ministers took their seats.

The military censor was seated offstage at a special console beyond the view of those in the audience.

The way the scene had been arranged made him little more than a stage prop, thought Eli. He was the man from whom the entire country and a significant part of international public opinion was waiting to hear. The listeners were ready to disbelieve him, the storyteller, whose tale was so far-fetched. Many pundits had already concluded that the Ferguson story had been concocted only so this infernal government could come out vindicated – or at least less soiled.

Eli felt utterly alone as he looked out through the eyelets of the hood at the flimsy partition of cameras, wires and boxes, the teleprompter and the blinding stage lights that stood between him and the lions, the press corps, who waited hungrily for the opportunity to rip his words to shreds. It was hot under the burlap and he had begun to sweat, the briny moisture burning his eyes and blurring his vision.

Elaborate press kits were distributed to the journalists and the conference began. In the end, the ministerial one-upmanship resulted in Eli being introduced by the minister of internal security, a fanatic Eli recalled from the days when Israel was the sole authority in Judea and Samaria. "Mr. Hot Pursuit," the press had dubbed him then as he gratuitously ordered roundups of Palestinians for interrogation long after the army had captured all fugitives wanted on terrorism charges.

Mr. Hot Pursuit spoke at length about how thoroughly the investigation had been conducted by Superintendent Mordechai Carmi, his now departed protégé. The minister praised the late policeman for "tireless and heroic efforts, day and night, to break the Sons of Gideon case." He was sure that Carmi would be proud that his efforts had led to the arrest of the Gideons. Then the minister called upon the superintendent's "right hand man" – Eli – in the investigation, to explain how the affair had been brought to a close.

The show then began in earnest and the spotlight was on Eli.

"When did you first join the investigation and in what capacity, that is, on behalf of which agency?" was the first question asked.

Eli looked for the light on the teleprompter. It took him a few seconds to find it, and even though it was green, he turned toward the censor, waiting for an affirmative nod.

"I was called in immediately after the murder of Fatima Abed, the elderly woman killed in Jaffa, which was the first crime for which the Sons of Gideons took credit. As for the agency with which I am associated, I am a former senior field agent with the Shin Bet currently assigned to the office of the..." Seconds after he uttered the words "Prime Minister's security advisor," Eli heard his own words voiced-over. "Agent Aleph is not at liberty to elaborate further," metallically uttered the military censor.

A correspondent from the Agence France-Presse asked the second question. "According to the cabinet's press statement, the suspect is a 47-year-old male who we have been told is American-born and has been resident in Israel over the past three years. He is said to suffer from mental imbalances, specifically from multiple personality disorder. The official line is that he acted alone. Agent Aleph, can you please tell us more about this man?"

"What more do you want to know?" Eli replied awkwardly. It was increasingly uncomfortable under the heat of the studio lights.

"Some more particulars about his background would be helpful," the Frenchman asked with an unmistakable dash of derision. Skepticism was running high among members of the foreign press.

Eli sighed, then recited the facts he had painstakingly assembled on note cards in preparation for the press conference. "Mr. Ferguson was born in Bangkok where his father, an American intelligence professional, was stationed. He spent parts of his childhood and youth in Bonn and Tokyo and attended high school in McLean, Virginia. He was known as a loner and had many, many problems adjusting to his family's frequent moves. He applied for and was admitted to West Point, the U.S. Army Military Academy, but was dismissed from the Academy under dishonorable circumstances, which we have learned were related to behavioral problems.

"Using the assumed name James McSimmons, he enlisted for service in the American military in 1990, and volunteered for and was inducted into the U.S. Army Special Forces. He saw action in the Persian Gulf and was incriminated there for committing acts of violence against civilians. He was discharged on psychiatric grounds."

The next question referred to an accusation that was gaining increasing currency in the international press.

"Is there any truth to rumors of Ferguson's past links with Israeli intelligence? What exactly were his ties with Israel?"

Eli had heard the rumors. He was going to be damned if the security services were going to be dragged through the mud.

"The suspect was never employed by Israeli intelligence nor did he serve in the Israeli military. He had been granted an exemption on the grounds that he was a full-time yeshiva student. As for his connection with our country, the story is a complicated one." He paused and took a drink of water before he continued.

"From what we have been able to determine, Mr. Ferguson entered Israel via Egypt in June 2003, using the identity of Eric Gelbson, whose occupation he listed as a student of Biblical archaeology. Ferguson participated in digs in the West Bank and Jerusalem. In March 2005, the Israel Police arrested Gelbson for illegal possession of firearms and explosives, and he was placed under house arrest pending trial. For reasons still under investigation, Ferguson was able to flee the country shortly afterwards, under circumstances we are still trying to reconstruct.

"Ferguson reentered Israel in February 2007, posing as a new immigrant, under the name of Samuel Franklin Borne of Auburn, Massachusetts, U.S.A., where he had purportedly converted to Judaism. At that time, he adopted the name Moshe Ben-Avraham. During the ensuing period, he left the country twice more, returning as Shimon Ya'akov and then as Sandra Jacoby, who subsequently became known as Shoshana Ya'akov. These identities were used by the prisoner in carrying out many of the attacks launched in the name of the Sons of Gideon."

Several moments passed while the journalists recorded his remarks in a frenzy of scribbles and laptop clatter. Eli's frank presentation suggested that this was not some propaganda session. Still, doubts remained.

"How could a man as ill as you claim Mr. Ferguson is be able to elude capture for so long? Moreover, if the individual is so sick that he is unfit to stand trial, how is it that he masterminded and executed such hideous crimes?" asked an Australian correspondent.

Dr. Almog took the question, the ministers tripping over each other for the opportunity to introduce her. The psychiatrist described Ferguson's psychopathology as resulting from a familial predisposition triggered first by the frequent displacements he had experienced in childhood and various adjustment problems he encountered as an adolescent and teenager. His highly traumatic service in Kuwait and Iraq served as a trigger in subsequent years. Dr. Almog revealed that her team was in communication with psychiatrists and psychologists who had treated Ferguson in the U.S. They had provided considerable insight regarding a number of key points that led to the resolution of the case, including the genesis of many of the personalities assumed by Ferguson, which played a part in the Sons of Gideon.

Dr. Almog also discussed how one of Ferguson's personalities, Eric Gelbson, befriended and manipulated people who shared his own gender confusion. He had developed a small network of vulnerable souls, who in return for his pretensions of caring, sexual liaisons and in some cases drugs or cash, unknowingly provided support for Sons of Gideon operations.

The press listened attentively as Eli described one of Ferguson's confederates, a clerk at the housing ministry who had burgled files and destroyed documents relating to Ben-Avraham, Jacoby and Ya'akov. When the censor disallowed a series of answers Eli had given regarding the enlisted man who had enabled Ferguson to pilfer ordnance from army stocks, Eli bitingly asked the censor if he would perhaps like to take over for him.

"Can you give us more information about whoever Gideon is and Ferguson's connection to him?" one of the journalists asked.

"Ferguson was raised in the Church of Latter Day Saints," Eli answered. "Apparently the reference is to a general by that name in the Book of Mormon."

After ninety minutes of questioning, Eli's and Dr. Almog's forthright answers were gradually winning credence. But Eli responded sharply to one particularly obnoxious question.

"I'm not about to let you try me as if I were a criminal," he shouted at the caustic reporter. "This investigation was in full swing from the moment Fatima Abed was slain. Do you know how many hours of my time and that of others in Israel's security services have gone into this case? How many sleepless nights? I haven't had a day off in months. I cannot remember the last time I got more than four hours of sleep in one go."

The ministers then began to enter the fray and engaged in verbal fisticuffs with the press. After one particular demagogic harangue by the public information minister following a subtle though venomous accusation by a Russian reporter, Eli rose from his chair and said, "If you ask me, what has gone on here this evening is a circus. I have had enough."

The remark provided the moderator with an excuse to end the press conference. After he did so and the television cameras had been turned away, Eli tore off the hood and turned contemptuously toward the cabinet members. "Sirs," he declared, "you are a bunch of jokers in a government that is a burlesque show. Have mercy on the country and resign while you still can get your pensions!"

As he was being led behind the stage curtains back to the waiting vehicles, the defense minister hurried toward him and, extending his hand and smiling smugly said, "You gave a solid performance out there. You served us well..." Eli gazed at the man in disbelief, then scorn.

"They still don't realize that the people have had enough," Eli sputtered as Amos spirited him away from the ministers to a waiting car. "They don't understand that the show is over, that the people of Israel, all of us, demand better," he added.

On the morning following the Jerusalem vigil and Naftali's, Issam's and Carmi's deaths, the chief rabbinate, like the government, was forced to take note of the people's will. In a statement dictated by Rabbi Ben-Yishai, the two chief rabbis issued a joint edict condemning the Sons of Gideon and forbidding Jews to give them aid or succor. While the concession would lead to the discontinuation of Rabbi Ben-Yishai hunger strike, it was otherwise without effect since at that same hour in a bar in south Tel Aviv, Eli and his men were taking down William Connely Ferguson. There were, thereafter, no Sons of Gideon left to whom aid or succor might be given.

During the previous week, Rabbi Ben-Yishai's Sackcloth Marchers and the other Spiritual Warriors had established five tent cities, Na'aleh One through Five, outside of Jerusalem, Beersheva, on the road between Rishon LeTzion and Modi'in, just north of Haifa and on the outskirts of Kiryat Shmona. There, Na'aleh hosted teach-ins and public debates. Performers appeared and poets recited on hastily built stages, as crowds of Israelis from all sectors of the society flocked to the centers. Those days of protest, learning and music were a veritable citizen's holiday: throngs of people participating in the general strike called by the Labor Federation and parts of the business community gathered to usher in the new Israel.

Eli's characterization of the government ministers as a "bunch of clowns" had become a sound bite that accompanied a photo of him gazing contemptuously at the defense minister after the press conference. The utterance and image became iconic and went viral, twittered and otherwise transmitted along the social networks. It reflected the mood of the public: resolute, defiant and insistent on the government's dissolution and new elections.

In the days following the press conference announcing Ferguson's capture and the apparent end of the Sons of Gideon terror, dozens of salon meetings were called by Na'aleh. The gatherings were conducted as part of the Movement's FORUM, the Framework for Reconciliation, Unity and Mutual Understanding. The popular will of the country had been vastly expressed by the assembly at the Jerusalem vigil, and it had hardened with the deaths of Prof. Naftali Kedem, Dr. Issam

Halaby and Chief Inspector Motti Carmi. In the course of the salon meetings, prominent academics, business leaders, civil servants and intellectuals prepared position papers on a myriad of issues. They were networked across the Web and consolidated into *A Charter for Israel's Renewal* that outlined the program the successor government to the Nationalists would be expected to follow.

The *Charter* called for fundamental changes in Israeli society and greater participation of the public in the life of the country. "Responsive Governance," it was called. The document recognized that Israel served as the center of Jewish civilization while upholding the equality of all citizens – Jews, Arabs and all others in matters of personal standing and opportunity.

It was affirmed that while religion could inspire the society, clerical influences on the functions of state were to be abolished.

There was no issue of public life that went unaddressed. The *Charter* was a people's manifesto for remaking the country after the ruination caused by the decades-long Nationalist rule.

The *Charter* demanded elections within forty-five days. It called for a final status agreement with the Palestinian authorities and the rehabilitation of Israel's foreign relations. Efforts to advance coexistence and partnership with Israel's newly democratic neighbors and other countries in the Middle East would be given top priority.

The Charter would be known as *Rise for Israel's Renewal*.

The Nationalist-led government tottered and fell by Passover. In the ensuing months, rapid change was seen everywhere after elections had been held and the New Democrats and their allies formed a stable government. It toiled under public scrutiny to meet the expectations expressed in the *Rise* charter.

With the coming of spring, a new, fresher breeze redolent with hope returned to the Land of Israel. One American newspaperman described the revived spirit of the country as "reminiscent of a barn raising, the entire country, Jews, Moslem and Christian Arabs, and Druze seeming to recognize their common interest in the revival of an old-new society, rebuilding justly. From daycare centers to retirement villages, the peoples of Israel are nailing a new roof on the national home of the Jewish people, one that would be extended to include the 'stranger that dwells within,' the Arab and other minorities, who would become 'an integral part of the House of Israel' while maintaining their distinct identities. 'A new harmony,' was building" the author wrote approvingly.

Harmonious would not be the way that Lilah would describe her state in the months after Naftali's death. His passing had been a hammer blow, the strongest one in a series she had suffered over the year since her return to Israel. She did not know how she would pick up the pieces now that he was gone.

The car bomb that had shattered all hope for the renewal of her relationship with Naftali had taken its toll on her ties with her son as well, at least for now. Staggered by his father's murder, Ido had sequestered himself in an apartment he rented in Kiryat Shmona near his base on the Golan Heights. He needed his time and place away from the great tragedies that were associated with 3 HaGaon Street. Lilah accepted that, not with ease but with respect. The rebuilding of her friendship with Michal had also been disrupted by the bombing. Following the slayings, Michal had withdrawn into herself. She isolated herself in Acre, remaining at home in deep mourning for Issam.

Deprived of Naftali and with Ido and Michal out of reach,

Lilah found herself talking a great deal with Eli. She felt at ease with him and trusted him implicitly. In their conversations, Eli had drawn from her the realization that she had duly "atoned" for the thirty years she had estranged herself from her country. If any debt could have been levied her for that, she had more than repaid it by becoming a participant, a leader, in the society's rebirth.

He also helped her understand that in order to cope with the new realities of her life, she needed to regain her sense of self, recover her balance. She found herself agreeing but realized that to do so, she had to withdraw from the public spotlight. She and the Na'aleh Board concurred that it was no longer appropriate for the movement to operate out of her apartment. Both parties had outgrown that arrangement. Na'aleh took up quarters in a modest suite of offices downtown. Lilah would continue to lend her name to its activities but would quietly withdraw from its leadership.

The success of *Women of the Ports*, newly published, critically acclaimed and selling well enabled Lilah to wrangle an agreement from her publishers to publish a photo essay, *In Search of Phantoms*, comprised of the photos she had taken in pursuit of the Sons of Gideon. She designated Na'aleh as the recipient of all profits from the project, the revenues to be earmarked for scholarships and projects to be awarded in memory of Naftali. That would be Lilah's final contribution to the Movement. It was time to let it go.

What Lilah worked the hardest at was accepting that for all its potential, all the love and caring and effort, the single relationship that had most eluded her, that with Naftali, would never be fully realized. Destiny was a notion that she had never fully embraced. But now, faced with the cavernous emptiness and finality left by Naftali's death, she began to realize that some things are not fated to be. She ached, as though a rib had been removed from her and left a cavity behind. Little by little, she came to realize that in that vacated place near her heart, there was room that could, should, be filled.

CB ❖ ED

In late June, an international commission invited by the new government to evaluate the results of the Sons of Gideon investigation confirmed its conclusions: The principal suspect and his confederates had been apprehended and what and how the events had transpired had been determined. With the investigation concluded and the experts convinced that there was little prospect of rehabilitating William Connely Ferguson, his parents petitioned the State of Israel to allow them to take him home. The American authorities warranted that he would remain all his days under heavy guard in an appropriate federal facility. Thereafter, the erstwhile Gideon was transferred to an institution in Virginia and became an American problem, no longer an Israeli one.

The case and its burdens behind him, Eli began realizing how physically and mentally spent he was. He felt there were matters that he had been caused to neglect and that affected him deeply. He was concerned about his father's health and he missed not spending time with his nephew Lior. There was also the issue of surgery on his injured hand; it was overdue.

Eli had begun confiding these things to Lilah and listened to her counsel: that he needed to take time off. When Eli approached Amos with the idea, he readily agreed stating that Eli had more than earned a leave of absence and that he encouraged him to take one. Amos committed in writing that a senior position in the security community would be waiting for Eli on his return.

Eli took the leave.

Relieved of her public responsibilities, Lilah spent the

summer shooting, developing and compiling photos, some for *Phantoms*, but most with no clear purpose other than creative fulfillment. Eli would sometimes accompany her; both he and Lilah began to look forward to these outings. They would leave early and drive to the selected site. They would pass the day together.

Eli had surgery in August. It would be the first in a series of operations intended to restore as much functionality as possible to his hand. He would never have full use of it and there would always be some measure of pain, a perpetual keepsake of the Sons of Gideon affair.

With the rehabilitation progressing and an increasing urge to return to work, a position as a senior analyst in the intelligence community was tailored for Eli, which he would begin after Rosh Hashanah. He would have an office in the capital with his own staff and spend less time in the field. He found a comfortable apartment in Beit HaKerem and was given time to resume his doctoral studies at the Hebrew University computer faculty.

All of this was in Jerusalem, not Tel Aviv, where Lilah continued her residence at 3 HaGaon Street. As the months progressed and the time they wanted to spend with each other grew more than the distance would accommodate, they considered how they might overcome the problem, in time.

Gradually, Lilah felt Eli was filling the emptiness that Naftali's passing had left behind. She allowed herself to grow toward Eli.

And he toward her.

There was something natural about their melding, a complement of parts. They were made of very different shapes and textures, their life trajectories – until the last year – having been so disparate. But during the Year of the Gideon – which is how the pundits had begun to refer to the period during which Ferguson wreaked havoc on the country — they had tread across the same landscape and had then exited it together. Their lives had converged.

Throughout the autumn months, their affections deepened. By winter, as the mourning year for Naftali drew to a close, it was apparent to them that something approaching love had come out of the carnage they had survived.

During the winter following the end of the Year of the Gideon, the rebuilding of Israeli society was drawing kudos from citizens and foreign commentators alike. The rising esprit de corps coupled by the final status agreement reached with the Palestinians brought a certain buoyancy bordering on elation to the society.

It was not perfect, but things were definitely getting better – save for the situation on the northern and eastern fronts. Israel faced a tier of hostility from Teheran westward, a solid wall of militarized hate fueled by religious zeal. It loomed large across the border. The changes in the society had not succeeded in changing that.

Lilah felt foreboding.

In the period following the slaying of his father, Lt. Col. Ido Kedem, eager for a new challenge, agreed to take command of a unit of elite infantry that engaged in special missions, often deep within enemy territory.

Nearly a year to the day of Naftali's death, Lilah became restless and unsettled after a week of not hearing from Ido. "Call it a mother's intuition," she said to Eli as they drove home after visiting a still-grieving Michal in Acre. "It's not like him to be out of touch for so long."

After making inquiries, Eli learned that Ido was "in the field and incommunicado." When he tried to find out what that meant, the answer his contacts at the IDF headquarters gave was only that the operation was listed as classified.

Eli pressed Amos to get more specific information about Ido's whereabouts. Within hours, Amos paged Eli and asked him to come to his office.

Amos was tight-lipped, the situation requiring him to be vague. He told Eli that Ido was well outside of Israel, somewhere in a country to the north and the east. Ido's unit had been sent on a highly sensitive mission, something to do with disrupting an arms transfer to terrorists. The mission had been completed but something had gone awry, and Ido's unit had not rendezvoused with the helicopters that had been sent to bring them home.

"The best units in the IDF and every intelligence resource we have at our disposal have been mobilized to find Ido and his men. I promise you that. I have requested that I be updated concerning developments, and I will pass on whatever I know to you," he assured Eli. "But," Amos went on to appeal, his face looking creased and worn, "this must all be kept in-house. This whole matter is black-boxed, nothing about it can get out. There is much at stake."

Eli nodded his understanding, but pressed, "Is there any room for optimism about their return?"

Amos looked Eli squarely in the eyes and said, "I don't know. They have been missing for eleven days. That's a long time in such situations."

The visitor to 3 HaGaon Street, a young woman named Amalia arrived early one morning.

Lilah was showering after another night of sleeping in patches, her sixteenth since Eli brought her the news about her son being missing, an Israeli parent's worst nightmare. She was distressed every waking minute now that she had been caught up in the "waiting game." That's what it was called by the IDF social worker, a specialist in supporting families of missing, wounded and dead soldiers, who had been assigned to Lilah.

Lilah had become immersed in a new community, much different than the activist Na'aleh, the movement that had fundamentally changed the face of Israel. In the new community of which Lilah had become an unwitting member, there was little to do but wait. They, those forced to play the waiting game, were few in Israel, their commonality being the singular woe of living in limbo not knowing if they would ever again see their sons dead or alive.

Amalia knew even less about Ido's whereabouts than Lilah did. She was not a "recognized" family member and had received no briefings. She knew only that he was missing after he had left for a military operation. She had been coping with the waiting game alone.

In the two hours that Amalia visited Lilah, she told her how she had met Ido several months after Naftali's death. Their romance was an intense one and they were planning a future together. When Lilah expressed hurt that Ido had told her nothing about the relationship, Amalia explained that he struggled with clashing feelings, a budding romance while still mourning his father. He wanted to resolve the conflict before sharing the news of their relationship with his mother.

Lilah liked Amalia. She was a kind of flower child, fresh-faced and dreamy, an idealist. The young woman was lovely in appearance: light auburn hair that hung down her back, aquamarine eyes. She was petite, her body firm and lithe, and her face fresh full of light. She wore a simple pullover of deep purple and a long skirt with many folds that clung to her waist and embraced her protruding belly.

Lilah noticed the bulge of Amalia's midsection only when the young woman got up from the kitchen table and took their tea mugs to the sink.

Lilah's eyes lingered there. Amalia noticed and said, "This is what I wanted to tell you about. It's why I came."

ଔ ❖ ଛ

The living room at 3 HaGaon Street was crowded with people who had come to brainstorm on the next steps to be taken to get the missing soldiers home.

With Amalia's due date approaching, it was Rabbi Shaul Ben-Yishai who proposed the name, Ma'ayan, for Ido's son.

Amalia thought the name incomplete. "Spring?" she asked. "Spring of what?"

Lilah and Eli were sitting on the living room couch. When Amalia posed the question, Lilah sprung out of Eli's arms and exclaimed, "Ma'ayan Chaim," as if it was obvious, "Spring of Life!"

Amalia agreed to the name. It was fitting, she decided.

That was also the consensus of those surrounding her. They had gathered at 3 HaGaon Street after receiving word that the negotiations had resumed –whether the men were still alive or not had not been established. The Jihadists were refusing to say.

The group that had assembled in Lilah's home included Na'aleh activists, well-connected strangers with influence abroad, friends and supporters.

They were determined to bring the father home to his soon-to-be-born son.

They had chosen to believe in life, that being the way of their people.

Finally, Lilah felt she had arrived home.

CPSIA information can be obtained at www.ICGtesting.com
Printed in the USA
BVOW070518160412

287701BV00001B/6/P